Gender and Learning in Rwanda

Edited by
Shirley Randell, Hilary Yerbury and
Astrid Escrig-Pinol

UTS ePRESS
University of Technology Sydney
Broadway NSW 2007 AUSTRALIA
epress.lib.uts.edu.au

Copyright Information
This book is copyright. The work is licensed under a Creative Commons Attribution
Non Commercial-Non Derivatives License CC BY-NC-ND

http://creativecommons.org/licenses/by-nc-nd/4.0

First Published 2021
© 2021 in the text and images, the author/s of each article
© 2021 in the book design and layout, UTS ePRESS

Publication Details
Gender and Learning in Rwanda
ISBN (Paperback): 978-0-9775200-7-7
ISBN (PDF): 978-0-9775200-9-1
ISBN (EPUB): 978-0-9945039-6-1
ISBN (MOBI): 978-0-9924518-0-6
DOI: https://doi.org/10.5130/aag

Peer Review
This work was peer reviewed by disciplinary experts.

Declaration of conflicting interest
The editors declare no potential conflicts of interest with respect to the
research, authorship, and/or publication of this book.

Funding
The editors received no dedicated financial support for the
research and publication of this book.

UTS ePRESS
Manager: Scott Abbott
Books Editor: Matthew Noble
Book and Cover Designer: Megan Wong
Cover photographer: Karina Glasby
Enquiries: utsepress@uts.edu.au

For enquiries about third party copyright material reproduced in this work,
please contact UTS ePRESS.

OPEN ACCESS
UTS ePRESS publishes peer reviewed books, journals and conference proceedings
and is the leading publisher of peer reviewed open access journals in Australasia.
All UTS ePRESS online content is free to access and read.

Suggested citation
Randell, S., Yerbury, H. and Escrig-Pinol, A. (eds.) 2021. *Gender and Learning in Rwanda*. Sydney:
UTS ePRESS. DOI: https://doi.org/10.5130/aag. License: CC BY-NC-ND.

 To read the free, open access version of this book online,
visit https://doi.org/10.5130/aag
or scan this QR code with your mobile device:

Gender and Learning in Rwanda

Edited by
Shirley Randell, Hilary Yerbury and
Astrid Escrig-Pinol

Contents

Acronyms	xi
Preface	xv

Part I: Academic Reflections — 1

Establishing the Centre for Gender, Culture and Development at the Kigali Institute of Education
Shirley Randell — 3

The Challenges of Using a Feminist Pedagogical Approach
Sharon M. Meagher — 17

Feminist Research in Rwanda: Challenges and Importance
Anita Clair Fellman — 27

Thinking and Acting; Towards a Gendered Scholarship
Hilary Yerbury — 43

Teaching Gender Research Methods for Leadership: Reflections from Rwanda
Jaya Dantas — 53

Teaching Transitional Justice: Towards a Political and Personal Transformative Journey
Gertrude Fester-Wicomb — 65

The Importance of Educating Girls and Women in Sciences
Verdiana Grace Masanja — 77

The Framing of Gender-Based Violence Discourses in Mainstream Development: From a Human Rights Violation to a Development Barrier
Astrid Escrig-Pinol — 93

Part II: Graduate Stories — 107

The statements of the students and graduates from the first cohort of the Masters in Gender, Culture and Development.

Adeline Uwamahoro	109
Aline Mukantabana	113
Allen Cyizanye	117
Angelina Muganza	121
Anne Abakunzi	125
Aquiline Niwemfura	129
Claudine Murindahabi	133
Donatha Gihana	137
Edouard Munyamaliza	143
Egidia Rukundo	149
Egidie Murekatete	153
Emmanuel Bimenyimana	157
Ernestine Narame	161
Ernestine Uwimpeta	165
Fidèle Ndamyeyezu	169
Fidèle Rutayisire	173
Françoise Uwumukiza	177
Grace Igiraneza	185
Irenée Umulisa	189
Jane Umutoni	193
Janvière Mukantwali	197
Jean Damascène Gasasira	201
Josephine Kobusingye	205

Josephine Mukakalisa	209
Jovia Kayirangwa	215
Jules Sebahizi	221
Landrade Umuraza	227
Laurence Uwera	231
Leonie Mujawayezu	235
Marie Odette Kansanga Ndahiro	237
Mediatrice Mukeshimana	241
Monica Kirabo	245
Natacha Kaneza	249
Oda Gasinzigwa	253
Odette Bagitengire	259
Odile Muhayimana	261
Patrick Mico Ntunga	265
Radegonde Bayisenge	269
Regine Abanyuze	273
Shamsi Kazimbaya	277
Sidonie Uwimpuhwe	283
Sifa Bayingana	287
Simon Nsabiyeze	291
Violet Kabarenzi	295
Viviane Kalumire Furaha	299
Index	**305**

Acronyms

AF	African Feminism
Africare	American NGO that provides development aid for Africa
ARBEF	Association Rwandaise pour le Bien-Être Familial
AusAID	Australian Agency for International Development
AWID	Association of Women in Development
CCE	Certificate of Continuing Education
CGCD	Centre for Gender, Culture and Development
CGS	Centre for Gender Studies
COPE	Community-based Orphan care, Protection and Empowerment
DRC	Democratic Republic of Congo
EU-28	European Union's 28 countries
FAWE	Forum for African Women Educationalists
FEMNET	African Women's Development and Communication Network
FGM	Female Genital Mutilation
Gacaca Courts	A system of community participatory justice
GBV	Gender Based Violence
GCD	Gender, Culture and Development
GD	Gender and Development
GDP	Gross Domestic Product
GEM	Global Education Monitoring

GEWE	Gender Equality and Women's Empowerment
GMO	Gender Monitoring Office
GoR	Government of Rwanda
HIV/AIDS	Human Immunodeficiency Virus infection and Acquired Immunodeficiency Syndrome (HIV/AIDS)
HR	Human Resources
Imbuto Foundation	A project under the Office of the First Lady with programmes in health, education, youth and economic empowerment
INGO	International Non-Government Organisation
IT	Information Technology
KIE	Kigali Institute of Education
KIST	Kigali Institute of Science and Technology
MDGs	Millennium Development Goals
MIFOTRA	Ministry of Public Service and Labour
MIGEPROF	Ministry of Gender and Family Promotion
MSocSciGD	Master of Social Science (Gender and Development)
NCSES	National Center for Science and Engineering Statistics
NGC	New Generation Connect
NGO	Non-Government Organisation
NORAD	Norwegian Agency for Development
NUR	National University of Rwanda
ODU	Old Dominion University
OVC	Orphans and Vulnerable Children
P1	First year of primary education
PACFA	Protection and Care for Families with AIDS
PCF	Post-Colonial Feminist
PEPFAR	US President's Emergency Plan for AIDS Relief
PhD	Doctor of Philosophy

PSC	Public Service Commission
RAUW	Rwanda Association for University Women
RPF	Rwandan Patriotic Front
RWAMREC	Rwanda Men's Resource Centre
RWPF	Rwanda Women's Parliamentary Forum (FFRP)
S1	First year of secondary education
SA	South Africa
SDGs	Sustainable Development Goals
S&E	Science and Engineering
SNV	Netherlands Development Organisation
SSA	Sub-Saharan Africa
STEM	Science, Technology, Engineering and Mathematics
TJ	Transitional Justice mainstreaming Gender
TRC	Truth and Reconciliation Commission
UIS	UNESCO Institute of Statistics
UN	United Nations
UNDP	United Nations Development Program
UNESCO	United Nations Educational, Scientific and Cultural Organization
UNHCR	United Nations High Commissioner for Refugees
UNICEF	United Nations Children's Fund
UNIFEM	United Nations Development Fund for Women
UR	University of Rwanda
USA	United States of America
USAID	United Stated Agency for International Development
VAW	Violence Against Women
VRA	Vice Rector Academic

Preface

This book celebrates a significant initiative supporting social change in Rwanda, the introduction of a master's program in gender, culture and development, and in so doing acknowledges many of those pioneers involved in its inception in early 2011. These include graduates who were part of the first cohort of students as well as academics involved in developing and offering subjects in the first weeks of the program.

Many thousands of women took on the role of heads of household and key community leadership positions after the death, imprisonment and escape of men during and immediately after the Rwandan Genocide in 1994. Laws, policies and practices in place at the time favoured male children over female, and men over women, in most aspects of social and domestic life. Legislative changes to support equal status for women, for example in the inheritance of land, began to be implemented in the early years of the 21st century and required a significant shift in administrative processes as well as in societal attitudes. Similarly, the importance of education for girls and the need for practical measures, such as dedicated toilet facilities and safe transport to school, became a key message in Rwanda, echoing a message promulgated by the United Nations Educational, Scientific and Cultural Organization (UNESCO). At the same time, gender-based violence was recognised as a major deterrent to the development of a nation espousing principles of equality.

In this context, the Kigali Institute of Education (KIE—now part of the national University of Rwanda—UR) supported the development of a master's program in gender, culture and development (now MSocSciGD) to be offered beginning in early 2011. This was designed not only as an awareness raising program, giving ideas for policy development and implementation, but it was also to be a program of education, based on feminist pedagogy, instilling the value of evidence-based practice. More than forty students were admitted to the first cohort, each keen to contribute to the societal change inherent in these legislative and policy changes, and on graduation determined to be involved whether at a local, national or international level.

The idea of documenting the background and aspirations of these students as a record of a point in time arose in the first instance from discussions with them. In 2011, all but one of the enrolled students agreed to be interviewed or to write their own profile and most agreed to be photographed. The structured interviews sought information on a range of topics, sensitive to the reality that questions relating to family and schooling would be distressing to some students, who would prefer not to provide those details. The topics covered included biographical details, family and roles, schooling experiences, professional career, research interests, future plans, role models and mentors and perceptions of leadership. The intention was always to make these public in some way and in so doing, allow the stories of these inspirational people to emerge as tales of leadership. At the time, funds were not available for the production of a book, and so the possibility of creating this valuable historical record seemed to recede.

Then, in 2017, Professor Shirley Randell, the foundation director of the program, saw the possibilities that online open access publishing offered. Following discussions with her colleague Dr Hilary Yerbury, one of the first academic volunteers to teach the program in Kigali, who also has experience in online open access publishing, the seeds for this book were sown. It would place the stories of the first cohort of students and graduates within a conceptual frame that included the accounts and learnings of the academics involved in subject development and teaching in the first weeks of the program in 2011. Thus, the book presented here comprises two sections: the first comprises eight chapters, covering the genesis of the program of education, reflections from academics on feminist approaches to education and their implications, as well as a glimpse of the contested nature of feminist scholarship and of the international policy debates on girls and women in education; the second comprises the stories of the first students and graduates first told in 2011.

The updating of the students' and graduates' stories and their preparation for publication was a lengthy process, begun in 2017, pursued during 2018 and finalised in 2019 and 2020. The students, now graduates, are dispersed, not just in Rwanda and neighbouring countries, but also in Europe, North America and other parts of Africa. Some have retained close ties with each other and with Professor Randell, whereas others have not; some are active in social media and others leave no trace; a few are public figures, and some have disappeared from the radar. The stories presented here carry the date they were developed and validated by the individual; whilst some chose to present their story from 2011, others included revisions right up to the deadline of 1 August 2019, with a couple beyond that date. Each story is annotated to give its provenance.

Thus, this book presents an unparalleled mix of aspiration and achievement, of feminist theory and practice. It does not claim to be complete or final, nor is it a snapshot of a single point in time. All the contributions are informed by a set of common experiences, but each writer presents her (or his) own perspective. This is clearly evident in the short chapters written by the women who brought their diverse scholarly backgrounds together in their passion for the development of other women and men, in an empowering, feminist, educational experience. This mix of experiences and the diversity of writings make the book a challenging read and an invaluable resource for anyone interested in research-based approaches to social change, the weaving of personal experience into scholarly reflections and in insights into leaders working towards gender equality, a policy area which affects social relationships throughout a society, including at the most intimate level.

Shirley Randell
Sydney

PART I

Academic Reflections

Establishing the Centre for Gender, Culture and Development at the Kigali Institute for Education

Shirley Randell

Abstract

This chapter describes the establishment of the Centre for Gender, Culture and Development at the Kigali Institute of Education in the Rwandan context of strong support from the President, Government and international development agencies for gender equality. The Centre and its graduates have played an important role in national development and Rwanda's achievement of the UN Millennium Development Goals (MDGs).

The Context

Rwanda is well known around the world for its high level of participation of women in economic and democratic development. Rwanda's enviable reputation has arisen largely because of the extraordinary political will for gender equality and women's empowerment (GEWE) in Rwanda led by President Paul Kagame. He recognised the part women played in the 1990–94 struggle for Tutsis in the diaspora to return to Rwanda. After the genocide against the Tutsis and moderate Hutus in 1994, the social structure across the country was in disarray. Over 70 per cent of the population were women, with men killed, in prison or fled. The destruction of social arrangements pushed Kagame to acknowledge

---

How to cite this book chapter:
Randell, S. 2021. Establishing the Centre for Gender, Culture and Development at the Kigali Institute of Education. In: Randell, S., Yerbury, H. and Escrig-Pinol, A. (eds.) *Gender and Learning in Rwanda.* Pp. 3–16. Sydney: UTS ePRESS. DOI: https://doi.org/10.5130/aag.a. License: CC BY-NC-ND.

that it was critical that Hutu and Tutsi women take over the work carried out previously by their husbands, fathers and brothers, and work together in reconciliation and for the reconstruction of Rwanda.

In 2019, Rwandan women were 61 per cent of parliamentarians, heading the world in parliamentary representation, and women hold many senior roles in the public service and non-government associations (NGOs). Rwanda also has a Constitution that requires 30 per cent of all decision-making positions to be held by women and a gender monitoring office to monitor progress towards gender equity (Republic of Rwanda, 2008a). There is a Gender Policy published by both the Ministry of Education (Republic of Rwanda, 2008b) and the Ministry of Gender and Family Promotion (Republic of Rwanda, 2010a) and a Girls' Education Implementation Strategy (Republic of Rwanda, 2010b). Government departments employ gender officers, and universities and other educational institutions appoint students as Ministers of Gender to deal with gender issues. International NGOs (INGOs) have gender units and ensure gender equality in their programs. President Paul Kagame makes frequent pronouncements on gender equality and advocates that women and men have to work together for their country's development. In November 1999 at the official opening of a gender-training workshop for Parliamentarians, he said:

> The question of gender equality in our society needs a clear and critical evaluation in order to come up with concrete strategies to map future development, in which men and women are true partners and beneficiaries. My understanding of gender is that it is an issue of good governance; good economic management; and respect for human rights. (Izabiliza, 2004, p.3)

It was partly in response to that call for evaluation, and so that other countries might learn from Rwanda's unique situation, that in 2007 UNIFEM (the United Nations Fund for Women) gave a grant to the Rwandan Women's Parliamentary Forum (RWPF) to conduct an International Conference on 'Gender, Nation Building and the Role of Parliaments'. The attendance consisted of over 400 delegates from across the world. The women Parliamentarians of Rwanda commissioned me as Netherlands Development Organisation Rwanda (SNV)'s senior gender advisor to prepare a comprehensive report for delegates that would review Rwanda's progress towards GEWE. I worked with my Rwandan colleague, Ambassador Joy Mukanyange, to critically examine gender progress in all sectors. The late Judith Kanakuze, then President of RWPF, organised for the review to be published 'because it has proved to be an excellent assessment of what we were able to achieve, with Government commitment and collaboration from all of our Parliamentary colleagues, both men and women, over the last ten years' (Randell & Mukanyange, 2007, p. viii). Indeed, the late Senator Aloisea Inyumba, the first Minister for Gender and Social Affairs in Rwanda, a distinguished Parliamentarian, carried the report with her, referring to it as her 'second Bible' because of the comprehensive data it made available on the contribution that women at all levels had made to nation building in Rwanda.

At the end of 2007 when my three-year contract with SNV Rwanda was completed and I had planned to retire to Australia, Kanakuze and Inyumba on behalf of RWPF invited me to consider returning to Rwanda to work with them to establish a centre for excellence in governance in the Parliament. They planned to allocate the unexpended UNIFEM funds committed for the conference to this project, so I agreed to a second assignment in the country I had grown to love. Unfortunately, following my return to Kigali, and after we had prepared a concept note and budget, UNIFEM failed to approve the transfer of conference funds to a consultancy. They prepared a request to the United Nations in New York for the new position to be approved. Knowing this would be a lengthy process, the alternative of establishing a centre for gender studies in one of the universities was proposed by RWPF.

Genesis of the Centre for Gender Studies

The concept of a gender studies centre was appealing to all of the universities approached but only one had both the commitment to support an additional centre and funds immediately available for a director. Dr George Njoroge, Rector of the Kigali Institute of Education (KIE), (now Principal of the College of Education, University of Rwanda (UR) was aware that KIE was fundamentally charged with the development of teachers as transformative agents who must be in the forefront in championing social justice. The establishment of specialised research centres was also allowed for in KIE's statutes. Further, Dr Njoroge had recently released an expatriate position in the institution's education faculty, so an academic position was available. During an informal conversation between us at a KIE graduation ceremony, he indicated interest in the concept of a centre for gender studies with a research program. He invited me to discuss the proposal with him and his management at an early meeting.

One of the powerful women's associations in Rwanda at this time was the Rwanda Association of University Women (RAUW). I was its first Secretary General and I invited three RAUW members to accompany me to the meeting with the Rector to discuss the importance of a gender studies centre in Rwanda. Dinah Musindarwezo, RAUW Awards Coordinator, had completed a Master of Gender at Sussex University, UK on a Chevening Scholarship; Alice Bamusiime, RAUW Program Coordinator, had completed a Bachelor of Gender at Makerere University in Uganda; and a RAUW member, Donatha Gihana, had completed her Bachelor of Education at KIE where she was the student Minister for Gender. They spoke convincingly to the Rector of the need for a centre and assured him that there would be many interested students with practical experience in gender units who would seek academic qualifications in the subject. The Vice Rector Academic (VRA) at the meeting said it was important, if a centre were established, to begin with a diploma and bachelor's degree before considering a master's degree. However, the rector was committed to initiating research in KIE and determined that a master's degree in gender would be a priority. He also recognised that a centre for gender studies would stimulate research in an area to which the government was fully committed. He invited me to take up the vacant position and I began the next day in April 2009 as an associate professor of education in the faculty of education to plan for the development of a gender development centre. On 1 June 2009, the KIE Academic Senate approved the establishment of the Centre for Gender Studies (CGS) with me as its first Director and with plans initially for 50 master's degree graduates/Gender and Development researchers every year from 2011. This chapter covers the establishment of the Centre over the period 2009–12, from its inception until my three-year contract was completed and the first cohort of students graduated after three semesters of study.

The Vision of the new CGS was determined with Kanakuze and Inyumba. The goal for the centre was to be an internationally known centre of excellence, producing professionally qualified academics and leaders for the public service, the private sector and civil society, in a high-quality strategic and applied research environment that engaged in policy development, multicultural exchange and community service. The Mission was to be responsive to the needs of individuals, communities, government, employers and other stakeholders in Rwanda. In addition to the development of gender expertise in academics and practitioners, it would stimulate research and documentation in key gender issues and help to build the international, regional and national networks and partnerships needed to promote GEWE, cultural exchange and sustainable development in Rwanda and eventually in the Great Lakes Region.

Garnering Support

This approval for the establishment of the centre did not mean the commitment to funding or supporting the centre. Such a centre requires people to carry out the many tasks involved in getting the centre set up as an organisation, the curriculum prepared and learning resources available and establishing a dedicated location. It also requires a significant injection of funds.

Following my appointment, I immediately began an extensive period of consultation and networking both within Rwanda and internationally to seek academic and funding support for the Centre. Gihana and I began a program of visits to the diplomatic missions, development partners, and INGOs in Kigali. While all expressed interest, no funds were forthcoming until an approach was made to the Norwegian embassy. Musindarwezo was a gender adviser for the Norwegian Agency for Development (NORAD) and a keen advocate for the Centre. It was a huge relief when funds for gender, culture and development

(GCD) were declared to be one of NORAD's 2009 priorities and our bid for support in establishing a Centre for Gender, Culture and Development (CGCD) in Rwanda was approved. The grant of USD 254,000 for implementation and development of the first master's program was successful; this included provision for 25 half scholarships for students, salaries for support staff, laptop computers and materials. Subsequently, applications to the Australian Agency for International Development (AusAID) for a USD 50,000 communication grant and USD 5,000 for the first CGCD's 2009 International Conference on Gender Centres in Africa (Nevin & Randell, 2013) were successful. The Embassy for South Africa also attracted funds from the South African Government to fund gender experts to attend and present their work at this conference.

In 2009, after weeks of persistent representations from my small office in the education faculty, the Centre was allocated a large room in the International Documentation Centre building. This gave space for the international and national volunteers who worked with me on planning, although as Director of the Centre, I was still without a private office at the end of 2009. This was my first experience of the considerable challenge that KIE administrative procedures—especially frustrating delays in recruitment, information technology (IT), finance and procurement—was to become.

The NORAD grant provided adequate funds for planning the Centre's establishment, including advertising for staff and students, after which it was expected that student fees would cover staff costs and other expenses. KIE's advertisement for staff eventually appeared once in the major Rwandan newspaper *The New Times* and resulted in no eligible applications. This limited advertising, which did not make use of the NORAD funds, was clearly insufficient, both in terms of time and the spread of newspapers in the region and I supplemented it with an advertisement for qualified gender lecturers emailed to my extensive gender network within Africa and across the world. Four staff were selected from among the most competent of those responding to my request: Dr Sipora Kisanga from Kenya, Professor Gertrude Fester-Wicomb from South Africa, Dr Anne Marie Hilsdon from Western Australia and Dr Venera Zakirova from Russia. For a variety of reasons, these appointed lecturers did not arrive in Kigali until six weeks after the teaching semester had begun in 2011 and students were already in classes.

Advice on best practice was sought from directors of gender centres and women's studies departments in the United States of America (USA), Uganda, Australia and India, and was readily forthcoming. My approaches were welcomed and led to the influx of volunteer lecturers and interns from the USA, Australia, Afghanistan, Canada, Ireland and Slovenia who visited CGCD, beginning almost immediately in 2009.

The CGCD Annual Report of 2009 documents the history of the first year (KIE, CGCD, 2009) and is elaborated upon here, with a summary of the support of volunteers, staff, students and the Centre's scholarly impact over the next three years recorded in this chapter.

The Support of Volunteers

The Centre greatly benefitted from the help and practical support of Rwandan and expatriate volunteers, including academic staff, with 31 national, regional and international volunteers from Rwanda, Uganda, Nigeria, the Netherlands, Slovenia, Italy, Australia, USA and Canada serving from 2009-12. The volunteers carried out a range of tasks, including curriculum development, cataloguing library materials, assisting with conference organisation, conducting desk research, preparing publications and supporting grant applications and consultancies. Without the support from volunteers, the development of the Centre and its programs would have been almost impossible to achieve.

Some of the early international volunteers were gender experts in their universities. In particular, Dr Jennifer Fish, Chair of Women's Studies, Old Dominion University (ODU) and Dr Sarah Ryan, University of Texas-El Paso, with four of her master's students, greatly assisted with the development of module descriptions and program specifications for undergraduate, postgraduate and certificate programs. The Master of Social Science: Gender and Development (MSocSciGD) and the Certificate for Continuing Education (CCE) program modules and specifications we had prepared were immediately accepted by KIE's Academic Board. They were validated internally and externally, approved by the KIE Senate at its September 2009 meeting and confirmed in November 2009. Final approval was given by the Higher Education Council of Rwanda, the Minister of Education and the Cabinet of the Government of Rwanda (GoR) to allow courses to begin in 2011.

The administrative staff necessary for the ongoing running of the Centre and for support to the Director were almost all volunteers. Justine Mbabazi, Esq, founder of New Generation Connect (NGC) allocated one of her staff to be an administrative volunteer every year. Two of the most valuable volunteers were Josephine Musabyimana, a legal graduate with experience as a district mayor, who undertook the role of my executive assistant for 12 months without pay. Prisca Iraguha, a teacher, was another who worked as an unpaid administrative officer and research assistant. Both of these women have since completed the MSocSciGD as recipients of a Shirley Randell scholarship. Help in managing the complex accounts was provided pro bono by local professionals for some considerable time until it was possible to provide some reimbursement. Funding for the positions of Administrative Assistant, Communication Officer, Secretary and Finance Officer was available through the NORAD grant, but the establishment of the positions themselves was not supported by the management of KIE.

The KIE library had very few gender resources prior to 2009. Significant donations were received by CGCD to establish a large collection of GCD resources, comprising over 1,000 books, 150 learning packages and 10 audio-visual items that were housed in the KIE library. Emerita Professor Anita

Clair Fellman PhD, who had recently retired as Chair of Women's Studies ODU, donated a substantial proportion of her entire personal library on gender, including complete runs of gender periodicals. Professor Lee Slater, also from ODU, and her husband, and the Rotary Club of Tyson's Corner, Virginia, organised discounts and donations and paid for the transport of a large number of these resources from the USA to Rwanda. Other materials were received from the World Bank, the USA Department of State, Washington DC, from the International Women's Tribune Centre, New York, and from individual academics and authors. Western University, Canada, made major contributions to the Centre's gender collection through a book drive. Scranton University donated its GEWE print journals which were no longer required because they were available electronically to their students. As the cataloguing services available to the KIE library were inadequate, the CGCD relied on the services of two volunteer librarians from the USA who began cataloguing donated materials and gave advice about journals. They were ably supported by Rwandan volunteer library assistants, members of RAUW and NGC, who registered the library materials and began the labelling process.

We were ready to start teaching students in the first intake into the MSocSciGD in January 2011 but the contracts for the four appointed staff were not yet finalised. This meant a reconsideration of how to offer the program. Fortunately, several gender experts were able come to Kigali and teach the classes for the first six weeks of the year. Instead of teaching subjects across the whole semester, three subjects were taught intensively for two weeks each. I had already organised for Dr Sharon Meagher, Director of Women's Studies at Scranton University, USA, accompanied by a staff colleague and 11 master's students, to visit the Centre. She came for the first two weeks of 2011 to teach the first module on Masculinities and Femininities. Her students participated in the classes which became a particularly stimulating environment for both groups, as discussed in Chapter 2. A friend from Curtin University, Dr Jaya Earnest (now Professor Jaya Dantas) with previous experience in Rwanda, conducted the next two-week module on Gender Research Methodology, and her reflections and analysis can be seen in Chapter 5.

I was particularly keen for students to study a unit on Gender and Religion given the constraints religion, culture and tradition exerted on GEWE in Rwanda. When I became aware of a recent publication on this topic, I telephoned the author, Professor Tamsin Bradley at the London Metropolitan University, UK, with an invitation for her to refine our draft module and teach it. She welcomed the opportunity but as she could only be away from her own teaching for one week, she organised for a colleague to teach the second week.

Students

Advertising for students was a challenge, similar to that involved in advertising for academic staff. Finally, KIE management agreed to advertise in all Rwandan newspapers and on television. The incentive of a 50 per cent reduction in fees for students who won the NORAD scholarships meant that over 200 applications were received. Although an intake of 25 students would have been a manageable number for the first year of a new master's program, the VRA was determined we should take 50. Selection criteria for eligible students were competence in English and IT, completion of an undergraduate degree, and evidence of contribution to GEWE. After English and computer literacy tests were administered to eligible applicants, interviews were held with the top students to assess their commitment to study and consider their experience with GEWE. Four of the final top 50 selected withdrew because of financial and health problems and four forfeited their scholarship very early, including one to take up an MGD program offered overseas and two others who accepted employment offers. Finally, 42 students were offered places in the first cohort to begin the MSocSciGD program; of these, 21 were given NORAD scholarships, with the other four scholarships being distributed later to three students from the second cohort, and one from the third cohort.

The quality of students in the first cohort was extremely high. Their ages ranged from 29 to 59. The majority were mature age with families and were in full-time employment as well as full-time students, which put them under great pressure. Many of the students had been refugees living in Uganda, the Democratic Republic of Congo (DRC), Kenya or Tanzania after their parents had fled the 1994 genocide against the Tutsi and moderate Hutus, or even before then after discrimination and earlier persecution against Tutsis. They had overcome significant trials, succeeded with their undergraduate studies, and were hungry for more education, particularly to inform their gender knowledge so they could contribute more effectively to their nation's development. The cohort included seven men, two of whom were leaders of the Rwanda Men's Resources Centre, two female parliamentarians, two doctors, the Chair of the Public Service Commission, the Chief Gender Monitor and three of her staff, one bank manager, one entrepreneur and several who held positions as gender advisers or gender consultants in their workplaces. The determination of all of them to make the most of this opportunity might be best illustrated by one large woman who broke her leg prior to the first week of the course. She was carried to and from her car to the classroom and the washroom by fellow students for six weeks until the plaster was removed. Another had HIV but was committed to her professional development and excelled in the program.

The Centre and Its Scholarly Impacts

My international and regional networks were of great benefit in creating and sustaining academic partnerships, with regular contact being made with academics and gender centres around the world, sharing publications and news, and through the Centre's Facebook page. I engaged in a vigorous lecturing program, speaking and giving presentations about Rwanda, KIE and the Centre's progress towards GEWE in Johannesburg, Kampala, Nairobi, Lagos, Senegal and Accra in Africa; in Sydney, Melbourne and Perth in Australia; in New York, Washington, Scranton, Philadelphia and Norfolk in the USA; in London and Ottawa in Canada; in Manchester, London and Sussex in the UK; in Ljubljana in Slovenia; in Mexico in Central America; and in Geneva, Switzerland. All expenditure for these overseas and regional events were either self-funded or covered by inviting organisations. Memoranda of Understanding were developed with several universities. A great disappointment to me and the international scholars and centres who supported my application at UNESCO's request for the CGCD to become a UNESCO Centre of Excellence in Gender and Education—at first submitted with support from the Rector KIE and then from UNESCO Rwanda—was not followed through because of an adverse report by KIE's internal auditor.

Several master's, PhD and postgraduate students from USA, Canada, Israel, United Kingdom, Slovenia and Italy were affiliated with KIE and CGCD while researching their theses in Rwanda. They used the Centre as a base, had access to the Centre's resource collection, consulted the KIE library, acknowledged the Centre's support, and deposited their theses and articles in the library after completion. Professor Sarah Ryan, who also taught a CCE course, made a preliminary report on the students and proposed to research our first master's students when they were in place. This was intended as a NORAD-funded research and evaluation project, titled Measuring MSocSci—seeking attitudes and practices in Rwanda and assessing the first *MSocSci Program in Gender, Culture and Development Studies*. However, because KIE had not paid the University of Texas at El Paso for her first visit, Professor Ryan was not given approval by her university to travel to Rwanda for a second time.

CGCD initiated a program of regular public lectures by visiting professors and lecturers to the Centre in order to expose staff and students from all KIE faculties and the Kigali community to gender issues. These were well attended by both staff and students of KIE, and students in particular took part in the question-and-answer sessions following each lecture. The lectures covered general subjects like 'The State of the World's Women' and 'Gender and Development in Theory and Practice' and more specific topics like 'Gender, Sex and Violence: Africa on Screen'. Other public lectures were prepared by visitors such as Professor Ryan, Sarah Morison and Victoria Trabosh from the USA; Justine Mbabazi Esq from Afghanistan; and Dr Marion Gibson from Ireland but could not be integrated into an already full KIE lecture schedule. These were then hosted by RAUW.

Three research grants were won by CGCD. The National University of Rwanda (NUR) Gender Consultancies (NUR/Sweden grant) produced two reports that were well received by the university: *The Final Reports of the Gender Consultancies for the National University of Rwanda: Part 1: NUR Gender Baseline Survey 2010, NUR Gender Audit 2010, NUR Strategic Plan 2011-2015, NUR Action Plan 2011-2015 and Part 2: NUR Gender Policy* (Randell, 2010). The second grant was for the Forum for African Women Educationalists (FAWE) Regional Program for *Strengthening Gender Research to Improve Women and Girls Education in Africa: Impact of child friendly schools on girls' education in Rwanda* (Randell & Asemota, 2011a). The third, funded by the Embassy of the USA, was on *Gender Issues from Primary 6-Secondary 3 in Rwanda: A Kigali Institute of Education Interdisciplinary Study* (Malu et al., 2011).

Graduates have gone on to play an important role in their various fields of endeavour, including in national development and the achievement of the MDGs and these stories should be told. Graduates are serving in key positions in the government, private and NGO sectors within Rwanda, as well across the African Continent, with others more broadly around the world. Their success and the diverse areas they have influenced can be seen from their statements in Part 2 of this book.

An initial objective of the Rector of KIE to develop research graduates has, however, been slow to achieve. We both were keen to see Rwandans writing and publishing research about their country and hoped the MSocSciGD would stimulate this. There have been a few small steps. One graduate has published her thesis and another is jointly with her supervisor writing a research paper based on her thesis. One graduate finished a PhD in 2019 and several graduates have applications for postgraduate study in train. To date, only a few have been able to continue to do and publish research. One of the medical doctors and another graduate have been involved in very successful Rwandan and INGO research teams and have contributed to a number of scholarly published papers.

Gender expertise was provided at scores of national seminars and validation workshops conducted by government and NGO agencies, including the Ministry of Gender and Family Promotion, Ministry of Finance and Economic Planning, Rwandan National Police, Rwanda National Institute of Statistics, Gender Monitoring Office, Institute of Policy Advice and Research, UN Women, One UN, Norwegian Peoples Aid, Transparency International, Zonta International, and the Associations Defending Human Rights in Rwanda. Dr Venera Zakirova and I delivered a training program for the Rwanda National Police. This project was won competitively and conducted successfully with representatives of police, army and corrections services from 14 countries. Both the training and the resultant publications by Randell and Zakirova (2011) were well received by the Rwanda National Police and regional delegates.

An active scholarly publications program was also developed. Eleven CGCD research reports were prepared and are listed on www.shirleyrandell.com.au. The reports and other articles that were published in overseas journals are also included there. Four conferences were organised successfully by the Centre: AusAID funds supported an *International Conference on Gender Centres in Africa* in December 2009 (Nevin & Randell, 2013); an *International Conference on Women's Empowerment through Community-Based Tourism and Cultural Exchange: chances and challenges of grassroots development projects* was held in November 2010, with support from the University of Ljubljana, Slovenia (Umutesi, 2010); *Focus on Rwanda - Work in Progress; An international Conference on Gender Research and Activism in Rwanda*, took place in March 2011 with support from Old Dominion University, USA (Fellman & Randell, 2012); and AusAID supported *The National Conference on Education and Employment in Rwanda: Applied Gender Perspectives* in October 2011 (Randell & Asemota, 2011b). NORAD funds were available for a national conference to report on the first cohort's master's theses before the end of 2012, but with the change of Director and staff at that time, was not implemented.

Plans for the Future

In a handover report to the incoming Director, Dr Jolly Rubagiza, in 2012, I made several suggestions for her consideration. The master's program needed revision to provide more time for student reading. A bridging English/Computer program would greatly benefit some students returning to learning, especially those from a Francophone background. In 2011, the module descriptions and program specifications for a bachelor's degree in gender and development, prepared in 2009–10, was approved by the KIE Senate but was still to be implemented at the end of 2012. Proposals for a PhD program and a Post-Graduate Diploma in Gender and Education (PGDGD) were prepared but put on hold by KIE management. The delay of PhD program development was particularly disappointing to six prospective students, one of whom had already completed a full proposal. A course proposal developed in consultation with UN Women for capacity building programs for women Parliamentarians was partly written by the end of my term as Director.

Conclusion

A great deal was achieved in the first three years of the establishment of CGCD, and in the years since then. At the time of writing in 2019, the Centre will enrol its ninth cohort of students. Much remains to be done in relation to ensuring its sustainability, financial accountability, and publicising its work. The Centre is now well known internationally, regionally and nationally and receives many visitors and researchers, including both interested individuals and organisations.

The biggest challenge for the CGCD over the 2009–12 period was how to manage efficient implementation with a centralised bureaucracy and frustrating delays in decision-making. Looking back, it is clear that there was a kind of clash of cultures, between the systems of KIE and the ways of working of other organisations, especially ones based overseas, but it is not clear how this could have been resolved at the time. Even though the appointment of Dr Rubagiza—a Rwandan Director who had experience of KIE's administration as head of department and supervisor of a key project—was an excellent one, she experienced many similar challenges from management that were faced in the first years.

With the amalgamation of all public universities in 2013, including KIE into the national University of Rwanda (UR), and the renaming and repositioning of CGCD to Centre of Gender Studies in the reorganised Faculty of Arts and Social Sciences, College of Education, the Centre is on track to continue to fulfil its vision and mission and achieve its objectives. This will need the ongoing support of the UR Vice Chancellor, the College Principal, Dean and executive and the continuing generous support of national, regional and international partners. The graduates from the first and following cohorts continue to lead progress in GEWE in Rwanda with many of them spreading the reach of the Centre across the African continent and internationally. The stories of the students in the first cohort, which are the main feature of this publication, alongside reflections from some of the first academic leaders of the Centre, provide insights into the passion for scholarship and social change which drove its inception.

References

Fellman, A and Randell, S (eds) 2012, *Focus on Rwanda: A Conference on Gender Research and Activism: Proceedings*, 11–12 March 2011, SRIA Rwanda Ltd, Kigali, Rwanda. Available at: http://www.millennia2015.org/files/files/Publications/Conference_Rwanda_Research_and_Activism_EntireProceedings_final_for_printing_2012.pdf [Accessed 03/27/20].

Izabiliza, J 2004, *The Role of Women in Reconstruction: Experience of Rwanda*, http://www.unesco.org/new/fileadmin/MULTIMEDIA/HQ/SHS/pdf/Role-Women-Rwanda.pdf [Accessed 03/27/20]

Kigali Institute of Education, Centre for Gender, Culture and Development 2009, *Annual Report 2009*, KIE, CGCD, Kigali, Rwanda.

Malu, KF, Randell, S, Buhigiro, L, Mahuku, R, Niyomugabo, C and Yanzigiye, B 2011, *Re-Imagining Re-Search at the Middle Level: School Dropouts and Sanitary Pads in Rwanda—Implications for the United States and other African Nations*, KIE, CGCD, Kigali, Rwanda.

Nevin, C and Randell, S (eds) 2013, *Focus on Gender Centres in Africa: Proceedings of an International Conference*, 7–8 December 2010, SRIA Rwanda Ltd, Kigali, Rwanda.

Randell, S 2010, *Final Reports of the Gender Consultancies for the National University of Rwanda: Part 1: NUR Gender Baseline Survey 2010, NUR Gender Audit 2010, NUR Strategic Plan 2011–2015, NUR Action Plan 2011–2015 and Part 2: NUR Gender Policy*, KIE, CGCD, Kigali, Rwanda

Randell, S and Asemota, O 2011a, 'The impact of child friendly schools in Rwanda', in *Strengthening Gender Research to Improve Girls and Women's Education in Africa, FAWE Research Series* Vol. 2, pp. 62–89, Forum for African Women Educationalists, Nairobi, Kenya, 2012. https://issuu.com/fawe/docs/fawe_research_series_-_volume_2__fu [Accessed 03/27/20]

Randell, S and Asemota, O 2011b, 'The FAWE/KIE/CGCD Project on strengthening gender research to improve girls' and women's education in Africa: Impact of Child Friendly Schools on Girls' Education in Rwanda' delivered at the Symposium on Education and Employment in Rwanda: Applied Gendered Perspectives, CGCD, Kigali, Rwanda.

Randell, S and Mukanyange, J 2007, 'Gender, nation building and the role of Parliaments', *The 2007 Women Parliamentary International Conference, 22–23 February 2007*, SNV Rwanda and Rwanda Women's Parliamentary Forum, Kigali, Rwanda.

Randell, S and Zakirova, V 2011, The Role of Security Organs in Prevention and Response to Gender-Based Violence and Peacekeeping in Africa and International Level: Part 1: Analytical Review of Existing Data, Policies, Reports and Legal Frameworks; Part 2: Gender Analysis of the Role of Security Organs in Prevention and Response; Part 3: Security Organs Action Plan. SRIA Rwanda Ltd, Kigali, Rwanda

Republic of Rwanda 2008a, *National Constitution*, Kigali, Republic of Rwanda.

Republic of Rwanda Ministry of Education 2008b, *Girls' Education Policy*, Kigali, Republic of Rwanda.

Republic of Rwanda Ministry of Education 2010a, *Girls Education Implementation Strategy*, Kigali, Republic of Rwanda.

Republic of Rwanda, Ministry of Gender and Family Promotion 2010b, *National Gender Policy*, Kigali: Republic of Rwanda.

Umutesi, D 2010, 'Tourism: Women empowerment in light of community based tourism', *The New Times*, Kigali, Rwanda, 24 November. https://www.newtimes.co.rw/section/read/96083 [Accessed 03/27/20]

Contributor Biography

Professor Shirley Randell AO, PhD was the founding director of the Centre for Gender, Culture and Development at the Kigali Institute of Education. After over 20 years of senior policy and administrative work at Commonwealth, State and Local Government levels in Australia, she has provided specialist technical assistance to governments and agencies in Africa and the Asia Pacific Region over the last 20 years. She is a leading expert in public sector and institutional reform, teacher education, gender mainstreaming and human rights in developing countries.

The Challenges of Using a Feminist Pedagogical Approach

Sharon M. Meagher

Abstract

The introduction of a pathbreaking new master's degree in Gender, Culture, and Development required a pedagogy to match its program contents. Since the aim of the program was to cultivate the next generation of leaders with the knowledge, vision, and skills to not only implement the United Nations Millennium Development Goals (UN MDGs) but to set the future goals and agenda, students needed to experience an educational setting that was empowering. As such, we introduced feminist pedagogy into the first seminar, defining feminist pedagogy as the 'extent to which a community of learners is empowered to act responsibly toward one another and the subject matter and to apply that learning to social action' (Shrewsbury, 1997, pp. 166–173). But how do we introduce feminist pedagogy in a large class where many students had previously been subjected to the passive, rote memorisation teaching utilised in most educational systems in which adult students would have participated, especially given the popularity of what Paolo Freire would call the 'banking method of education' in colonial regimes? We responded to that challenge by being as transparent as possible in our teaching, and by modelling feminist pedagogy in all that we did.

I had the privilege of being invited by Professor Shirley Randell to work with a team of talented feminist professors to develop the curriculum for the new master's degree in Gender, Culture, and Development at the Kigali Institute

---

How to cite this book chapter:
Meagher, S. 2021. The Challenges of Using a Feminist Pedagogical Approach. In: Randell, S., Yerbury, H. and Escrig-Pinol, A. (eds.) *Gender and Learning in Rwanda*. Pp. 17–25. Sydney: UTS ePRESS. DOI: https://doi.org/10.5130/aag.b. License: CC BY-NC-ND.

of Education (KIE). The introduction of this path-breaking new master's degree required a pedagogy to match its program contents. Since the aim of the program was (and remains) to cultivate the next generation of leaders with the knowledge, vision, and skills to not only implement the UN MDGs but to set the future goals and agenda, students needed to experience an educational setting that was empowering. As such, we introduced feminist pedagogy into the first seminar, defining feminist pedagogy initially as the 'extent to which a community of learners is empowered to act responsibly toward one another and the subject matter and to apply that learning to social action' (Shrewsbury, 1997, p. 166). But how do we introduce feminist pedagogy in a large class where many students had previously been subjected to the passive, rote memorisation teaching utilised in most educational systems in which adult students would have participated, especially given the popularity of what Paolo Freire would call the 'banking method of education' in colonial regimes (1970; 1993, pp. 72–75)? We responded to that challenge by being as transparent as possible in our teaching, and by modelling feminist pedagogy in all that we did.

One important way to both model feminist pedagogy and to develop and strengthen a feminist learning community was to bring students and instructors together to learn from one another. I travelled to Rwanda a few times; during the first visit, I offered an introductory lecture to introduce key concepts in feminist thought and their relevance to global development to Professor Randell's colleagues and some prospective students at the Kigali Institute of Education. I then returned with a group of undergraduate students from the University of Scranton (where I directed the Women's Studies program at the time), who joined the Rwandan student cohort for the first two weeks of the first course in the new master's degree program. Some of the instructors hired to teach the remainder of that course as well as future courses in the new master's degree also sat in on the classes. The University of Scranton undergraduates contributed to the class, in that they were used to the expectations of active participation and student ownership of knowledge that feminist pedagogy demands. They therefore modelled it for the students, particularly in small group discussions. An additional benefit was that Rwandan students who were not native English speakers had the opportunity to practice with fluent English speakers, as English was the official instructional language. Scranton undergraduate students learned side-by-side their Rwandan counterparts. While the Scranton students had a stronger background in feminist theory and had native English proficiency, they lacked 'real world' experience, especially in terms of how gender issues affect people and policies in the developing world. The KIE master's degree students were all working adults with a great deal of real world experience, but some of them needed assistance, either in their introduction to gender theory or (in the case of those trained in francophone systems) with English language proficiency.

The faculty teamed together to employ feminist participatory pedagogies in which students taught and learned from one another as well as from faculty members. Working with an international group of instructors hired to teach in the program ensured that we developed some consistent vocabulary and feminist pedagogical practices that could be carried forward throughout the entire degree program.

So just what vocabulary and practices did we introduce, and how? The first course for the first cohort of the master's degree in Gender, Culture, and Development was called 'GCD 601: Theories of Masculinities and Femininities' and was offered in January 2011. The course description in the syllabus read as follows: 'This foundation course will explore various theories informing social assumptions about masculinities, femininities, sexualities, and transgender identities as they are understood in specific development contexts. Concepts such as sex, gender, sexual orientation, and gender identity will be the groundwork for students' theoretical knowledge that will inform the research component of their graduate studies. Gender Studies as a field aims that both male and female students make strong personal connections between classroom material and their own experience while developing an understanding of and respect for cultural diversity. Students will present individual research on theories of masculinities and femininities using technology and oral communication skills.' One key to feminist pedagogy is the ability to make connections between course material and personal experience. Another is for students to take ownership of their learning.

We aimed to accomplish both by being transparent with the students about these key goals, first by noting them in the syllabus itself and second by structuring assignments in ways that required active learning, independent and collaborative thinking, and connection making between course content and the lives of the men and women enrolled in the class. Making such connections entailed taking seriously the feminist claim that the 'personal is political' (and explaining what that phrase means), but it also encouraged reflection on how theory can and is translated in social and political practices that can make a difference in both socio-economic policy and our everyday lives. One learning objective noted in the syllabus was that students would learn 'to understand connections between specific gender theories and diverse forms of social action in women's and men's movements, both in Africa and internationally'. The initial readings also focused on feminist pedagogy itself so that students could reflect on how and why the course and its assignments were structured as they were.

While these are pedagogical strategies that I employ in all of my teaching, they took on particular relevance in the context of the launch of the new master's degree program, given the challenges presented. First, most of the Rwandan students had no knowledge or experience of any type of active learning teaching methodologies, including feminist pedagogy. While most school systems around the globe employed what Paulo Freire called 'the banking method', that was acutely true in the colonial school systems where most of the students had studied prior to enrolment in this new master's degree program. 'The banking method' refers to any teaching methodology that holds that the teacher is the owner of all knowledge and that the students are empty vessels. Lecturing is the primary mode of teaching, as the teacher pours his or her knowledge into the empty vessels. Rote memorisation is emphasised over critical thinking and reflection (Freire, 1970; 1993, pp. 72–75).

I began the first class by assigning Carolyn Shrewsbury's article 'What is Feminist Pedagogy?' and bell hooks' 'Toward a Revolutionary Feminist Pedagogy' (1989, pp. 49–54). I noted that Shrewsbury argues that feminist pedagogy 'begins with a vision of what education might be like' (1997, p. 166). I take seriously bell hooks' admonition that 'In the feminist classroom, it is important to define the terms of engagement, to identify what we mean when we say that a course will be taught from a feminist perspective. Often the initial explanations about pedagogy will have a serious impact on the way that students experience a course' (1989, p. 48). And so I defied student expectations that I would just lecture at them, asking the students to join me in developing that vision for the master's program, asking them, 'What are your hopes and goals for this course and for your overall master's program?' Based on their contributions, we then discussed three key concepts: power, community, and leadership.

If, following Freire as well as bell hooks, we define power in terms of energy rather than domination, what does it mean to be empowered (in the classroom and outside of it)? bell hooks argues that '… to teach in a way that liberates, that expands consciousness, that awakens, is to challenge domination at its very core. It is this pedagogy that Paulo Freire calls "education as the practice of freedom"' (1989, p. 50). Shrewsbury argues that the feminist commitment to the empowerment of students commits us to a set of classroom strategies and pedagogies that: 1) encourage students to develop individual and collective goals; 2) 'develop the students' independence'; 3) make everyone 'stakeholders'; 4) develop skills; 5) 'reinforce and enhance self-esteem'; and 6) 'expand knowledge of the subject matter' (Shrewsbury, 1997, pp. 168–9). The initial question began the process of asking students to develop their own goals and to make them all stakeholders.

Following Shrewsbury, we discussed community, and what it meant to create a learning community within the cohort, arguing that we had to balance community and individual rights (1997, p. 170). These claims provided an opening for us to discuss rules of engagement in the classroom that were noted in the syllabus (but also open to discussion and revision): 'Creating a positive learning environment is the responsibility of all students. Students should: freely share their ideas during discussion; listen respectfully to all students in order to understand their points of view; allow others time to express themselves without disruption; feel free to debate issues and disagree respectfully; value the worth of each individual student, acknowledging that others' worldviews and beliefs may be different from yours but no less valuable'. Students also were asked to use gender-inclusive language. One way that we summarised the aim of feminist pedagogy was to talk about the ways the feminist pedagogy encourages and promotes leadership. 'Leadership is the embodiment of our ability and our willingness to act on our beliefs' (Shrewsbury, 1997, p. 171).

Although many students were not used to working in small groups or taking leadership in the classroom, most of the students held leadership positions in their work in Rwanda. With the help of facilitators, groups developed their own goals for the course and for the master's degree program, which were then shared with the whole class. The class agreed on the following goals for the course: 1) understand gender theory and its relation to practice; 2) understand feminism; 3) strengthen capacity in gender and women's issues; and 4) share diverse experiences with the class. The class agreed on the following goals for the master's degree program: 1) understand gender theory and its relation to practice; 2) become qualified as a gender expert; 3) get certified as a gender expert; 4) become role models for gender justice in community to make positive change; 5) understand feminism; 6) strengthen capacity in gender and women's issues; 6) and empower ourselves through acquisition of skills and knowledge so that we can affect others.

Although the students wanted to become certified as gender experts through their completion of the master's degree program, few students had had any prior knowledge of feminist theory and practice. Building a learning community therefore entailed a great deal of initial focus on the introduction of key concepts on gender and feminism generally, as well as their link to global development issues. We began with several readings that introduced the concepts of 'gender', 'gender inequality', 'gender roles', and 'feminism'.

Many students resisted the idea that any aspect of gender might be socially constructed rather than 'God given'. I was not surprised by this reaction, as I had encountered it in the initial program lecture I had made at KIE the year before, and in classrooms in the United States too. At that lecture at KIE, there were students from several sub-Saharan nations. When they challenged the claim that at least some aspects of gender were socially constructed, I invited them to think about gender roles, and to tell me things that were 'naturally' women's work and things that were 'naturally' men's work. One woman immediately replied, 'well, construction is definitely men's work!' But others were perplexed by that claim, saying, 'in my country, the building of the thatched roofs on our homes is definitely women's work, as it is akin to weaving, and THAT is women's work!' I shared this story with the class, and there were knowing nods. They then volunteered other examples where gender roles vary culturally. These counterclaims helped to make my point, that the ascription of gender roles varies from culture to culture, but that we take engrained cultural practices as givens and therefore assume them to be natural.

Feminist pedagogy demands active listening on the part of the instructors as well as the students. Such listening requires attentiveness and respect for other cultures and for students' own knowledge. By encouraging examples from their own knowledge and experience, students were able to themselves see the social constructions that had previously been invisible to them. I then asked the students to reflect on what difference gender roles make. Students were then able to make sense of an assigned reading that linked gender and development. If gender rather than talent and ability determines type of work and workload, then gendered roles create a hierarchy of valued and non-valued work: 'in every country the jobs done predominantly by women are the least well paid and have the lowest status' (Momsen, 2010, p. 3) and women are more likely to do unpaid work than are men. The gendered division of labour affects economic development policies and practices such that men and women often are affected differently by development.

While I wanted to place points made in a global context, I also used and encouraged students' use of examples from Rwanda. While mainstream development theories and practices often have resulted in gender inequities that cause greater negative impact on women, the empowering aspect of feminist analysis is that it provides not only a critique but also points us towards solutions. For example, if we are attentive to the questions: Whose knowledge? Whose development? Then development planning and processes can ensure that appropriate knowledge and expertise informs policy and practice. While gender roles often lead to inequalities, role differentiation also creates differential knowledge and expertise that can be tapped rather than ignored. I found a great positive example in Rwanda. Gender differences in knowledge of plants is an example of the gender division of labour. In Rwanda, 'researchers used the knowledge of women farmers to develop new varieties of beans' which produced a consistently higher yield 'than those of male farmers' partly because of the women's knowledge of the local farming ecosystem' (USAID, 2001, quoted in Momsen, 2010, p. 148).

We studied the UN MDGs and their alignment with Rwanda 2020, the national economic and political development plan. Students were justly proud of the fact that they were part of a country that had embraced goals that could reverse gender inequities and promote development by embracing the knowledge and abilities of both men and women. Yet I also raised a critical question for their consideration. In Rwanda Vision 2020, there are both goals to move away from subsistence agriculture and to eliminate gender inequality. I asked whether these goals might potentially conflict, given that the majority of subsistence farmers in Rwanda were women. Certainly, having the goal of gender equality would help place a focus on the possible displacement of women as a consequence of the goal to eliminate subsistence farming, but how could such be assured? Burn argues that there is social science evidence that shows that men's status has usually risen as economies move from subsistence agricultural systems to 'settled', market-based systems (2005, p. 21). Could Rwanda buck that trend?

As an instructor who is a US native and white, I had to examine my own privilege daily, working to be as attentive to my students and their needs as possible. It also was important for students to understand privilege and how it works in social systems. Like students in the United States, many Rwandan students shared the misconception that feminism was about male bashing, as they failed to understand that feminism is a critique of systems of oppression rather than individual persons. I assigned Stephen Johnson's essay on the systemic nature of patriarchy to help us think through the complex relationship between the roles that individuals can and do play in perpetuating oppressive systems and ways that they can disrupt them as well. Johnson uses the metaphor of playing the board game *Monopoly* to explain how oppressive systems such as patriarchy provide the rules of the game, and that so long as we play the game and fail to question the rules, we will perpetuate the game. Just as well-meaning people can become greedy players when playing the game *Monopoly* because they are 'just following the rules', so we are often complicit in systems of oppression when we fail to question the rules of the system that oppresses (Johnson, 2014, pp. 26–47). Although not all of the Rwandan students were familiar with the board game, they quickly found other metaphors (including another game, but I can't remember its name) that helped them understand the concept.

My challenge as a feminist instructor is to help students move beyond popular misunderstandings of feminism to a more nuanced view that is not focused on the solipsistic individual. Feminist pedagogy aids in this challenge, as it calls on instructors to engage students in ways that counter individualist as well as authoritarian teaching methodologies; it demands that students be co-learners and take responsibility for their learning.

There was a high degree of mutual learning, as we worked from the premise that 'We can say that all feminists agree that women suffer social and/or material inequities simply because of their biological identity and are committed to challenging this, but the means by which such challenges might be made are many and various' (Pilcher & Whelehan, 2004, p. 49). The cross-cultural class composed of international faculty, Rwandan students (many of whom had lived abroad), and US students created opportunity for meaningful dialogue to explore this claim. How are gender inequities play out differently in different cultures? And yet what are the points of commonality that bound us in that class to one another across national and cultural differences? How could we learn from one another and create community?

We examined the Gender Equity Index. In 2007 two countries of the Global South, Barbados and Rwanda, were in the top ten on the Gender Equity Index demonstrating that national wealth is not necessary to achieve gender equity (Momsen, 2010, p. 230). National wealth is not a predictor of a nation's ranking.

In fact, Rwanda ranked 3rd after Sweden and Finland, while the United States ranked 25th (Social Watch, 2009, p. 1). The students from the US and those from Rwanda were invited to reflect on what factors they thought accounted for the differences in ranking between the two countries.

Rwanda is often rated in the top three in terms of various global gender equity indices because of its constitutional commitment to women's participation in governance and gender equitable public policies. Indeed, Rwanda's formal commitment to gender equity far outpaces that of the US. Yet on informal measures of women's empowerment in the workplace and the household, the US measures significantly higher. These differences created much material for fruitful dialogue between the American and Rwandan students. The combination of readings, class discussion, and educational field experiences encouraged students to examine how various factors impact both the perception and experience of gender equality and the quality of women's lives. We asked questions such as: To what extent do formal declarations and goals of gender equality positively affect women's lives? What are the causes of women's relatively low status and power? What are the solutions?

Of course, we could not answer all of those questions in one course, but the entry course set an agenda for the master's degree program, and as you will learn from other reports and interviews in this volume, shaped both the research and post-degree work of many program graduates. Neither I nor any of the other instructors claimed to have all the answers. The task of the students was to find their own answers, and to use the lens of feminism to help them see what may have been hidden to them before. Formal goals such as the UN MDGs demand local interpretation and implementation if they are to have transformative power in the actual lives of local girls and women.

In this sense, I think that we can say that feminist pedagogy travels well because it entails a commitment to mutual learning and respect. The juxtaposition of the examples of the US and Rwanda both illustrated what we needed to learn from one another about how to best achieve gender equality but also the global challenges in doing so. Cultural differences as well as differences in age and experience were bridged through dialogue. Although many of the Rwandan students were initially motivated to enrol in the program to get credentialed so that they could obtain a new position and were sceptical about both feminism and feminist pedagogy, the course goals that they developed in the first two weeks of the course demonstrated the fact that they were opening up to new possibilities, new ways of understanding and seeing the world—ways that connected their own experiences to social, political, and economic policy in a way that empowers them to lead to transform Rwanda.

References

Burn, S 2005, *Women Across Cultures*, A Global Perspective, McGraw-Hill, New York.

Freire, P 1970; 1993, *Pedagogy of the Oppressed*, 30th Anniversary Edition, Trans. Myra Bergman Ramos. Intro Donald Macedo. Continuum Press, New York.

hooks, bell 1989, 'Toward a revolutionary feminist pedagogy', in *Talking Back: Thinking Feminist, Thinking Black*, South End Press, Boston, pp. 49–54.

Johnson, A 2014, 'Patriarchy, the system: An It, Not a He, a Them or an Us', in *The Gender Knot: Unravelling Our Patriarchal Legacy*, 3rd edn., Temple University Press, Philadelphia, pp. 26–47.

Momsen, J 2010, *Gender and Development*, 2nd edn., Routledge, New York.

Pilcher, J and Whelehan, I 2004, 'Feminisms', *50 Key Concepts*, Sage, London, pp. 48–51.

Shrewsbury, C 1997, 'What is Feminist Pedagogy?' *Women's Studies Quarterly*, vol. 25, no. 1/2, pp. 166–173.

Social Watch 2009, *Gender Equity Index 2009*. http://www.socialwatch.org/node/11562 [last accessed 03/27/20].

Contributor Biography

Sharon M. Meagher, PhD is Professor of Philosophy and former Vice President for Academic Affairs and Dean of the Faculty at Marymount Manhattan College in New York City. Her prior appointments include Dean of the College of Arts & Sciences at Widener University in Chester, PA (USA) and Chair of the Department of Latin American Studies and Women's Studies at The University of Scranton (PA, USA). She served as a Visiting Professor in the Centre for Gender, Culture, and Development, Kigali Institute of Education, Kigali, Rwanda, 2010–2011.

Feminist Research in Rwanda: Challenges and Importance

Anita Clair Fellman

Abstract

The building of a feminist scholarly tradition, never easy, is especially challenging in a traumatised, post-conflict nation like Rwanda with under-resourced young universities. So much about Rwandan women's lives, past and present, has still to be learned, but pressing needs for economic development and poverty alleviation help determine research topics, as does the government's distrust of alternative narratives of recent history. Many of the Centre's students were already responsible for implementing gender policies in both government and NGOs, so it was essential to help them acquire skills of gender analysis and knowledge of feminist scholarship to facilitate coherent policymaking.

No doubt there is truth in the adage 'A little knowledge is a dangerous thing'. At times though, it is that 'little knowledge' that permits us to take on tasks that wiser heads shy away from.

When I went to Rwanda as a Fulbright Specialist in 2011, I had a fairly good knowledge of the existing scholarship on women and gender in Rwanda but had been to the country just once before for 10 days and had done no research there. I had perceived from the scholarly literature that there were many aspects of Rwandan women's history and current lives that had not been studied and

---

How to cite this book chapter:
Fellman, C. 2021. Feminist Research in Rwanda: Challenges and Importance. In: Randell, S., Yerbury, H. and Escrig-Pinol, A. (eds.) *Gender and Learning in Rwanda.* Pp. 27–42. Sydney: UTS ePRESS. DOI: https://doi.org/10.5130/aag.c. License: CC BY-NC-ND.

certainly not from a feminist perspective. Since I was to be associated with the new Centre for Gender, Culture and Development (CGCD) at the Kigali Institute of Education (KIE), which hoped to become a central locus of feminist research in Rwanda, it made sense to me to take on as my Fulbright project the organising (with the aid of the staff at the Centre and the administration of KIE, as well as the financial and strategic support by the Provost of Old Dominion University (ODU) and the Chair of its Women's Studies Department) of what would be the first interdisciplinary conference on gender research in Rwanda, to both highlight and encourage a wider range of research projects.

'Focus on Rwanda: A conference on gender research and activism', which took place on 11–12 March 2011 in Kigali, included presentations, not only by those doing traditional scholarly research, but also by people who were working 'on the ground' on gender issues, whether in government ministries, civil society groups or nongovernmental organisations (NGOs). The hope was that the two camps would feed each other, providing observations and data for researchers on the one hand and on the other, inspiration for the gender activists to think about systematising their data gathering in future so as to produce formal research. Another somewhat unorthodox inclusion was a plenary session devoted to encouraging creative writing: how to free the writer within and find both support and publication outlets. Members of the inaugural class of students in the Master of Social Science (Gender and Development) program based at CGCD made a substantial contribution to the conference as presenters, moderators and volunteers. Enthusiasm was high by the end of 'Focus on Rwanda' (Fellman & Randell, 2012). We anticipated that the students would build on this experience to participate in other conferences as published feminist scholars, and that the conference itself could serve as a model for an ongoing series of such events, emanating from CGCD.

Now, eight years later, it does not seem that these hopes have been fulfilled to any marked degree in Rwanda. Under current leadership the renamed Centre for Gender Studies no longer has a strong research profile and no other entity in the country seems equipped to spearhead feminist research colloquia.[1] Trying to figure out why this is so, beyond an acknowledgment of my naivety and my implicit North American assumptions, leads us onto the complicated terrain of the challenges to doing feminist scholarship in Rwanda—and to its necessity.

Coming from a North American academic setting, I had blithely assumed that a gender studies centre would be feminist in perspective. Professor Shirley Randell, the founding director, as well as the faculty she brought in to design and teach the modules comprising the curriculum, were all feminists, but almost certainly KIE had another model in mind: that of development studies. Even in a centre for gender and development in a nation whose leaders had shown a strong commitment to gender equality, such a course of study does not necessarily signal a feminist perspective to those supporting its establishment or to those applying for admission. Indeed, at the beginning of their studies in

2011, very few of the master's students identified themselves as feminists and some in the class believed feminism to be unRwandan, a common perception. (S. Randell, 2018, personal communication, 22 Nov; Warner, 2018).

Education has been accorded an important role in Rwanda. Vision 2020, the development plan of the Government of Rwanda (GoR) launched in 2000, proposed to propel the country from poverty to a knowledge-based middle-income country in twenty years. The government is forthright in its determination to 'transform the Rwandan citizens into skilled human capital for the socio-economic development of the country' (Republic of Rwanda, 2016, p. 1). That clearly requires a rapid increase in general literacy and a larger body of university educated citizens. Toward that end, the government has eliminated tuition fees for schooling up to the level of upper secondary (save for the 'hidden' expenses of school uniforms and school supplies) and has succeeded in seeing the enrolment of girls surpass that of boys at all levels from primary to upper secondary. President Paul Kagame has proved to be an enthusiastic proponent as well of investment in tertiary education, albeit especially in science and technology. University attendance in Rwanda has had especially large gaps to overcome; by the mid 1980s, the National University had graduated only 2000 students (Mellow & Katopes, 2009, p. 55). In 2016, total enrolment in tertiary education in the nation was 90,803, divided between public universities (39,208) and private degree and diploma granting schools (51,595)(Republic of Rwanda, 2016, Table 7.1, p. 54).

Almost certainly from the government's perspective, the MSocSciGD, fits right into the plans to use an educated citizenry to help propel the nation's economic growth. Given the considerable gender policy apparatus that had been established in Rwanda by 2010, a program to train the administrators of those government ministries, agencies and organisations in gender analysis must have seemed timely. Unlike the outcomes in primary and secondary schooling—substantial drop-off rates so that 64 per cent of 15–24 year-olds have not completed primary education—(Rwanda National Education Profile 2014 Update), and university education—assessment of student learning showing disappointing levels of critical thinking abilities—(Schendel, 2015, 2016; Niyibizi et al., 2018), the government may be getting more than it had hoped for with this master's degree. Although no one had requested that the master's students be taught feminist analysis and research methods by means of feminist pedagogy, nonetheless that is what characterised this cohort's graduate education at CGCD. Is the government (or the global banks or NGOs) prepared to use any critiques of development policies the graduates may have evolved as well as their expertise in implementing them?

One might ask, so what if the government is indifferent at best to the feminist education of this cohort? Look at what has been accomplished for women and by women in Rwanda without a feminist orientation but with gender equality as a cross-cutting theme in Rwanda's long-and medium term strategies. Why then is such a perspective needed? Is this not imposing Western assumptions on African contexts? Not according to African feminists who bristle at the idea that they have had to be tutored to perceive patriarchal institutions and policies and to fight against them. (Ali, 2018; Tripp, 2017; African Feminism (AF)). The Nigerian-British feminist scholar, Amina Mama (2003, p. 105) has written and spoken often about the necessity of gender activism to be embedded in:

> gender-competent theory, research, and analysis that are fully cognizant of African realities, extend across the disciplines, and offer resources for addressing the challenge of supporting the pursuit of equitable development, from the micro-politics of individual identities to the macro-politics of global economic policies and strategic interests.

To which she adds, 'We women are in no position to deprive ourselves of the intellectual tools that can assist us in pursuit of gender justice. The arena of the intellect has been used to suppress us' (2001, p. 63). Ten years later she revisited this topic with a sobering assessment of the challenges facing feminist research in African contexts. She identifies the systemic challenges, most especially the neoliberal discourses that dominate global policy, privileging the role of the market in development, and notes the challenges to academic freedom from unstable or undemocratic regimes, describing 'sustained climates of intimidation and threat that lead many scholars to censor themselves'. Gender and women's studies' units she characterises as isolated and under-resourced: 'The occasional international grants come in, with well-intentioned expatriate experts attached'. (Mama, 2011, pp. e4–6; Barnes, 2007). Ouch! So is there any purpose then in burdening students emerging from one of these centres with an intellectual perspective that is likely to be viewed with scepticism in the actual settings in which most of them work? I would argue, emphatically yes.

Mama's reference to development policies, most often based on free-market, neoliberal premises, is key here in regard to the importance of feminist perspectives. These policies, imposed by lending organisations and donors upon virtually all developing economies and adopted by many wealthy countries as well, have nowhere succeeded in bringing entire populations out of poverty, and in fact, have contributed to growing disparities of wealth within countries and between men and women—an ever-growing feminisation of poverty. In some countries the decimation of public health and education systems, a resurgence of child poverty and the removal of social and environmental protections have been its by-products and have affected women disproportionately. (Chepyator-Thomson, 2005).

It has been postcolonial feminist activists and scholars, paying close attention to how women have fared under development policies, including those intended to bring women into legal adulthood and full economic participation, who have served among its most trenchant analysts and critics (Kelleher, 2017). They have concluded that 'legal rights alone are insufficient to fundamentally transform gendered power systems' (Berry, 2015, p. 4) and that women's power 'cannot be defined by access to resources or rights; instead it is a question of control over these things' (Mason, 1986; Malhotra & Mather, 1997, quoted in Berry, 2015, p. 5). Many feminists in the Global South, in countries heavily dependent on development assistance, suggest that the prevailing policies have goals exactly reversed; instead of chasing economic growth on the presumption that people in poor nations will ultimately benefit, the policy should be to put resources into human development, and only then will sustainable economic growth follow (Aguinaga et al., 2013).

Some of the same negative development outcomes for women are present in Rwanda too, regardless of the 'strong political will to promote gender equality', which co-exists with a strong dependence (albeit state influenced) on private sector-led growth (Debusscher & Ansoms, 2013, p. 1117; Thomas, 2018, p. 56). Wealth inequality, made possible by robust economic growth, has markedly increased in recent years, but wealth concentrated within a very small segment of the population, with limited trickle-down potential, does not bode well for sustained development (Sindayigaya, 2012; Ansoms & Rostagno, 2012). Marie E Berry (2015, p. 2-3) describes, in regard to 'ordinary' Rwandan women:

> a depressing paradox: despite the world's highest percentage of women in parliament, some of the strongest state-led efforts to promote women, and an entire government apparatus designed with gender equality in mind, profound impediments to women's equality are deeply entrenched and appear unlikely to dissipate any time soon.

These impediments include strongly embedded patriarchal family structures, with women's worth, social adulthood and legal rights dependent upon marriage (not always easy with women 50.9 per cent of the population and men often too poor to marry), troubling levels of gender-based violence, including intimate partner violence (among all social classes) despite laws against it and mechanisms for reporting it (Abari, 2017), and conventional gender-instilling ideas in the schooling that increasing numbers of girls are accessing. Women dependent on male earnings cannot afford to report beatings at the hands of their partners (Berry, 2015). Their recently won legal right to inherit land means little when the holdings increasingly are too small to provide a living or when customary land rights favouring male land tenure persist. Giving a cow to poor women in the 'one cow per family' program offers scant help to a woman on her own in a community in which milking cows is culturally coded as a male activity (Kubai & Ahlberg, 2013).[2]

What accounts for these 'depressing paradoxes'? Feminist scholars of Rwanda, most often those living and writing outside the country, have pointed out that GoR attention to gender equality is instrumental rather than foundational, and as Debusscher and Ansoms put it, 'when gender equality concerns compete with economic development and societal modernisation objectives, as framed by the government, priority is given to the latter' (2013, p. 1120). As one example, they contrast the government's 'efforts to create a business-friendly environment and to attract large-scale capital-intensive projects' with their discouragement of 'small-scale, often rural-based informal sector initiatives', where women would have a better chance of participating and from which they would likely benefit more (Debusscher & Ansoms, 2013, p. 1120; Bigler et al., 2017; Ochieng, Ouma & Birachi, 2014). In its efforts to market itself to international lending agencies, donors and investors, the GoR portrays the nation as the upcoming 'Singapore of East Africa' with clean streets and tidily dressed citizens in modern garb. The prohibition of informal work— dirty, hard to monitor and control—is part of this picture. However, facing a serious lack of formal jobs outside the dominant agricultural sector, from necessity women gravitate to the informal sector, hawking small amounts of merchandise, doing casual domestic work or laundry or sex work, all prohibited and subject to strictly enforced restrictions resulting in arrests and jail time, thereby assuring that such women remain mired in poverty. As it happens, the low-skill industries in which men cluster, driving the ubiquitous moto taxis, selling phone credit, doing construction work, etc. are less often deemed illegal (Berry, 2015, pp. 18–19).

If we care about Rwanda's future and are to gain a clear-headed understanding of what is happening there, then we need to pay attention to those who are willing to probe behind the usual emphasis on economic development plans, societal modernisation and the impressive statistics on women in governance, and to look at the condition of the vast majority of Rwandan women so as to understand the rising levels of economic inequality and potential discontent. It is these scholars who have drawn our attention to the GoR's neglect of 'invisible labour' performed by women in subsistence agriculture and care work. Their traditional responsibility for producing staple crops, combined with labour-intensive reproductive work, puts women at a disadvantage to men who are more able to participate in government-promoted agricultural modernisation and marketisation ventures, seen as one of the engines of growth. Similarly, these multiple responsibilities make them more vulnerable to exploitation as casual on-field agricultural workers in wealthier farmers' fields (Debusscher & Ansoms, 2013, p. 1122; Bigler et al., p. 25; Mutandwa & Wibabara, 2016).

Care work (household tasks and care for family and community) is similarly allowed to remain invisible. The work of maintaining a rural household in Rwanda is formidable. Only 10 per cent of households nationwide have running water, and in rural areas 55 per cent of households require travel of 30 minutes or longer to obtain water. Household electricity, while spreading in urban areas, is only to be found in 23 per cent of households overall and in only

12 per cent of rural households. Virtually no one uses electricity for cooking. Wood is the most common cooking fuel, especially in rural households (77 per cent), with another 14 per cent using some combination of straw/shrubs/grass. The labour of either women or children is required to provide these materials (NISR, 2015, pp. 21, 23–4, 25). The substantial number of women with male relatives in prison or labour camps have yet additional burdens; not only have they lost male labour, 'but have the added responsibility of trekking to prisons, bringing their husbands, brothers or fathers food and other basic necessities' (Purdeková, 2011, p. 491). Debusscher and Ansoms (2013, p. 1122) conclude that 'the Rwandan government does not question the unequal division of care work in Rwandan society, nor is care work explicitly valued. Although unpaid and informal care workers are subsidising the economy, this contribution is excluded from the definition of work in national accounts and its implications for inequality are not discussed'. When asked about including domestic labour in the GDP, one of their interviewees (2011g), a male member of Parliament, responded that the idea was '"discussed", but that it is too complicated"' (2013, p. 1122).

The unpaid appropriation of care work extends to civil society groups as well. In common with less progressive countries elsewhere in the Global South, the Rwandan government has allowed civil society groups—often but not exclusively composed of women volunteers—to provide basic care services for the elderly, bedridden and for victims of rape, domestic violence, etc. without any recognition or support. This puts the groups in a bind: 'although service delivery is critically needed in a country with so many people lacking basic services, this practice is taking civil society's energy and attention away from its research and advocacy role' (Debusscher & Ansoms, 2013, p. 1126). The government's tolerance for the continued existence of these groups sometimes depends upon the alignment of their goals with government programs, thereby discouraging autonomous actions (Ryan, 2011). This may be one of the reasons that a feminist social movement has not arisen. Women are encouraged to think about the service they can provide their country, rather than their own rights.

There are also other challenges to creating a homogeneous women's movement in a nation still struggling with forgiveness and reconciliation. In the years immediately following the genocide of 1994, Tutsi and Hutu women came together to do the basic work of cleaning up a devastated country without a functioning government. In those years 'women's organisations were some of the only cross-ethnic entities in the country, and they took the lead caring for orphans, rebuilding communities, and creating care groups for psycho-social support' (Burnet, 2012, quoted in Berry, 2017, p. 839).[3] At the same time, however, organisations created to provide support and care for victims were often specific in their categorisation, and since only Tutsi were considered officially to be victims, this allowed the groups to become ethnically homogenous. Tutsi-led organisations were better able to access international funds and to create lasting structures, accomplishments much harder for Hutu women, given the lack of funding and distrust of Hutu organising in public spaces. (Pottier, 1996, quoted in Berry, 2017). Berry, inferring from her interview subjects their ethnicity (now illegal to discuss in Rwanda), concluded that the dozens of Hutu women she interviewed 'had little social space in which to mobilize around their interests' (Berry, 2017, p. 838). Berry also draws attention to another difficult-to-discuss divide between women: that between Tutsi 'survivors' (present during the genocide) and 'returnees' (those who grew up in exile and returned to the country after 1994), with the returnees better positioned to flourish from the policies of an administration led by returnees. When combined, she concludes, 'with the regime's tight control over civil society, these hierarchies have limited women's ability to sustain cross-ethnic and cross-class collective action around shared interests, such as access to financial capital or protection against gender-based violence' (Berry, 2017, p. 839). This is in contrast to the situation elsewhere in the Global South where 'feminist praxis lays emphasis on developing counter-publics or the space of civil society. Women's groups have emerged as vital counterforces to free market programs', whether as formal organisations or spontaneously formed groups (Simon-Kumar, 2004, p. 498).

Many women's and human rights groups across the world submitted critiques of the UN's proposed 2030 Agenda for Sustainable Development (SDGs) that were to replace the Millennium Development Goals (MDGs), set to expire in 2015. One major global women's coalition argued that the report establishing the framework for the new goals did not go far enough in 'identifying how women and girls face unequal and unfair burdens in sustaining the well-being of their societies and economies in both the wage and the care economy' or their 'deeper experiences of poverty, deprivation and social marginalization' (AWID, 2013; Abelenda, 2015). Rwandan women's voices are missing from critiques like these, which resulted in some changes to the SDG's final form.[4]

Linked to the constrained role for independent civil society groups in Rwanda is the very limited scope for ordinary women to participate in creating gender policy (Debusscher & Ansoms, 2013, p. 1128). Not only control but even information flows downward more often than it moves up from the grassroots. Mechanisms of accountability, such as *imihigo* (public pledges of performance) are used to extract compliance with government policies at all levels rather than to offer officials realistic appraisals of the population's needs and responses (Purdeková). This means that even well-meaning government policy may not be understood or accepted by the majority of the population who live in rural settings. It also means that rural people's concerns and dissatisfactions (potentially regime-destabilising), not to mention their possibly helpful observations and ideas, are not solicited.

The most easily accessible far-reaching critiques of the current administration in regard to the disconnect between formal gender policies and the actual situations of poor and marginalised women, have come from feminist scholars living and writing outside the country. Even with the scholarly domination of Western feminists, not all such researchers are able to get research permits. This is partly because the GoR is rightly determined that outsiders should not build their careers on Rwandan data with no benefits to the nation, and instead encourages Western scholars to find Rwandan research partners and co-author publications with them, thereby helping Rwandans get regional and international exposure (Motlafi, 2018, pp. 15–16). At other times, if a proposed topic has the potential to contradict the government's dominant narrative about Rwanda, the foreigner may be refused a research permit or have it withdrawn midway through the research project. (Motlafi, 2018, pp. 17–18; Thomson, 2010).

Might this happen to Rwandan researchers too? It is hard to know whether scholars in Rwanda self-censor themselves in response to an authoritarian regime that prefers to set its own parameters for permitted criticism. It is no secret that there is intolerance of dissent within the country (and even from Rwandans in diaspora) as well as a curtailing of civil liberties. Regardless, the domination of feminist scholarship on Rwanda by Westerners is not healthy or desirable. Clearly, Rwandan ownership of scholarly discourses would be preferable, both because of the ethical and practical problems of 'speaking for others' and because wide-ranging and free-wheeling research by Rwandans on all aspects of their society and history could lead to better policy and to bringing the marginalised out of the shadows. There is still so much to learn about Rwandan society, past and present, from feminist perspectives; the research should not be left solely to the handful of Western scholars able to attain research permits.

Let's return now to those graduates from that inaugural cohort of master's students. Might they be the ones to spearhead a robust tradition of feminist scholarship on Rwanda? To be of the most use to their country, shouldn't they be allowed to turn their feminist gazes upon it? Just one of them has become a university lecturer or full-time researcher thus far, but at least one other of that first cohort will have completed a PhD by the time this book is published, and others are either enrolled in PhD programs or hope to be shortly. Many of the group, while not employed in academic settings, are fully engaged in feminist praxis in Rwanda, throughout Africa and beyond. By their own reckoning, they have been marked by what they learned about the social construction of gender in the Gender and Development curriculum, as well as by the gender analysis frameworks, the transitional justice module, as well as the feminist research and ethnographic methodologies, especially the art of respectful and ethical listening to their subjects. A few of the graduates sought the master's degree for credentialing purposes, having discerned from work that they had done for international NGOs, that gender was a criterion of interest to these organisations. More, however, entered the program because they already had a passion for human rights work and for correcting gender inequities that they had experienced or observed. Some had lived through the genocide of 1994 and others had been spared that only to experience the violence of 1996 in the Democratic Republic of Congo (DRC). Almost all of them have lived or worked outside Rwanda at some point in their lives, thus have had access to broader perspectives. Their master's theses, virtually all focusing on development issues, reflect what they learned in the program and what interested them, modified, of course, by what was possible to do given time and mobility constraints. These show them to be well-attuned to the poverty experienced by their countrywomen, since almost a quarter of the students chose to write on some aspect of poverty or on women's self-help efforts. Another quarter of them focused on gender-based violence, HIV/AIDS or sexuality concerns. Others focused on schooling, reproductive health, and on male socialisation and male–female household dynamics, among other topics.

These concerns are reflected in their work lives too, as described in their essays in this book. Some of them are frank in acknowledging that the few in Rwanda have been helped while the poorest are neglected, or that in order for development to be sustainable, it must include vulnerable children and single mothers, or that civil society in Rwanda needs to grow and strengthen. Many of the program's first graduates have been working persistently to deal as best they can with various facets of the gender inequities and human rights violations they see. These efforts are taking place, not only in Rwanda, but more broadly around Africa. There are some from the cohort who work or have worked for the government, but many more have taken the NGO or INGO path, either as employees or consultants, moving from organisation to organisation, sometimes elsewhere in Africa in senior positions with many people working under them. They have faced daunting situations, dealing with refugees in conflict areas or combatting Female Genital Mutilation in male dominant societies or working with traumatised survivors of atrocities. Often their self-described mode of leadership is participative and empowering—one might even say feminist.

Some have made presentations based on their work at international meetings. A few of the cohort have started their own NGOs and some of the deeply transformative projects in which these organisations have been involved have led to scholarly publications for class members (Doyle et al., 2014; 2018). Many of the gender practitioners among the cohort have fallen in love with research, seeing it as the essential complement to the practical focus of gender organisations and as a powerful tool of effective advocacy. Just one of the class—a male—has expressed a desire to be an academic. That more of them do not seem interested, at least at this time, is understandable. The women may be aware of the special challenges for female academics as highlighted in a recent article on the University of Rwanda website (UR, 2018). Perhaps they all have some inkling of how hard it is to do research as overworked lecturers in African universities starved for research funds.[5] Most of the cohort are married and they all have children. It is hard to imagine their giving up their relatively well-paid jobs as gender administrators, consultants and trainers for the poorer pay of academia.

In fact, whether or not more of them go on to study for their PhDs, if they are able to build probing feminist research into their lives as gender practitioners, then they will become what Rwanda needs most: scholar-activists.[6]

Notes

[1] In November 2017, the International Monetary Fund, the Rwandan Ministry of Gender and Family Promotion, UN Women and the Uogonzi Institute convened a peer-learning event, 'Gender equality from theory to practice', in Kigali. This was not devoted to feminist scholarship but to 'spreading best practices in promoting gender equality beyond the dissemination of theoretical approaches'. (IMF, 2017).

[2] Mann and Berry characterise programs such as the 'one cow per family', rural land reform, free primary education and the Mutuelles de Sante health care system as 'wealth sharing mechanisms' designed to defuse dissatisfaction and unrest among a peasantry that is otherwise not benefiting from development policies under which the urban elites have prospered (Mann & Berry, 2016).

[3] It should also be pointed out that the women's movement, however broadly or narrowly based, strongly advocated for the pioneering gender legislation in Rwanda: 'the 'inheritance law' of 1999, the ratification of the new constitution in 2003, the land policy of 2004, followed by the organic land law of 2005, and the proposal on gender-based violence (GBV) which became law in 2009'. (Debusscher & Ansoms, 2013, 1115).

[4] There appears to be nothing written in Rwanda comparable to the South African Master's thesis, 'A Postcolonial Feminist Critique of the 2030 Agenda for Sustainable Development: A South African Application'. (Struckmann, 2017), which is reprinted in an issue of the South African journal *Agenda: Empowering women for gender equity*, devoted to feminist examinations of the SDGs. At least one Rwandan feminist, Dinah Musindarwezo, actively participated as a critic of the proposed SDGs and published an essay in that same issue of Agenda. At the time she was Director of FEMNET (the African Women's Development and Communication Network) and was living in Kenya. (Musindarwezo, 2018).

[5] It has been estimated recently that 'sub-Saharan Africa accounts for 13.5% of the global population but less than 1% of global research output' (Fonn et al., 2018, p. 1163).

⁶ With the GoR's recent policy shift to promotion of a domestic manufacturing sector, the controversial imposition of tariffs on imported second-hand clothing and the courting of Chinese garment factories to set up shop in a Special Economic Zone, yet another fruitful area for feminist research has opened up (Behuria, 2017; Lyu, 2018).

References

Abari, N 2017, 'Rwanda's path to gender equity', *Berkeley Political Review*, 18 Oct. Available at: https://bpr.berkeley.edu/2017/10/18/rwandas-path-to-gender-equity/ [Accessed 03/27/20].

Abelenda, A 2015, 'Make watered-down SDGs work', *Alliance*, vol.20, no.4. Available at: https://www.alliancemagazine.org/feature/make-watered%E2%80%91down-%E2%80%A8sdgs-work/ [Accessed 03/27/20].

African feminism (AF) Available at https://africanfeminism.com [Accessed 03/27/20].

Aguinaga, M, Lang, M, Mokrani, D and Santillana, A 2013, 'Development critiques and alternatives: a feminist perspective', in Langand, M and Mokrani, D (eds) *Beyond Development: Alternative Visions from Latin America*, Transnational Institute, Amsterdam, pp. 41–59.

Ali, A 2018, 'We're African women and we're feminists', *Open Democracy 50.50*, 23 Jan. Available at: https://www.opendemocracy.net/5050/aisha-ali/african-women-african-feminists. [Accessed 03/27/20].

Ansoms, A and Rostagno, D 2012, 'Rwanda's Vision 2020 halfway through: what the eye does not see', *Review of African Political Economy*, vol.39, no. 133, pp. 427–450. Available at https://doi.org/10.1080/03056244.2012.710836. [Accessed 03/27/20].

AWID (Association for Women's Rights in Development) 2013, *Some reactions to the HLP Report on the Post-2015 Agenda from a women's rights perspective*. Available at: https://www.awid.org/news-and-analysis/some-reactions-hlp-report-post-2015-agenda-womens-rights-perspective [Accessed 03/27/20]).

Barnes, T 2007, 'Politics of the mind and body: gender and institutional culture in African universities', *Feminist Africa*, vol. 8, pp. 8–25. Available at: http://www.agi.ac.za/sites/default/files/image_tool/images/429/feminist_africa_journals/archive/08/fa_8_feature_article1_0.pdf [Accessed 03/27/20].

Behuria, P 2017, 'The tentative developmental state in Rwanda: from anti-manufacturing to recapturing the domestic market, *International Development LSE Blog*. Available at: http://blogs.lse.ac.uk/internationaldevelopment/2017/02/17/the-tentative-developmental-state-in-rwanda-from-anti-manufacturing-to-recapturing-the-domestic-market-2/ [Accessed 03/27/20].

Berry, ME 2015, 'When 'bright futures' fade: paradoxes of women's empowerment in Rwanda', *Signs: Journal of Women in Culture and Society*, vol. 41, no.1, pp. 1–27. Available at https://doi.org/10.1086/681899. [Accessed 03/27/20].

Berry, ME 2017, 'Barriers to women's progress after atrocity: evidence from Rwanda and Bosnia-Herzegovina', *Gender and Society*, vol.31, no.6, pp. 830–853. Available at https://doi.org/10.1177/0891243217737060. [Accessed 03/27/20].

Bigler, C, Amacker, M, Ingabire, C and Birachi, E 2017, 'Rwanda's gendered agricultural transformation: A mixed-method study on the rural labour market, wage gap and care penalty', *Women's Studies International Forum*, vol. 64, pp. 17–27. Available at: https://doi.org/10.1016/j.wsif.2017.08.004. [Accessed 03/27/20].

Chepyator-Thomson, JR (ed.) 2005, *African Women and Globalization*, Africa World Press, Trenton, NJ.

Debusscher, P and Ansoms A 2013, 'Gender equality policies in Rwanda: public relations or real transformations?' *Development and Change*, vol. 44, no. 5, pp. 1111–1134. Available at https://doi.org/10.111/dech.12052. [Accessed 03/27/20].

Doyle, K, Kato-Wallace, J, Kazimbaya, S and Barker, G 2014, 'Transforming gender roles in domestic and caregiving work: preliminary findings from engaging fathers in maternal, newborn, and child health in Rwanda', *Gender & Development*, vol.22, no. 3, pp. 515–531. Available at https://doi.org/10.1080/13552074.2014.963326 [Accessed 03/27/20].

Doyle, K, Levtov, RG, Barker, G, Bastian, GG, Bingenheimer, JB, Kazimbaya, S, Nzabonimpa, A, Pulerwitz, J, Sayinzoga, F, Sharma, V and Shattuck, D 2018, 'Gender-transformative Bandebereho couples' intervention to promote male engagement in reproductive and maternal health and violence prevention in Rwanda: Findings from a randomized controlled trial', *PLOS ONE*, 4 April. Available at: https://doi.org/10.1371/journal.pone.0192756 [Accessed 03/27/20].

Fellman, A and Randell, S (eds) 2012, *Focus on Rwanda: A Conference on Gender Research and Activism: Proceedings*, 11–12 March 2011, SRIA Rwanda Ltd, Kigali, Rwanda. Available at: http://www.millennia2015.org/files/files/Publications/Conference_Rwanda_Research_and_Activism_EntireProceedings_final_for_printing_2012.pdf [Accessed 03/27/20].

Fonn, S, Laban, P, Cotton, P, Habib, A, Mulwa, P, Mbithi, F, Mtenje, A, Nawangwe, B, Ogunbodede, E, Olayinka, I, Golooba-Mutebi, F and Ezeh, A.2018, 'Repositioning Africa in global knowledge production', *The Lancet*, vol.392, no.10153, pp. 1163–1166. Available at: https://doi.org/10.1016/S0140-6736(18)31068-7 [Accessed 03/27/20].

International Monetary Fund 2017, *Gender Equality from Theory to Practice: A Peer Learning Experience*. Available at: https://www.imf.org/en/News/

Seminars/Conferences/2017/10/30/peer-learning-conference-on-gender-equality [Accessed 03/27/20].

Kelleher, F 2017, 'Disrupting orthodoxies in economic development—An African feminist perspective', *Feminist Africa*, vol. 22, pp. 128-38. Available at: https://www.agi.ac.za/sites/default/files/image_tool/images/429/feminist_africa_journals/archive/22/fa22_critical_reflection_3.pdf [Accessed 09/25/18].

Kubai, A and Ahlberg, BM 2013, 'Making and unmaking ethnicities in the Rwandan context: implications for gender-based violence, health, and wellbeing of women', *Ethnicity & Health*, vol. 18, no. 5, pp. 469-482. Available at https://doi.org/10.1080/13557858.2013.832012 [Accessed 03/27/20].

Lyu, T 2018, 'Chinese garment firm helps promote "made in Rwanda"', *New China*, 2 May 2018. Available at: www.xinhuanet.com/english/2018-05/01/c_137149281.htm [Accessed 03/27/20].

Mama, A 2003, 'Restore, reform but do not transform: the gender politics of higher education in Africa', *Journal of Higher Education in Africa*, vol. 1, no. 1, pp. 101-125. Available at: https://www.codesria.org/spip.php?article561&lang=en [Accessed 03/27/20].

Mama, A 2011, 'What does it mean to do feminist research in African contexts?', *Feminist Review Conference Proceedings*, e4-20. Available at https://doi.org/10.1057/fr.2011.22.

Mann, L and Berry, M 2016, 'Understanding the political motivations that shape Rwanda's emergent developmental state', *New Political Economy*, vol.21, no. 1, pp. 119-144. Available at https://doi.org/10.1080/13563467.2015.1041484 [Accessed 03/27/20].

Mellow, GO and Katopes, P 2009, 'A prescription for the emerging world', *Change: The Magazine of Higher Learning*, vol. 41, no. 5, pp. 55-59. Available at https://doi.org/10.3200/CHNG.41.5.55-61 [Accessed 03/27/20].

Motlafi, N 2018, 'The coloniality of the gaze on sexual violence: a stalled attempt at a South Africa-Rwanda dialogue?', *International Feminist Journal of Politics*, vol. 20, no. 1, pp. 9-23. Available at https://doi.org/10.1080/14616742.2017.1358908. [Accessed 03/27/20].

Musindarwezo, D 2018, 'The 2030 Agenda from a feminist perspective: No meaningful gains without greater accountability for Africa's women', *Agenda: Empowering women for gender equity*, vol. 32, no. 1, pp. 25-35. Available at: https://doi.org/10.1080/10130950.2018.1427693 [Accessed 03/27/20].

Mutandwa, E and Wibabara, S 2016, 'Natural resources and household incomes among rural women: Analysis of communities domiciled near national parks in Rwanda', *Journal of International Women's Studies*, vol. 17, no. 4, pp. 79-90. Available at: http://vc.bridgew.edu/jiws/vol17/iss4/6 [Accessed 03/27/20].

National Institute of Statistics of Rwanda (NISR) [Rwanda], Ministry of Health (MOH) [Rwanda], and ICF International 2015, *Rwanda Demographic and Health Survey 2014-15*, NISR, MOH, and ICF International, Rockville, Maryland. Available at: https://dhsprogram.com/pubs/pdf/FR316/FR316.pdf [Accessed 03/27/20].

Niyibizi, E, Sibomana, E, Niyomugabo, C, Yanzigiye, B, Ngabonziza, A, Jean de Dieu, A and Perumal, J 2018, 'Assessment in a Rwandan higher education institution: a quest for aligned assessment to promote socio-economic transformation', *Assessment & Evaluation in Higher Education*, vol. 43, no. 7, pp. 1166-1182. Available at https://doi.org/10.1080/02602938.2018.1436688 [Accessed 03/27/20].

Ochieng, J, Ouma, E and Birachi, E 2014, 'Gender participation and decision making in crop management in Great Lakes region of Central Africa', *Gender, Technology and Development*, vol. 18, no. 3, pp. 321-362. Available at https://doi.org/10.1177/0971852414544007 [Accessed 03/27/20].

Purdeková, A 2011, ' "Even if I am not here, there are so many eyes": surveillance and state reach in Rwanda', *Journal of Modern African Studies*, vol. 49, no. 3, pp. 475-497. Available at https://doi.org/10.1017/S0022278X11000292. [Accessed 03/27/20].

Republic of Rwanda 2016, *2016 Education Statistical Yearbook*, Ministry of Education, Kigali. Available at: http://mineduc.gov.rw/fileadmin/user_upload/pdf_files/2016_Education_Statistical_Yearbook.pdf [Accessed 03/27/20].

Ryan, S 2011, 'The dilemmas of post-identity organizing: unmaking feminist ties in southern Rwanda', *Women & Language*, vol. 34, no. 2, pp. 61-78.

Schendel, R 2015, 'Critical thinking at Rwanda's public universities: Emerging evidence of a crucial development priority', *International Journal of Educational Development*, vol. 42, pp. 96-105. Available at: https://doi.org/10.1016/j.ijedudev.2015.04.003 [Accessed 03/27/20].

Schendel, R 2016, 'Adapting, not adopting: Barriers affecting teaching for critical thinking at two Rwandan universities', *Comparative Education Review*, vol. 60, no. 3, pp. 549-570. Available at https://doi.org/10.1086/687035 [Accessed 03/27/20].

Simon-Kumar, R 2004, 'Negotiating emancipation: the public sphere and gender critiques of neo-liberal development', *International Feminist Journal of Politics*, vol. 6, no. 3, pp. 485-506. Available at: https://doi.org/10.1080/1461674042000235627 [Accessed 03/27/20].

Sindayigaya, A 2012, 'Rwanda: Wealth inequality, an impediment to sustainable human development', *Insightful Quotient*, Available at: http://insightfulquotient.com/rwanda-wealth-inequality-an-impediment-to-sustainable-human-development/ [Accessed 24 Nov 2018].

Struckmann, C 2017, A postcolonial feminist critique of the 2020 Agenda for Sustainable Development: A South African application. Master of Arts Thesis, Stellenbosch University. Stellenbosch, South Africa.

Thomas, P 2018, 'Whose Vision 2020? The World Bank's development and educational discourse in Rwanda', *Development Studies Research*, vol. 5, no. 1, pp. 50–58. Available at https://doi.org/10.1080/21665095.2018.1469422 [Accessed 03/27/20].

Thomson, S 2010, 'Getting close to Rwandans since the genocide: Studying everyday life in highly politicized research settings', *African Studies Review*, vol. 53, no. 3, pp. 19–34. Available at: https://doi.org/10.1017/S0002020600005655 [Accessed 03/27/20].

Tripp, AM 2017, 'How African feminism changed the world', *African Arguments*, 8 March, Available at: https://africanarguments.org/2017/03/08/how-african-feminism-changed-the-world/ [Accessed 03/27/20].

University of Rwanda 2018, *UR female academics meet to reflect on challenges preventing them to thrive*. Available at: webcache.googleusercontent.com/search?q=cache:qRVUE_5kIRAJ:https://ursweden.ur.ac.rw/?q%3Dnode/536&hl=en&gl=au&strip=1&vwsrc=0 [Accessed 03/27/20].

Warner, G 2018, 'Rwanda ranks in the top 5 for gender equity. Do its teens agree?' *National Public Radio*, 10 Jan. Available at: www.npr.org/sections/goatsandsoda/2018/01/10/577018509/rwanda-ranks-in-the-top-5-for-gender-equity-do-its-teen-girls-agree. [Accessed 03/27/20].

Contributor Biography

Anita Clair Fellman is Professor Emerita of Women's Studies and former Chair of the Women's Studies Department at Old Dominion University in Norfolk, VA. Her most recent book is *Little House, Long Shadow: Laura Ingalls Wilder's Impact on American Culture* (2008, paperback. 2016). In 2011 she was a Fulbright Specialist at the Kigali Institute of Education where she worked with staff members at the Centre for Gender, Culture and Development to organise 'Focus on Rwanda: A Conference on Gender Research and Activism'.

Thinking and Acting; Towards a Gendered Scholarship

Hilary Yerbury

Abstract

Scholarship is inextricably linked to education and development, yet often, when most needed, it is a resource difficult to come by and often the voices of women scholars are under-represented. This chapter reflects on resources available to support scholarship and how a gendered approach to these resources can foster the development of informed policymakers and female scholars and through this, the growth and development of scholarship itself.

Introduction

Imagine creating a master's program in a new field of study, with the intention of developing a curiosity-driven culture which will lead to policy innovation and to scholarly research. On the checklist would be the questions about resources and about the capabilities of the students, taking into account the approaches to learning determined by the epistemological approach and by the field of study. Academics in a western university tradition will be familiar with this process, and will recognise that their university will probably have procedures in place to remedy gaps and weaknesses identified in providing the

---

How to cite this book chapter:
Yerbury, H. 2021. Thinking and Acting; Towards a Gendered Scholarship. In: Randell, S., Yerbury, H. and Escrig-Pinol, A. (eds.) *Gender and Learning in Rwanda*. Pp. 43–51. Sydney: UTS ePRESS. DOI: https://doi.org/10.5130/aag.d. License: CC BY-NC-ND.

adequate resources and in developing the capabilities required of students for successful engagement in the program.

Now imagine starting this program without being able to complete this checklist, without being able to attest to the strength of the library's collection in the field and without being able to respond on the capabilities of prospective students; but prompted by a belief in the importance of curiosity-driven social change and the capacity of students who are passionate about social change to overcome many obstacles.

Such were some of the challenges facing staff and students when the master's program in Gender, Culture and Development began at what was then the Kigali Institute of Education (KIE) in Rwanda in early 2011. This chapter frames those challenges alongside a number of other challenges, as a series of realities to be confronted. Some of these will exist in the development of many programs of postgraduate education aimed at policy development and social change, whereas others will be particular to the context of this program of study. Among these challenges are the return to study of mature aged students including the balancing of work life, social life and study for the students; learning in a language which had not been the language of earlier education; the use of digital resources; the development of a scholarly to professional practice in an environment unfamiliar with such an approach; and the use of a feminist methodology in conceptualising the program of study.

The Significance of Language

Rwanda had been a Belgian colony and after independence in 1962, French had continued to be the official language, alongside Kinyarwanda, the local language. In 2008, prompted by the return after the genocide of many educated Tutsis and moderate Hutus from Uganda as well as by political considerations, the government introduced English as the medium of education in schools and in 2011—the year in which the Master's in Gender, Culture and Development was to begin—KIE adopted English as its medium of instruction and deliberation. English became another official language, and many people in public administration managed to communicate in spoken English. However, in spite of reasonable facility with spoken English, written English was a challenge for some; in this way, the language of previous education and some associated cultural aspects had a significant effect on the students enrolled in the master's program, providing a clear reminder of the past for each student. A seemingly trivial example provides evidence of the distinction between those educated in French and those educated in English. Each student was to be provided with a notebook to document their career goals, an associated learning contract and their progress in completing the learning contract, as a kind of portfolio. The only shop selling notebooks of the kind anticipated did not have in stock enough notebooks with lined pages for each student to have one; to make up the number it would be necessary to buy some books with squared pages. When the books were distributed, the books with squared pages were readily taken up by the students whose previous education had been in French, as they had learned to write using the grid system of these pages and were more comfortable using them than using the books with plain lines.

More seriously, as Pennycook has noted (2001, p. 120), is that language use is linked to agency and thus to power. A challenge in class discussion was to support those not used to speaking in English so that their voices were not muted, and in assignment tasks to recognise that lack of facility with written English was likely to hamper the exploration of ideas and the presentation of thought and argument. The study groups established in the first weeks of the program, including Anglophone and Francophone students, and the coincidental ability of one of the teaching staff to speak French, and thus to act as a cultural and academic interpreter, helped to create a context where students were more able to demonstrate their agency equitably, at least during the period when they were settling in to their roles as learner and future scholar.

Language use and power are also linked to the topic of communication. The content of the master's program was designed to be challenging and at the same time to normalise the discussion of topics fundamental to gender equity and social change. The students appeared to take on this challenge with gusto. Early in their program, they had to carry out a small scale research project, including collecting and analysing data and report on it to an audience of their peers: the academic staff of the program and the small number of senior scholars who accepted an invitation to attend. One group presented an investigation into the work and aspirations of women bus conductors—a bus company operating from the nearby bus station had recently employed two women conductors. The aspiration of one of these women to become a bus driver provoked an outburst from one of the invited members of the audience, for whom the thought of women driving was anathema, as 'everyone knew that there were times of the month when a woman was not rational and would be a danger to all'. Here was clearly a topic where there was much to be done in the society to normalise discussion of such issues and work towards the social change which would accept the women as competent to work in many new jobs.

Not Finding Their Voice

Rwanda is a country which has prioritised access to internet-based services, completing a fibre-optic cabling project in 2011. Ownership of mobile telephones is high, with many people having phones linked to at least two out of the three networks. When the master's degree program commenced, KIE had effective internet access and the city of Kigali itself had a number of internet hotspots, although at the time access to the internet was relatively costly. Personal computers were not commonly owned. KIE, however, had relatively stable access to the internet and all of the buildings had Wi-Fi. This included the classrooms and the library. Access to a library was not a part of everyday life for most Rwandans. Most schools had no library and they would certainly not have had librarians. The Kigali Public Library was about to open when the program began. Thus, most students were unfamiliar with the range of services that an academic library could be expected to provide to support postgraduate education and research. The library at KIE (as noted elsewhere in these chapters) had a small collection to support the program, mainly consisting of donations from retiring scholars from overseas. However, it did have access to a significant number of electronic databases, a number of which provided access to the full text of journal articles and reports. Sessions with the chief librarian were invaluable in giving students skills in the searching of these online bibliographic databases. Other sessions helped the students gain skills in skimming and scanning journal articles and making notes from their reading.

The approach to education from the past, which for many had been an examination-based system, relying on the ability to remember and reproduce lectures and notes provided by the academic, encouraged many students to take their readings verbatim and include them in their classwork and their assessment tasks. From this, the lack of a broader understanding of information literacy was clear. Information literacy goes well beyond the finding and evaluation of relevant sources, to encompass the ethical practices of scholarship and research, including practices of references and citation. A significant challenge in overcoming what an Australian university would consider plagiarism arose, not because students deliberately sought to pass someone else's words off as their own, nor because they did not grasp the conventions of referencing, but because they were concerned that their use of English was not polished enough for the ideas they wanted to express. The importance for each student to develop his or her own voice, in order to express agency, was a new concept.

Not Finding Other African Voices

A significant issue which affects much scholarship across the continent of Africa is that there are comparatively few articles and books written by African scholars. In 2007, Ondari-Okemwa published a study that demonstrated the paucity of African voices in the scholarly literature. In 2006, more than 100,000 articles were published by scholars in the United States, a number which bore no relationship to the output of countries in sub-Saharan Africa; in Rwanda in 2005, according the UNESCO Science Report (2015), the number of scholarly articles published was 13, a figure which had risen to 143 in 2014. There are many reasons for this low level of publishing. A key factor is that knowledge production through scholarly processes is a cumulative process; each scholarly article builds on existing scholarship. The legacy of problems with access to scholarly resources in libraries will affect scholarship for some time to come

(Lor & Britz, 2005). A second issue is that local knowledge about Africa is overwhelmed by Western knowledge about Africa (Jackson et al., 2008). These systemic issues with scholarly publications should not be taken as evidence that African scholars do not write up the work that they do. It is the case that many African scholars produce reports and technical papers that have significant local impact, but which do not become part of the formal publishing record and are thus much more difficult for those not involved in the local community to access (Abrahams et al., 2008). It is also the case that there may be discrimination by the editors of some journals against African scholars. The editor of the Lancet, a major British medical journal, is reported to have said that 'if he chose to publish African authors, this might reduce the citation impact of his journal', leading to a situation that he described as 'a racist culture in journal decision-making' (Gray, 2010, p.10).

A fourth issue relates to the gendered nature of publishing. It is well documented that women scholars are seen to be less productive than their male counterparts. There is also anecdotal evidence indicating that women scholars may be more interested in achieving change in policy or in professional or social processes, so that they do not publish in the journals read by other scholars, but focus on professional journals and magazines, read by policy-makers and practitioners. The consequence is that the particular concerns of women scholars may be less well represented in the literature and that their research approaches potentially are seen as having less validity.

Windows and Mirrors

This lack of representation in the literature indicates a marginalisation of the research interests, especially for women scholars. This is particularly significant in a context intending to raise awareness of issues of gender-based discrimination and to prepare people to be researchers attuned to the complexities of these issues in a country such as Rwanda. Galda (1998) writes of the windows and mirrors through which identity is constructed. This metaphor indicates the power of scholarly literature in providing insight into the worlds of others, and even into our own worlds, through the perception of others—these are the windows that give perspectives onto realities and also on to possibilities of other ways of acting. The metaphor of the mirror is perhaps more powerful as it functions at two levels. First it enables scholars and researchers to have the potential of seeing themselves reflected in the work of others, at least at an inspirational level. Secondly, it enables scholars and researchers to recognise in the work of others, something of their own situation. This is not the 'generalisability' of positivist research, where someone else's findings are relevant to one's own situation. Rather, this is a deeper recognition of something shared, the acknowledgement of a kind of imagined community, giving strength to the individual scholar who can glimpse that there are others working from a similar position. This metaphor of the importance of windows and mirrors is inherent in feminist scholarship.

Feminist scholarship itself presents a number of challenges to students and to researchers. It is, fundamentally, political, seeking a profound institutional change in society, from changes in the everyday use of language that has privileged the male over the female, to changes in attitudes and everyday practices, to changes to law and policy. Recognition of social problems is a starting point, but it is important for feminist scholars to recognise that in these social problems are broader, conceptual problems, problems in sociology, its concepts and theories. In other words, feminist scholarship must always seek to go beyond exposing inequalities in society. Early work in the western literature often focussed on economic inequalities, focussing on limitations in work opportunities, but this approach can constrain the understanding of the systems, structures and beliefs that prevent women from achieving economic equality. Several students expressed a concern with practices that they saw as gender-based violence, where men controlled economic resources in the family to the detriment of women. They noted that this was not necessarily an issue arising from the woman's lack of participation in the paid workforce, or even an issue arising from poverty as significant anecdotal evidence related to women who might be considered members of a social elite. It had been a tradition, and recent changes to legislation were difficult to implement when neither men nor women had learned any other way of managing the economic resources of the family. Societal beliefs and lack of practical experience were perceived as barriers to implementing solutions to this problem. Standpoint theory has been useful in positioning the importance of the point of view of women in the exploration of issues and problems—it highlights the inequalities that women suffer by presenting the analysis of a situation from the perspective of women. Yet, in a society seeking a fundamental shift in gender relations, there is the risk that feminist scholarship based on standpoint theory may marginalise the men who are working in support of societal change, by muting their voices.

In a context where the literature which might have provided windows and mirrors for the students enrolled in the first intake of the master's program was scarce and difficult to access, an obvious response was to create those windows and mirrors. Teaching staff selected readings that would go some way towards creating those windows that might provide perspectives in other realities and on ways of confronting these realities, especially through policy approaches and through approaches arising from community-based actions. Importantly, the learning activities themselves went some way towards creating the mirrors through which students as beginning scholars could recognise themselves and the issues of concern to them. Locally based investigations began a process of going beyond a recital of the facts of a situation, interpreting the findings in the light of the theoretical and conceptual underpinnings of the topics; students not only worked in groups to carry out these small-scale investigations, they were required to present them to their fellow students and sometimes to wider audiences. Even in this modest way, they began the scholarly process of creating new, conceptually based understandings of everyday realities, and considering the possibilities of this leading to institutional change.

Gender Studies centres elsewhere in Africa have identified similar problems with a lack of locally grounded material as a focus for discussion (Focus, 2009). Setting up some kind of publishing program was a common solution to the problem. More solidly established centres have been able to establish scholarly journals; as an example, the African Gender Institute in the University of Cape Town, was able to support a peer reviewed journal, *Feminist Africa*, and a significant website. Other centres placed an emphasis on producing working papers. This was the approach taken at the Centre for Gender, Culture and Development at KIE, which used the Centre's Facebook page to make these papers available. The use of the Facebook technology removed the barriers to access created by paywalls, registration and subscription. Conferences, with at least summaries of the papers in lieu of a full proceedings made available online, was another avenue through which research materials local to Rwanda were made public.

Another problem in the production of locally grounded research materials was identified as the lack of local people trained to the level of doctoral studies. The introduction of the MSocSciGD was seen to be the first step in a long process of preparing people to undertake doctoral study. Several students in the first cohort expressed the desire to become researchers, but the obstacles they have encountered mean that doctoral education remains a dream for most.

New Ways of Thinking and Acting

In spite of the problems with language, with the gaps in resources, the lack of African voices and locally grounded research materials supporting the development of the students in this program, nonetheless, it is clear that much has been achieved. Small beginnings, emerging from ways of conceptualising situations as well as living them, have led to powerful changes. It should be said that most of the students in the first cohort of the master's degree program had the capacity for implementing societal change because of their employment, in government departments and in NGOs. The program of education, based on feminist scholarship, brought new ways of thinking and in turn facilitated the development of new approaches to solutions as they became informed policymakers. The real challenge in institutional change is rarely the passing of new laws. Instead, it is in the implementation of the policies needed to support the new legislation and in the awareness raising, education and practical assistance which helps people to adjust and change their behaviour. The gendered approach to the learning in the course was no doubt an important influence in both personal development and institutional change in the policy context. It also seems, in a simple and unpretentious way, to have begun the development of scholars informed by a gendered approach and this will eventually lead to the growth and development of scholarship itself.

References

Abrahams, L et al. 2008, *Opening Access to Knowledge in Southern African Universities*, Southern African Universities Regional Association.

Focus on Gender Centres in Africa: Proceedings of an International Conference, 7-8 December 2009, Le Printemps Hotel, Kigali, Rwanda.

Galda, L 1998, 'Mirrors and windows: Reading as transformation', in Raphael, T and Au, K (eds) *Literature-based Instruction: Reshaping the Curriculum*, Christopher-Gordon Publishers, Norwood, MA, pp. 1–12.

Gray, E 2009/2010, 'Access to Africa's knowledge: publishing development research and measuring value', *The African Journal of Information Communication*, no.10. Available at: https://journals.co.za/content/journal/10520/EJC-18cef220e5 [Accessed 03/31/20].

Jackson, S, Batcheler, A, Edwards, P, Bowker, G, Cisler, S & Starr, S 2008, *Extending African Knowledge Infrastructures: Sharing, Creating, Maintaining*. A Report for the World Bank Knowledge for Development Program March 2008. Available at: https://deepblue.lib.umich.edu/bitstream/handle/2027.42/61201/Jackson%20et%20al,%20Extending%20African%20Knowledge%20Infrastructures%20(March%202008).pdf;jsessionid=CE00AD9BC17C08D9CFE7826D73076748?sequence=1 [Accessed 03/31/20].

Lor, P and Britz, J 2005, 'Knowledge production from an African perspective: International information flows and intellectual property', *International Information and Library Review*, volume 37, number 2, pp. 61–76. http://dx.doi.org/10.1016/j.iilr.2005.04.003 [Accessed 03/31/20].

Ondari–Okemwa, E 2007, 'Scholarly publishing in sub–Saharan Africa in the twenty–first century: Challenges and opportunities', *First Monday*, vol. 12, no. 10, https://firstmonday.org/ojs/index.php/fm/article/view/1966/1842 [Accessed 03/31/20].

Pennycook, A 2001, *Critical applied linguistics: a critical introduction*, Erlbaum Associates, Mahwah, USA.

UNESCO Science Report: Towards 2030, 2015, https://en.unesco.org/unesco_science_report [Accessed 03/31/20].

Contributor Biography

Hilary Yerbury has worked on programs to support the development of researchers, both as students and as established academics. Appointed Adjunct Professor and formerly Associate Professor in Information Management at the University of Technology Sydney, she brings a diverse background in European social and political cultures, anthropology, librarianship and development studies to the important topic of the use of information in everyday decision-making and in social change. She is a passionate supporter of open access scholarly publishing and a mentor to young scholars. She has extensive experience in working with young people on development issues.

Teaching Gender Research Methods for Leadership: Reflections from Rwanda

Jaya Dantas

Abstract

This chapter discusses teaching and research undertaken by the author in Rwanda between 1997 and 2011. The author draws on her experiences of establishing and running an institution in Rwanda from 1997 to 1999, undertaking research for her PhD in 2000, visiting the country in 2007 to gain further insights into the reconstruction of education and in 2011 teaching at the Centre for Gender, Culture and Development. Using a gender lens, the author reflects on teaching gender research methods, the interactions with an amazing first cohort of students and the immense leadership potential shown by the students. The chapter concludes with some recommendations and implications.

The Personal and Professional Context of the Author

My interest in education in developing countries and educational reform in transitional societies is a result of working in countries where systems of education were being re-established after years of political turmoil. As head teacher of schools in Uganda and Rwanda, I have been part of education reform efforts and have often experienced the frustrations and the challenges associated with the rehabilitation and reconstruction process. My interest in development

---

How to cite this book chapter:
Dantas, J. 2021. Teaching Gender Research Methods for Leadership: Reflections from Rwanda. In: Randell, S., Yerbury, H. and Escrig-Pinol, A. (eds.) *Gender and Learning in Rwanda*. Pp. 53–63. Sydney: UTS ePRESS. DOI: https://doi.org/10.5130/aag.e. License: CC BY-NC-ND.

education, educational reform and sustainable education has evolved over the years and forms part of the background for this chapter.

I have lived and worked in five countries—India, Kenya, Uganda, Rwanda and Australia—and undertaken research and teaching consultancies in Pakistan, Kosovo, Timor-Leste, Sri Lanka, Singapore, Tanzania and South Africa. I thus had experiences as a teacher, head teacher, teacher educator, researcher and academic. I was educated and had worked in India and was always aware of the immense problems associated with an ever-increasing population, severe regional disparities in educational access and reduced opportunities for girls and women. In a country with a billion people, India also educates some of the leading scientists, doctors and software specialists in the world, but even today has millions of children with no access to primary and secondary schooling. Indeed, the problems of child labour and gender inequalities are still widely prevalent. With respect to education, India does not produce statistics as a whole because of severe regional disparities (Bhatty, Saraf & Gupta, 2017).

I moved to Kenya in 1990, where, in my second year as a school teacher, the country had elections which resulted in a severe economic collapse and a gradual breakdown in the social fabric of life with escalating crime, ethnic violence, the HIV/AIDS pandemic and an increase in street children (Ministry of Education and Human Resource Development, 1998). At that time, Kenya already had the support of a number of aid organisations and non-governmental organisations (NGOs)doing work in the areas of primary and secondary education, teacher training, science education and laboratory instruction (Aga Khan Education Services, AKDN, n.d.).

From 1993 to 1997, I worked as a headteacher in Uganda, rebuilding a school that had closed down in 1972 during the Idi Amin era. In the midst of gunfire at night, car hijackings and the AIDS pandemic where one in seven adults was infected with the AIDS virus, I witnessed a country dedicated to rebuilding the education system and bringing the same status to Makerere University (a well-known African Commonwealth University) that existed in the pre-Idi Amin era before 1972. I was impressed with the implementation of school improvement programs, the child-to-child program (a unique program that forges links between the child, the school and the community) and secondary science education programs and observed the return of educated Ugandan citizens who had left the country during the period of turmoil and now wanted to be part of the reconstruction process (Earnest, 2003, p. 4).

After Uganda, I spent two years in Rwanda and established a private school comprising nursery, primary and lower secondary classes. I witnessed first-hand a country recovering from the genocide of 1994, and never got used to seeing young armed soldiers on the streets, increasing numbers of war orphans and AIDS orphans, displaced children and the inherent poverty. During my time in Rwanda, the country implemented its new curriculum in September 1998 with a major thrust on science and technology, established an Institute of Science and Technology and an Institute of Education with the main aim of increasing the number of engineers, technologists and secondary science teachers (Ministry of Education, 1998).

In 2000, I spent several months in Rwanda, collecting data for my PhD thesis. During this period, I worked with a multi-lingual refugee teacher from the Democratic Republic of Congo who was also a survivor of the genocide, who acted as my interpreter. On completion of my PhD, I published a book chapter on Science Education Reform in Rwanda (Earnest & Treagust, 2004) and in 2006 published a 16-chapter book on Education Reform in Transitional Countries (Earnest, 2006; Earnest & Treagust, 2006). I went back to Rwanda at the end of 2007 and met with Rwandan colleagues and friends who continued to work in the education sector to further explore the changes in the education system and impacts on leadership. This led to the publication of a book chapter on challenges to school leadership in Rwanda (Earnest, 2013).

Teaching Gender Research Methods in Rwanda

I met Professor Shirley Randell in 2009 in Perth when she spoke on her work in Rwanda at a meeting of the Western Australian Branch of the Australian Institute of International Affairs. In early 2010, I invited her to speak at Curtin University on her experiences in Rwanda. Shirley reached out to me in October 2010, asking if I could come and help teach a class on Research Methods for the inaugural program in Gender, Culture and Development. I was honoured with the invitation, as it allowed me to draw on my experiences working with coursework master's students at Curtin University (in Perth, Western Australia) and my growing expertise in refugee and migrant education and health with a focus on women and youth. I was also skilled in participatory and community research using qualitative methods.

In consultation with Shirley, I developed a 10-week research methods unit with a focus on gender and feminist research methods. In order to support student learning each student was provided with a compact disk (CD) of course readings, comprising a selection of over 40 journal articles and book chapters on gender research. Presentations were delivered that provided the theory on the methods and methodologies of gender research methods and drew on feminist epistemologies. The next section provides a brief overview of feminist research that underpinned my teaching.

Feminist Research

Feminist research gives voice to marginalised and vulnerable populations and provides a platform for women to share their wisdom, experiences and opinions on issues that impact them personally. Gender equality, precipitated through the restructuring of traditional social hierarchies, is not only necessary for justice and human rights but is also vital for the establishment and sustainability of best practice research processes (The Lancet, 2019). Doucet and Mauthner (2007, p.42) argue that over the past three decades feminist scholars have made significant contributions to global discourse on 'issues of power, knowing, representation, reflexivity, and legitimation in methodological and epistemological discussions'. During this time, the international research community has seen the emergence and convergence of feminist epistemologies and methodologies resulting in the establishment of a new field of scholarship known as 'feminist research'. Feminist research refers to qualitative, quantitative and mixed method research that is instigated by, and directed towards, the desire to challenge social inequalities especially impacting women and girls (Doucet & Mauthner, 2007).

To ensure inclusivity and equitability, the need to diverge from traditional research practices has seen the field of feminist research introduce methodological approaches that challenge conventional data collection, analysis and dissemination (Doucet & Mauthner, 2007). Historically, quantitative, positivist research methods have dominated global development research. However, more recently, qualitative research methodologies have progressively gained acknowledgment as valuable tools for obtaining contextually rich data that is both female centric and culturally specific (Mack et al., 2005).

Supporting the feminist research ideology are the methodological approaches of participatory research and action research (Doucet & Mauthner, 2007). These processes strive for the inclusivity of participants and communities within a collaborative research context and have the potential to facilitate holistic, empowering and transformative outcomes (Coghlan & Brydon-Miller, 2014). My experience has shown that action and participatory methodologies, underpinned by a feminist research framework, enable research to not only be about women, but also to be conducted for women and with women (Doucet & Mauthner, 2007; Coghlan & Brydon-Miller, 2014) because it relates to the context of their every-day lives.

In this first semester of study for the students enrolled in the master's program, students were introduced to a range of research methods associated with feminist research: ethnography, life history, participatory research, action research, case studies and linked them to examples from published research undertaken by my students and myself. Through these research methods and the associated readings, students learned about empowerment, resilience, inequalities and complex human and socio-cultural issues in practice, concepts introduced to them in other theoretically based subjects.

The journal articles provided a glimpse of arranged marriages in South Asia, gender-based violence in Papua New Guinea, homosexuality and issues of gender differences. As part of the course assignment, students were assigned to groups and had to undertake a group PowerPoint presentation on a journal article of their choice. This analysis and critique of the work of established scholars was new to the students but they readily accepted the task. From this exercise, students began to understand the strengths and weaknesses of particular research methods and the ways they were implemented. This background and learning helped them develop their own knowledge base and gave them insights into feminist research which they could integrate into the research proposal they prepared, which would later form the basis of their master's projects.

It was a privilege to teach this passionate group. It was wonderful to see a cohort of mixed age students that included nine male students. Most of the students were mature age and nearly all were working full time, but all were keen to learn and felt privileged to be given the opportunity to be part of this exciting new master's course. Most students shared about their personal and professional lives, some had important government jobs, others worked in NGOs and some with international organisations. An exciting outcome from this learning experience was that in 2015, two of the students, now graduates, presented at the Commission on the Status of Women (CSW59) at the UN in New York, alongside Shirley Randell and me. One of the graduates went on to become the Minister of Gender in Rwanda in 2015 and I was privileged to meet her at CSW60 in New York and attend a session hosted by the Rwandan delegation to the CSW60 on Rebuilding in Rwanda and gender development.

My Reflections

Reflecting on my experiences of teaching the first cohort, I found that the students valued the mentoring and teaching provided in the classes. They proved to be resilient and empowered and their families played an important role in their development. Many of the students, both men and women, displayed leadership qualities and were passionate about making a difference in Rwanda and the world. The concepts of resilience, empowerment, leadership and mentoring with a focus on the student cohort have been examined in the next section. As noted earlier, these concepts underpin much of the scholarship developed through feminist research methods and were fundamental to the scholarly, professional and personal development of the students.

Resilience

The definition of resilience provided by Atkinson, Martin and Rankin (2009, p. 137) is 'the ability to recover readily from the extremes of trauma, deprivation, threat or stress'. Similarly, Rutter (2007, p. 208) states that resilience is observed when individuals have 'relatively good outcomes despite exposure to adverse life experiences'. According to Walsh (1996, p. 7) 'resilience is forged through adversity, not despite it'. Resilience is also considered a dynamic process that varies and evolves over time (Luthar, Cicchetti & Becker, 2000; Mullin & Arce, 2008). What binds these definitions together is that they suggest there is an element of recovery of the individual from difficult events (Bonanno et al., 2007) and include protective factors that may promote resilience at the individual level, such as good social support, family and good health. The students in the master's in gender classes were extremely resilient; most had lived as refugees, had experienced the genocide and were involved in rebuilding their country. They were all zealous about the desire to further their qualification so they could make a difference and become leaders. Studying in the program was not without its difficulties, with some students travelling long distances to attend classes, others having to balance domestic and work responsibilities, and others still coming to terms with studying in English, their third or fourth language.

Empowerment

Empowerment is inextricably related to and relevant for particular cultural and social contexts in which people live (Mohajer & Earnest, 2009). Freire (1999) describes empowerment as a cultural synthesis, where all involved in the empowerment process undergo change, and knowledge is shared equally. This knowledge has the power to enact social action and bring about change. Empowerment has been successfully incorporated into a variety of disciplines (social work, development, education and human rights) including participatory or action research. An all-encompassing definition of empowerment by UNESCO is: 'How individuals/communities engage in learning processes in which they create, share knowledge, tools and techniques in order to change and improve the quality of their own lives and societies' (Faccini and Jain, 2000.). The students in the first cohort were engaged in the new learning they were receiving, and empowered by it to further create new knowledge for leadership and change in Rwanda. They learned the value of evidence-based practice. Some were empowered very soon after the completion of the course to take their own new knowledge into broader scholarly and policy arenas, so that they or others could work towards implementing these new understandings, supporting changes to the quality of life for many Rwandans.

Family

The family has been known to serve as a protective or risk factor in an individual's life (Caplan, 1982; Wolin & Wolin, 1993). A separate body of research considers the family as an important unit of support (McCubbin et al., 1997; Patterson, 2002; Walsh, 1996). Family resilience has been described as how families use their strengths as a buffer in times of stress (Hawley & DeHaan,

1996). Strong connectedness and being able to seek reassurance and safety are all factors that can help increase family resilience. These strong connections, and the need for social and cultural cohesiveness are observed within the family (Brookes, 2010). Family played a vital role in the lives of all students. Nearly all were parents, with a couple of pregnant young women in the class, and most had significant support from their families. They shared information about their families, formally and informally, were proud of their children and wanted to be strong role models. They were also trying to find ways to live by the principles they were learning about, and sometimes portraying themselves through action research or auto-ethnographic projects.

Mentoring

Mentoring has been defined as a one-to-one relationship in which an experienced older career person guides and supports the career development of a new or early-career member. Sorcinelli and Yun (2007) have proposed a model that encourages a broader, more flexible network of support, in which no single person is expected to possess the expertise required to help someone navigate a career. In this model, robust networks are established by engaging multiple 'mentoring partners' in non-hierarchical, collaborative, cross-cultural partnerships to address specific areas of mentoring, such as research, teaching, working towards success and striking a balance between work and life. These reciprocal partnerships benefit the 'protégé' and also the 'mentor'. The tutors and visiting professors from around the world provided mentoring to the students, advising, sharing and providing valuable guidance from their own personal experiences. The students themselves, as noted above, were already highly experienced professional women and men, and their sharing of experiences and open discussions, especially in the clarification of the research questions for the thesis, enabled a mentoring among peers, as they workshopped their ideas and received comments and feedback from those with different perspectives and experiences.

Implications and Conclusion

In spite of the immense difficulties and constraints in education in Rwanda, the master's students provide a portrayal of human experience in this transitional society. In a recent article in *The Conversation*, Karangwa and Bayisenge (Feb 2018) point to a significant disconnect between Rwanda's international reputation for gender equality and the lived realities on the ground. While the focus of their article was on girls with disabilities, their call for unified policy approaches highlights the need for strong and proactive national strategies that involve multiple sectors (health, education, labour and youth).

The women from the first cohort of the degree in Gender, Culture and Development in Rwanda were passionate community advocates and played a supportive role in their communities. They displayed a strong social justice and human rights conscience. They presented great resilience and were involved in the rebuilding of their country. They took on the challenge of accepting senior government and NGO leadership positions often learning new skills on the way. The contribution of the men should not be overlooked. Their example in this research methods class was a constant reminder that a feminist research methodology is not the province only of women. Men, too, can strive for new scholarly knowledge and social change, leading to gender equality, using collaborative and inclusive research methods. My experience of teaching in Rwanda resonates with the vital and uncontested importance of education, the desire to be empowered, the capacity to be resilient and adaptive, and the importance of giving back to the community.

A key recommendation arising from this experience is to continue to provide women with avenues to feel empowered, to have opportunities to further their education, to offer adaptive structures and mechanisms that build resilience, and to grow strong communities where both men and women are engaged in a constant dialogue for growth. It is my hope that through transnational alliances and collaboration, we can bring about capacity building and transitional impacts and harness the immense leadership that women in Rwanda have.

The implications from this chapter provide a foundation for sustainable, relevant education and gender development in complex transitional societies. To successfully take advantage of emerging realities in Rwanda will depend on the quality of its educational and human resources. This is key to meeting Rwanda's pledge of removing all obstacles against women's development. The degree of success in this regard will depend on the abilities of Rwandans to critically understand, adapt and reshape their country through education that benefits all Rwandans.

References

Aga Khan Education Services, AKDN (n.d.), *The Aga Khan Foundation's Education Activities*, Available at: http://www.akdn.org/agency/akes.html [Accessed 03/31/20].

Atkinson, P, Martin, C and Rankin, J 2009, 'Resilience revisited', *Journal of Psychiatric and Mental Health Nursing*, vol. 16, no. 2, pp. 137–145, Available at: https://doi.org/10.1111/j.1365-2850.2008.01341.x [Accessed 03/31/20].

Bhatty, K, Saraf, R and Gupta, V 2017, *Out of school children in India: some insights on what we know and what we don't*, Working Paper, Center for Policy Research India, New Delhi. Available at: http://cprindia.org/

research/papers/out-school-children-india-some-insights-what-we-know-and-what-we-dont [Accessed 03/31/20].

Bonanno, G, Galea, S, Bucciarelli, A and Vlahov, D 2007, 'What predicts psychological resilience after disaster? The role of demographics, resources, and life stress', *Journal of Consulting and Clinical Psychology*, vol. 75, no. 5, pp. 671–682. Available at: https://doi.org/10.1037/0022-006X.75.5.671 [Accessed 03/31/20].

Brookes, G 2010, 'The multilayered effects and support received by victims of the Bali bombings: A cross cultural study in Indonesia and Australia', PhD thesis, Curtin University.

Caplan, G 1982, 'The family as a support system', in McCubbin, H, Cauble, A and Patterson, J (eds) *Family stress, coping, and social support*, Charles C. Thomas, Springfield, IL, pp. 200–220.

Coghlan, D and Brydon-Miller, M 2014. *The Sage Encyclopedia of Action Research*, SAGE, London.

Doucet, A and Mauthner, N 2007, 'Feminist methodologies and epistemology', in Bryant, C and Peck, D (eds) *21st Century Sociology*, SAGE, Thousand Oaks, CA, pp. 36–42.

Earnest, J 2003, 'Science education reform in a post-colonial developing country in the aftermath of a crisis: the case of Rwanda', PhD thesis, Curtin University.

Earnest, J 2006, 'Science education reform in a transitional society: the case of Rwanda', in Earnest, J and Treagust, D (eds) *Education Rebuilding in Societies in Transition: International Perspectives*, Sense, Rotterdam, pp. 129–145.

Earnest, J 2013, 'Challenges to school leadership in post-genocide Rwanda', in Clarke, S and O'Donoghue, T (eds) *School-level Leadership in Post-Conflict Societies: The Importance of Context*, Routledge, London, pp. 78–94.

Earnest, J and Treagust, D 2004, 'Science education reform in Rwanda: a window to understanding change through dilemmas', in Mutua, K and Sunal, C (eds) *Research in Education in Africa, the Caribbean, and the Middle East*, Information Age, Charlotte, NC, pp. 59–80.

Earnest, J and Treagust, D 2006, *Education Rebuilding in Societies in Transition: International Perspectives*, Sense Publishers, Rotterdam, Netherlands.

Faccini, B and Jain, M 2000, *Technology and learning: definitions*, UNESCO, Available at: https://unesdoc.unesco.org/ark:/48223/pf0000135410?posInSet=1&queryId=3f2fa233-444b-4e87-a5c4-0277499c4be4 [Accessed 03/31/20].

Freire, P 1999, *Pedagogy of the Oppressed*, Rev. ed., Continuum, New York.

Hawley, D and DeHaan, L 1996, 'Toward a definition of family resilience: Integrating life-span and family perspectives', *Family Process*, vol. 35, no. 3, pp. 283–298.

Karangwa, E and Bayisenge, J 2018, 'How Rwandan girls with disabilities are fighting sexism at school', *The Conversation*, 22 April 2018. Available at: https://theconversation.com/how-rwandan-girls-with-disabilities-are-fighting-sexism-at-school-94456 [Accessed 03/31/20].

Kenya, Ministry of Education and Human Resource Development 1998, *National Primary Education Baseline Report. The State of Primary Education in Kenya.* Nairobi, Kenya: Ministry of Education.

The Lancet 2019, 'Feminism is for everybody', *The Lancet*, vol. 393 no.10171, p. 493. Available at: https://doi.org/10.1016/S0140-6736(19)30239-9 [Accessed 03/31/20].

Luthar, S, Cicchetti, D and Becker, B 2000, 'The construct of resilience: a critical evaluation and guidelines for future work', *Child Development*, vol. 71, no. 3, pp. 543–562. Available at: https://doi.org/10.1111/1467-8624.00164 [Accessed 03/31/20].

Mack N, Woodsong C, MacQueen KM, Guest G, Namey E 2005, *Qualitative research methods: a data collector's field guide*, Family Health International, North Carolina.

McCubbin, H, McCubbin, M, Thompson, A, Sae-Young, H and Allen, C 1997, 'Families under stress: What makes them resilient', *Journal of Family and Consumer Sciences*, vol. 89, no. 3, pp. 2–11.

Mohajer, N and Earnest, J 2009, 'Youth empowerment for the most vulnerable: A model based on the pedagogy of Freire and experiences in the field', *Health Education*, vol. 109, no.5, pp. 424–438, Available at: https://doi.org/10.1108/09654280910984834 [Accessed 03/31/20].

Mullin, W and Arce, M 2008, 'Resilience of families living in poverty', *Journal of Family Social Work*, vol. 11, no.4, pp. 424–440, Available at: https://doi.org/10.1080/10522150802424565 [Accessed 03/31/20].

Patterson, J 2002, 'Understanding family resilience', *Journal of Clinical Psychology*, vol. 58, no.3, pp. 233–246, Available at: https://doi.org/10.1002/jclp.10019 [Accessed 03/31/20].

Rutter, M 2007, 'Resilience, competence, and coping', *Child Abuse & Neglect*, vol. 31, no.3, pp. 205–209, Available at: https://doi.org/10.1016/j.chiabu.2007.02.001 [Accessed 03/31/20].

Rwanda, Ministry of Education 1998, *Plan of action for education in Rwanda (1998-2000): Recovery and development.* Ministry of Education with support of UNDP and UNESCO, Ministry of Education, Kigali, Rwanda.

Sorcinelli, M and Yun, J 2007, 'From mentor to mentoring networks: Mentoring in the new academy', *Change: The Magazine of Higher Learning*, vol. 39, no. 6, pp. 58–61, Available at: https://doi.org/10.3200/CHNG.39.6.58-C4 [Accessed 03/31/20].

University of Rwanda, Available at: https://theconversation.com/institutions/university-of-rwanda-1960, [Accessed 03/31/20].

Walsh, F 1996, 'The concept of family resilience: crisis and challenge', *Family Process*, vol. 35, no.3, pp. 261–281. Available at: https://doi.org/10.1111/j.1545-5300.1996.00261.x [Accessed 03/31/20].

Wolin, SJ and Wolin, S 1993, *The Resilient Self: How Survivors of Troubled Families Rise Above Adversity*, Villard Books, New York.

Contributor Biography

Dr Jaya Dantas is Professor of International Health and Dean International in the Faculty of Health Sciences at Curtin University in Western Australia. Her research and teaching focusses on refugee and migrant health, the social determinants, health equity and gender. Professor Dantas has worked for 30 years in India, Kenya, Uganda, Rwanda, Australia, Timor Leste, Sri Lanka and Singapore. She is a passionate advocate for education of women and youth. As a migrant woman and global health educator and researcher, she has expertise in gender, health and education.

Teaching Transitional Justice: Towards a Political and Personal Transformative Journey

Gertrude Fester-Wicomb

Abstract

In reflecting on my teaching experience of transitional justice i realised that it was not just an academic exercise but a deeply spiritual, political and personal journal for many of my students and me. In introducing myself as a South African former political prisoner there was what i felt some immediate empathy and rapport. In this chapter i will trace sharing new learnings, apprehension, pain, celebration and hope. Intimately encountering the comprehensive spirit of reconciliation in my class and Rwanda, it encouraged a personal journey conjuring up courage to communicate with my torturer/interrogator exploring possibilities of reconciliation.

In reflecting on my teaching experience of Module 607 Transitional Justice mainstreaming Gender (TJ) i[1] realised that it was not just an academic exercise but also a deeply spiritual, political and personal journal for many of my students and me. This is evident from the responses of the students to the evaluation i conducted with them.[2] The official evaluation done by the university is also evidence of this. I will be quoting from my questionnaire and let the voices of the students be foregrounded. In introducing myself to

---

How to cite this book chapter:
Fester-Wicomb, G. 2021. Teaching Transitional Justice: Towards a Political and Personal Transformative Journey. In: Randell, S., Yerbury, H. and Escrig-Pinol, A. (eds.) *Gender and Learning in Rwanda*. Pp. 65–75. Sydney: UTS ePRESS. DOI: https://doi.org/10.5130/aag.f. License: CC BY-NC-ND.

the class as a South African, from the subsequent discussions and questions i straightaway sensed that they knew about the struggles in my country. There seemed to be an identification with me as also having experienced conflict and oppression. Most of them knew about Nelson Mandela and aspects of his life. In elaborating that i was a former political prisoner i felt immediate empathy.

In this chapter i will trace the sharing, new learnings, apprehension, pain, celebration and hope. Intimately encountering the comprehensive spirit of reconciliation in my class, just living in Rwanda and learning and exchanging perspectives with my students encouraged in me a personal journey conjuring up courage to communicate with my torturer/interrogator from Apartheid South Africa (SA) and exploring possibilities of reconciliation.

Firstly, i will highlight aspects of my lessons and the responses that i had had. Thereafter will be the students' evaluation according to my questionnaire. My approach was qualitative and hence more feminist in that the students could share their personal feelings and emotions. I will use the students' direct words and give each a number, not using their names even though they had given permission for their names to be used. I had committed that before i used their work with their names attached i would share it with them. Now it is not possible to share this writing with all of them, hence they will all remain anonymous. I also would like to stress that although i was the teacher/lecturer, the experience for me was one of profound reciprocation. I have learnt from them as much as they probably have learnt from me. For this i thank them. I also am grateful to Professor Shirley Randell for her vision and insight in almost single-handedly establishing this Centre for Gender. She also gave me the opportunity to be part of this wonderful experience of teaching in Rwanda. I will conclude with the summary of my findings and my analysis of them. Thereafter i will share my interaction with my interrogator/torturer and the subsequent events after my approaching him and then I will conclude.

My teaching methodology was mixed. It ranged from formal lectures and the use of PowerPoints to games, quizzes, panel discussions, presentations, drama, and i hoped that i was successful in implementing what Paulo Freire advocated in his *Pedagogy of the Oppressed*. I also often re-arranged the lecture style of the desks into a circle to facilitate communication more effectively with all the students facing one another. There also were some amazing magical moments when the class spontaneously burst into song and even did their elegant Rwandan dance.

For my very first lesson we stood in a circle and they each had to introduce themselves, do a movement if they felt comfortable and also share their favourite animal. One of the aspects that i was acutely aware of was that often some students did not feel comfortable with drama and movements in the class. Hence i always added that they should feel comfortable and participate as it suited them. It was during this exercise that i understood the importance of cows to Rwandans. Almost 90% of the class shared that the cow was their favourite animal.

I was conscious of the fact that most of the students did not have English as their first language. When i am excited i tend to speak fast. I mentioned this to them and appealed to them to please indicate when i speak too fast or whether they do not understand. This happened a few times that student brought this to my attention. However, in the evaluation there was one who commented on this. It may mean that i was not completely successful in slowing down altogether and that that this person did not feel comfortable in asking me to slow down. I acknowledge this weakness of mine.

In keeping with sound classroom management, the need for maximum empowerment, building of confidence of students and the Freirean education as a liberatory tool, i always endeavoured to encourage maximum class participation. Drama is well known to be an effective method to facilitate personal growth and development as well as confidence building. Hence this was used frequently and where appropriate, once again bearing in mind there may be those who would not like to participate. No one was ever compelled to participate in the drama. However, soon all of them were happily and actively engaged in their performances on some or other scenario around conflict and resolutions.

As stated earlier there were times that i had formal lectures as an introduction to the topic. Nonetheless, I preferred to have interactive exchanges. I would occasionally ask different students to comment or raise questions. Thus, during the early stages i one day asked a particular student a question. The entire class (or so it seemed) sniggered or burst out laughing. I was shocked at this behaviour and tried diplomatically to assess what the issue was. However, i was rather stern in my critique of their laughter. I reminded them that their behaviour went against the entire grain of TJ and the respect for the dignity and integrity of each individual. I then realised that this student was French and Kinyarwanda speaking and his English was minimal. I then repeated my question to him more slowly but there was no response. I reformulated my statement in various ways in order to simplify it. Eventually i restated my question as a statement. I then asked the student whether he agreed or disagreed with my statement. I further encouraged him by requesting: 'Just say "yes" or "no"'. He then said 'No'. In subsequent lessons i sometimes engaged this student in a similar fashion until i augmented the interaction to use further sentences. I added, 'Why do you agree?' This student gradually spoke extemporaneously, interacted actively in discussions and his presentations were well prepared.[3] He was one of the first students to complete and submit his thesis. I recall that during his viva he performed very well.

I was also mindful of the fact that our students had had a long day of work before coming to class at 6pm until 9pm. I heard that most places of work commence at 7am until 5pm. These long hours were of concern and that there was no time for relaxation or exercises. I then decided to institute some relaxation exercises like stretches or that we should maybe jog or walk briskly around the classroom block sometimes. There were a few who adamantly refused to participate. I tried to encourage them on the importance of exercises but to no avail. This i accepted. On the other hand, i also introduced meditation; both guided and unguided. I recall some students thanked me in the evaluation for introducing them to meditation.

Students' Reflections

The following is based on an evaluation for TJ for the class done on 29 July 2011. The written questions posed to the students were optional and they responded in writing to a questionnaire with open-ended questions. The quotations will be used verbatim. The references for each student are devised as follows: S for the group, then the group number followed by the students' comments which had been transcribed and numbered. Students were also given the option to write their names on the questionnaire. I will focus mainly on the responses to questions 3 and 4 as they directly link to the theme of this chapter.

Question 3 asked: *'Did you find the content sometimes upset you, made you angry or caused pain and anguish? In general how did it affect you emotionally?'*

The data from responses can be divided into the following themes: (1) not experienced any emotions; (2) very angry with what's happened and still is happening in some countries; (3) victim vs perpetrator; (4) questioning why is it important to learn and some gender implications.

Some general responses on each of these themes are presented below. Responses on theme one were as follows:

- The content did not affect me emotionally because as ... scholar(s) we have to do analysis. (S3.16).
- Not at all (S3.8).
- No, the content was very interesting (S3.14).

The responses above are the only three from the 38 students in the class to have used this theme in their response which meant that the majority of the class had been emotionally affected.

From theme 2, most of the students referred to the issue of justice hence the subject content made an impact on them. Some were affected by injustice even within TJ mechanisms and expressed this:

- I have been emotionally affected by the way injustice is still affecting millions of people all over the world despite efforts (S3.34).

- It did not affect my emotional status but sometimes when we were reading [about] other countries I was sometimes very upset by the way they are very unjust. (S3.29).

There was also some focus on the third theme, victim versus perpetrator:

- Studying about the elements of TJ like reparations ... and compensation remind me of the life between survivors and perpetrators ... sometimes it was a painful experience (S3.30).
- As a survival [survivor] of Genocide, I found teaching [reading] the way the persecutors are given money in Ugandan Amnesty Act and it made me think about what victims feels (S3.37).
- I was very upset and angry about the failure for TJ to benefit victims fully (S3.35).

Students understood the inequality of how victims and perpetrators had been unfairly treated. At one stage a student stated out of the blue that perpetrators are everywhere in the country, they only have not been exposed. He added: 'In fact here could be perpetrators right in this class'. There was an awkward silence and momentarily i was at a loss of what to say. On gaining my composure i referred to the remarkable success thus far in Rwanda and how Rwandans have inspired the world with their forgiveness and reconciliation. A discussion then followed regarding the way forward.

The follow-up part of question 3 asked: *'Why do you think it is important to learn about TJ?'* Some responses highlighted gender implications:

- I feel bad to know how war and post-war affect women differently with [from] men. (S3.3).
- Yes, TJ teaches me how to respect all people irrespective of status, e.g. gender, race, ethnic[ity] (S4.27).

Question 4 asked: *'Did you encounter that through learning about TJ you had to reflect on your own behaviour?'*

The data from the responses can be classified into the following five themes: (1) Yes, they reflected or (2) their behaviour changed; (3) expression of commitment to peace and gender issues; (4) awareness of being integral to TJ; (5) reflection on behaviour/revelation/ realisation.

Most responses were couched in general terms but one gave details of specific lessons. I used the song of South African singer, Vicki Sampson, 'My African Dream'. I played the song a few times so that they could clearly hear and understand all the words. The students then had to reflect on their Dream for Rwanda. Another lesson referred to was that of what type of Rwanda they want to work towards. They then had to write a letter to the children of Rwanda. To the question, one student wrote the following:

- Yes, [I reflected on my behaviour] several times and especially with the exercises of 'My Rwandan Dream' and 'A letter to the Children of Rwanda'. (S4.1).

Others made reference to peace building and gender issues:

- Yes, I found the opportunity to think about my own behaviour, what was my role in the process of peace and reconciliation in my country, and i discovered what i had to do in order to live (having) good relationships with others (S4.13).
- Justice is a prerequisite for sustainable peace and reconciliation and gender [analysis] is the only way as a human rights issue, but also as a way of ensuring success and sustainability (S 1.11).
- I am a peace builder every moment of my life at work when i resolve cases of gender-based violence between spouses, as a staff member of the gender monitoring office (S3. 12).

Students used the vocabulary of TJ like Justice, sustainable peace and were thus acquainted with the concepts, but they also applied these to their own lives at their places of work and their homes. Teaching TJ and being exposed to horrific situations which had occurred really shocked us all. Some students shared how they were emotionally affected:

- When we were analysing some articles such as human rights reports about the Rwanda Gacaca courts it was painful ... (S3.4).
- The content sometimes made me upset and caused pain (S3.12).

Some reflected on their behaviour and their role as change agents:

- I ... realise how I can be a peace builder wherever I am (S3.4).
- Yes, peace is first and foremost. As an individual obligation, the world's peace begins with me as an individual (S3.10).

Other examples of this reflection resulted in their commenting on working towards some change in their lives:

- This course of TJ helped me to reflect on my behaviour that I should avoid conflict starting with me in my home (S3.5).
- I learnt a lot from TJ. I had to think of my way of forgiving, peace building, reconciliation, etc. (S3.11).

- With the TJ Course, I got the chance to examine my conscience and realise I need to operate some changes in behaviour, respect ... others and [be] responsible (S3.15).
- Yes, I had always to reflect on my own behaviour—some exercises also required one to think about our own behaviour. Yes, I believe I treat [colleagues and workers] with respect (S3.19).

These responses reflect what i stated at the beginning of this chapter: That TJ was not just an academic exercise but a personal journey in many ways.

One of the key lessons we focused on was to learn to be critical and read texts critically. At various workshops in Kigali, Rwandan scholar, Phil Clarke, emphasised how polarised academics are about Rwanda and the progress developing: some called President Paul Kagame a dictator whereas others saw him as visionary. What we discovered when we did literature searches on the internet was that the majority of the texts on the internet or even in the library were written by non-Rwandans. This we discussed and came to the conclusion why it is important for Rwandans to publish their research. We discussed this as an epistemological issue. Some writers have never even been in Rwanda and used secondary data done by non-Rwandans. We looked at their research methodology and the periods that they actually did their fieldwork. Some had very small samples and most none at all, yet they made the most generalised comments in a most authoritative and confident manner.[4] The students were concerned about this:

- Yes, sometimes the content was making me angry because the articles and publications had different and inaccurate views (and) opinions about the Rwandan context (S3.17).
- Yes, negative and biased articles on my country and government upset me (S3.18).

This encouraged the students to realise the importance of publishing their research. The Centre had a workshop on publishing and some have already published their work.

My Reflections

As a South African i was impressed by the many positive things students exchanged and Rwandans were doing in general. This made me reflect and explore what we as South Africans could learn and emulate. One of the many events i had witnessed was the reconciliation between perpetrators and victims. Genocidaires (convicted prisoners guilty of genocide) built houses for the children of their victims. Poor women (both groups of victims and perpetrators) because of their poverty and need to feed their children, worked together to form cooperatives as Marie Odette Kansanga Ndahiro's and Jane Umutoni's data[5] reflected. This impressed me deeply.

During my interrogation while in solitary confinement in SA during apartheid my interrogator proudly announced he would serve in the new government that would inevitably happen as the signs were there that the apartheid regime's days were counted. I immediately mentioned the need for a Nuremberg type trial. He arrogantly retorted that no human rights violations have been committed in SA. I challenged him, highlighting the fact that he was an Afrikaner white male, which gave him great power and many privileges in apartheid SA. I added that he was either so obtuse or denied that he did not know that what he was doing to me was a human rights violation. Subsequently post-1994 in SA we had the Truth and Reconciliation Commission (TRC). He did not consider it necessary to go. As many will attest, despite being internationally lauded, it had mixed results. The Amnesty section worked more effectively than the Reparations one. Millions had suffered gross human rights violations, yet they are still not classified as victims. The TRC lasted for 10 years and identified only 1,700 of us listed with the TRC as victims. One of the key recommendations of the TRC is that the process of identifying victims of gross human rights should continue. This has not yet happened. Khulumani Support Group of which i was a board member is working towards and advocating for the incomplete work of the TRC to be finalised.

I am privileged to be one of the 1,700 that are classified as 'victim of gross human rights' and i receive a special monthly pension. Our treason trial of 14 persons is a microcosm of the new SA. Post-trial only six of us had privileged employment and four of these were as members of parliament and have had political appointments. Two were fairly comfortable within their families but the rest really struggled to get employment. One still has not have employment since the treason charges had been dropped in 1990.

The class discussions and witnessing the events in Rwanda made me realise the importance of reconciliation. Perpetrators met victims asking for forgiveness, shared experiences and worked towards reconciliation. I decided that during my holidays to SA i would try to speak to my interrogator. I had a few questions that i would like to pose to him and hoped that through this interaction some understanding and reconciliation would result. I was also encouraged about the possibility of meeting with him when i learnt about how another South African Apartheid Lieutenant Mostert (a very notorious Security Policeman during the 1980s) had approached political activist Johnny Issel to meet and asked for forgiveness. Johnny Issel was a grassroots political leader who had been terrorised by Mostert. When i learnt about the Mostert visit and apology i was heartened. I believed in sharing this news with the Captain, he may be encouraged to follow Mostert's example and agree to our meeting.

Captain Andre Du Toit did not want to meet or have any form of interaction with me. He justified through writing a three page email why he did not want to be interviewed. He gave me permission to use the email in my writing. Of course, i should forward my text to him before publishing. What is marked though is that as a beneficiary of apartheid and who worked to maintain the apartheid system, he does not make any reference to this or the negative implications of doing this. He believes he 'served both regimes faithfully, the former under the Nationalist apartheid Party and secondly under the African National Congress'. He is now 'doing his bit for the new SA' as he is *'lecturing mainly to blacks in Criminal Law'*. He further added: *Apparently I must have done some things correctly, as I was promoted to [a very senior] rank ... in the ... Province*. He has been promoted to general.

My responses: Immediately, i think of the enormous pension he gets. In terms of reparations and dignity of the victims, i think of my co-trialists and to what extent some of them are living in dire poverty and unemployment. What is also remarkable, though, like most beneficiaries of apartheid, he does not take any responsibility for the past. Instead he still refers to *'(the) involvement in the criminal actions you and others engaged in during the so-called Rainbow Trial'* (my emphasis). He refers to our 'criminal actions' even though none of us had been found guilty, as all the charges had been dropped in December 1990.

Conclusions

TJ was not an academic subject but gave my students and me an opportunity to explore the context of our lives, what was happening in our countries and what needed to be changed and resolved. The course material encouraged self-reflection and our roles and contributions to building a new society. What was remarkable was the fact that students mentioned their commitments to provide positive inputs into their homes, communities and the country in general.

According to the Kigali Institute of Education's (where the Gender Centre was housed) evaluation 94% strongly agreed that the learning outcomes were clear and that they had opportunity to actively participate in the module. In the overall evaluation, comments included: 'It is the most interesting module I learn in the master's' (p. 5); 'more time' (p. 5); 'I recommend this module for all university students' (p. 8). Other concerns were 'Too many assignments' (p. 8); 'Outline of course to be given before the course' (p. 8).

The fact that we did country cases and that i highlighted the parallels and polarities between Rwanda and South Africa gave an added irony to our analyses of these countries.[6] There were many positive experiences that South Africa could emulate; one being the structured memorial time as in Rwanda.

There are many positive aspects that can be learnt from Rwanda. Because of the *umuganda* tradition (monthly cleaning up) Rwanda is billed as the cleanest African country. The parents' evenings (*umuhira*) are devoted to parents discussing gender equality in the family. The *agaciro* (dignity) fund has been in place for some years. It is a project through which Rwandans all contribute to general development in order to lessen their dependence on external funding. But it was fast-tracked in November 2012 when countries like the United Kingdom, France, the Netherlands and the United States of America, amongst others, immediately stopped their funding because of Rwanda's alleged support of the rebel Congolese group, M23, in the Eastern DRC. This has since been disproved. Each person and public institution took decisions about how much they were to donate monthly. Most decided on 10% of their month's salary. In our case, our university decided on 30%. People still willingly continue to pay this. It has been an inspiring experience for me to teach and live in Rwanda.

Notes

[1] I consciously use the small letter for the first personal pronoun 'i' throughout this text. In Afrikaans which we speak, as well as many other languages, a small letter is used for the first person singular. I hence choose to follow this example as it also reminds me to remain humble. The exception is when i start a sentence with it i will use the capital letter.

[2] 29 July 2011.

[3] This process was protracted through a number of classes. I was mindful not to focus too much on the student for a long time during one lesson. This could also have been embarrassing to the student.

[4] Two of many possible examples include Senier (2008) and Rombouts (2004).

[5] Ndahiro (2012) and Umutoni (2012).

[6] In both countries April 1994 was a turning point in their respective histories; Rwanda experiencing the genocide until 4 July 1994 and South Africa the apprehension and later celebration of successful first democratic elections.

References

Kansanga Ndahiro, MO 2012, The 1994 Rwanda Genocide against Tutsi Memories and the lives of raped Tutsi Women. Thesis submitted to the Centre for Gender Culture and Development, Kigali Institute of Education, 2012.

Rombouts, H 2004, *Victim Organisations and the Politics of Reparation: A case study on Rwanda*. Intersentia, Antwerp.

Senier, A 2008, Traditional Justice as Transitional Justice: A Comparative Case Study of Rwanda and East Timor, *Praxis: Fletcher Journal of Human Security*, vol. 23, 67–88.

Umutoni, J 2012, Tools of Nurturing Women's Entrepreneurship and Promoting Reconciliation in Post-Conflict Rwanda: Buranga Women's Cooperative.

Thesis submitted to the Centre for Gender Culture and Development, Kigali Institute of Education, 2012.

Contributor Biography

Gertrude Fester-Wicomb, an anti-apartheid activist, was part of the Women's National Coalition that contributed to gender-sensitivity in the South-African Constitution. Like many political prisoners she was an MP in the new democratic government. Academic positions include Professor Extraordinaire (Western Cape University), Wynona Lipman Chair (Centre for American Women and Politics, Rutgers, USA), Professor in Transitional Justice (Rwanda) and Sociology (Sol Plaatje University). Currently PhD supervisor (Bishop Stuart University, Uganda) and Honorary Professor (Centre for African Studies, University of Cape Town).

The Importance of Educating Girls and Women in Sciences

Verdiana Grace Masanja

Abstract

For the past decades, focus on attaining gender equality in science education has attracted a lot of attention. Governments and international community believe that girls'/women's science education is a worthwhile investment; it has many direct effects on economic growth and human welfare. In this chapter, we discuss this view as a tool for development as well as the moral aspect of creating equality. We focus on what practically is being done to promote girls'/women's science education and why their participation continues to be low despite many efforts and heavy investment.

Emphasis on Science, Technology, Engineering and Mathematics (STEM) education has been a major focus of developing countries, based on the perception that the difference between poor and rich countries is seen to lie in their levels of generating scientific knowledge and innovations, applying STEM for socio-economic productivity and services and working productively in Science and Engineering (S&E) careers (Masanja, 2018). Additionally, it is reported that S&E careers are better paid and rewarding than non-S&E ones. Since fewer women than men attain education globally due to the numerous

---

How to cite this book chapter:
Masanja, V. 2021. The Importance of Educating Girls and Women in Sciences. In: Randell, S., Yerbury, H. and Escrig-Pinol, A. (eds.) *Gender and Learning in Rwanda*. Pp. 77–91. Sydney: UTS ePRESS. DOI: https://doi.org/10.5130/aag.g. License: CC BY-NC-ND.

barriers girls and women face based on gender biases and stereotypes, education for girls and women in general, and especially in STEM fields, has been a major concern for many decades (Masanja, 2018).

Before discussing why it is important to educate girls and women in science, I start by discussing why educational opportunity should be equal to all individuals. An educational opportunity is valued either for the intrinsic benefit of acquiring knowledge, or for its instrumental benefit, such as a greater chance of finding work (Masanja, 2018). To have this opportunity, a person should not face any insuperable barriers not directly related to a particular educational goal. Equal opportunity can be said to exist when to attend a selective school or college or university, all other things being equal, the only barrier they face is passing the entry examination. Equal opportunity does not exist if a female individual also faces other obstacles that the male individual does not.

In the next section, the discourse is presented from points of view raised by philosophers and legal practitioners in countries with stark educational disparities based on race, religion, gender and other social economic strata (Shields, Newman & Satz, 2017).

Why Educational Opportunities Ought to Be Equal

From the philosophical and legal points of views, it is widely accepted that educational opportunities for children ought to be equal (Alexander, 1985; Loury, 1987; Jacobs, 2010; Carnevale, Rose & Cheah, 2011; Sahlberg, 2011; Ryan, 2008, pp. 1232–1238; Reich, 2013). A significant assumption here is that a child's future should not be determined by so-called 'accidents of birth', such as the colour of their skin, the social or economic position of their parents or their gender. Education can have a significant influence on job opportunities, overall well-being and the possibilities of being a good citizen (Duncan & Murnane, 2011; and Shields, Newman & Satz, 2017).

Education is considered a highly valuable good; for individuals and for societies as a whole (Nussbaum, 1999). It has been argued that the main purpose of education is to develop the skills and talents of the individual, so that he or she can be fulfilled, contented and productive. In turn, there are advantages for the wider society in having educated people able to share their knowledge and skills, make informed decisions and participate in civil society.

A second purpose for education is to prepare people for the workforce. The education policies of many countries state that an instrumental goal of basic (primary and secondary) education is to support access to higher education and that a range of benefits accrue to the individual as a result, including access to interesting jobs, better health care, better decision-making skills and so on (Institute for Higher Education Policy, 1998). Research shows that the more education a person has, the wealthier he or she is likely to be and the more likely to enjoy good health. A child denied the opportunity of an education is unlikely to be productive and to enjoy these benefits (Carnevale, Rose & Cheah, 2011; Jacobs, 2010).

Education to participate in the workforce can have significant benefits for a country, for example leading to growth in Gross Domestic Product (GDP). In this context, education is a highly ranked good in today's exceedingly competitive labour market, leading to the call to ensure equal education opportunity to all. Equal education opportunity is a matter of justice and human rights, regardless of genders (Alexander, 1985; Reardon, 2011: p. 91; Reardon, Robinson-Cimpian, & Weathers, 2015).

Science Education a Human Right or a Development Tool?

Support for the importance of educating women and girls in science draws on two arguments, the right to education on the basis of non-discrimination and the contribution of women to economic and welfare development. The right to education, based on equality and free from discrimination is a recognised right under human rights law. Non-discrimination on the grounds of gender has been a critical concern in education, especially in STEM education and careers globally, and particularly in sub-Saharan Africa (SSA) countries. Women and girls lag behind in education; they face multiple obstacles to equal rights to quality education based on gender, and other factors, such as age, ethnicity, poverty and disability.

For decades, this became a global concern resulting in women's groups and feminist movements being established to advocate for education as a right, claiming for girls and women the right to education on the basis of non-discrimination and equality. By the 1960s the international community began to recognise the equal right to quality education and committed to achieving gender equality in education, through the acceptance of a number of UN and African Conventions (Convention against Discrimination in Education (CADE), 1960; International Covenant on Economic, Social and Cultural Rights (ICESER), 1966; Convention on the Elimination of All Forms of Discrimination against Women (CEDAW), 1979; Convention on the Rights of the Child (CRC), 1989; Article 12 of the Protocol to the African Charter on Human and Peoples' Rights on the Rights of Women in Africa (ACHPR), 2003) obliging governments legally to remove all discriminatory barriers and undertake positive measures to bring about gender equality in education.

In the 1980s, another argument began to emerge, advanced by development aid agencies, where gender and education became central elements in debates about development aid. It resulted in the inclusion of a gender perspective as a tool for development in all development aid agendas.

In gender and development, the most dominant view of the importance of female education is that investment in girls' and women's education is worthwhile due to the many direct effects it has on economic growth and human welfare (e.g. Bysiewicz, 2018; Madu, 2013). The image created by this view is that girls' and women's education is important when it has a positive effect on development. In other words, education has no use if girls and women do not use it for something that has an economic or human welfare effect. Such an emphasis has an implication that if it can be proved that girls' and women's lack of education would lead to economic growth and wellbeing, then action would be taken to ensure girls and women do not get education.

Women's and girls' education is often viewed by aid agencies and organisations which invest in female education as the solution for developing countries that will change everything, such as delivering them from poverty (e.g. Thousand Girls Initiative, 2018). This discourse dominated the Millennium Development Goals (MDGs) whose emphasis was on poverty reduction where arguments about educating women especially in STEM fields was on their contribution to economic development. Less emphasis was put on girls' and women's own right to education and thus to enjoy the benefits of education for themselves and to explore their full potential.

What do People Think about the Importance of Female Education?

Between October and November 2018, I conducted a short survey of various individuals to get their views on what they perceive to be the importance to educate girls and women in STEM. I sent the following two questions to 987 men and women who are on my various WhatsApp groups: Question 1: Do you think it is important to educate girls and women in STEM? Please pick one of the answers: yes or no or don't know. Question 2: If yes, explain why? The WhatsApp groups include fellow mathematicians from Africa; my current and former colleagues at universities where I worked full-time and part-time in Rwanda, Tanzania, Uganda and Kenya; family members; and members of some women associations in Africa. I received answers from 822 respondents. All said 'yes' to the first question, and all gave as many reasons as they wished to the second question. All their responses fall into the two categories discussed above: (i) it is a human right on the basis of equal opportunity and non-discrimination, and (ii) it is a development tool because of women's and girls' effect on economic growth and human welfare. In the following section, the responses are summarised.

'Female Education is a Human Right'

I summarise and cluster responses on female education as a human right into six most frequently advanced reasons:

1. Responses from about 86% (707 out of 822) can be summarised as follows: There is a massive gender imbalance that persists in STEM-related fields. According to the United Nations, Scientific and Cultural Organisation (UNESCO, 2017) ground-breaking report 2017, only 35% of STEM students in higher education globally are women, and differences are observed within STEM disciplines with Mathematics, Statistics and Computer Sciences being as low as 16%. This leads to having very few women in STEM related jobs in industry (hovering between 10% and 30%). Therefore, it is important to increase their representation in tertiary education.
2. About 65% (534 out of 822) responded that having a more equal combination of men and women in leadership and STEM jobs would improve creativity and innovation and consequently lead to sustainable positive economic and socio-cultural change. Therefore, it is important to increase women's representation in tertiary education.
3. About 55% (452 out of 822) contend that women are creators and problem solvers. The STEM fields help to create solutions and solve problems. Women's (girls') education in these fields will help further the already inbuilt skills and thus equip and empower them.
4. All 822 (100%) respondents are of the view that too many girls and women are held back by biases, social norms and expectations influencing the quality of the education they receive and the subjects they study. There is no evidence that girls are less capable in STEM fields, but rather that they often 'feel' less capable, partly due to stereotyping. Such self-perception contributes to girls and women missing out on STEM education. Through the biases and stereotypes which lead to women's (girls') low self-efficacy in STEM, girls and women are denied the chance to explore their potential in STEM and to capitalise on their inbuilt skill as problem solvers. This is a social injustice which must be rectified.
5. About 93% (764 of the 822) responded that there is a tendency for STEM jobs to be higher paid, meaning that the lack of women in these roles is contributing to the gender salary gap.
6. All 822 (100%) respondents said that the lack of women in STEM fields means having fewer female role models, both for current female STEM employees and for girls still forming choices, thus this necessitates increasing the number of women/ girls in STEM careers and studies.

'Female Education Creates Wealth and Health'

Below I cluster responses on female education as a development tool into three reasons:

1. Responses of nearly 23% (189 of 822) can be summarised as 'when you educate a woman, you educate the whole society, or the country, or the world'.
2. About 15% (133 of 822) said educating women in STEM has higher returns economically and socially.
3. Responses of about 8% (66 of 822) can be summed as 'if women are educated in STEM there will be less disease, less malnutrition and their families will be healthier'.

Although this survey cannot be termed a scientific study in the sense of research, these findings give an indication about current perceptions on why girls and women should get access to science education. The majority of responses hold the view that girls' and women's education is a human right. Very few respondents still hold the formerly widely held views that women's education is good when it has a positive effect on development and social welfare. Girls' and women's science education is important foremost because of their own right to the science education for them to enjoy its benefits for themselves and to explore their full potential and be able to also contribute to economic and welfare development.

In the next section, I explore whether the gender gap in STEM education (and careers) exists and if so, how wide the gender gap is.

Is the Gender Gap in STEM Education and Careers Narrowing?

Tremendous efforts have been made by various stakeholders to achieve gender equality in education, and female progress has been registered in education and the workplace during the past 50 years. Data from the UNESCO Institute of Statistics (UIS) for 110 countries with available data, show that women have made great strides in higher education, slightly outnumbering men overall at bachelor and master's level. In 2013, the share of female graduates with bachelor's degrees was 53%; that of female master's degrees' graduates was also 53%. However, that of PhD graduates dropped to 44%, and the share of women engaged in postdoctoral research dropped even more sharply to 28% (UNESCO Science Report, 2015, p. 86). Despite efforts to bridge the gender gap in STEM subjects, women remain underrepresented in STEM fields. For example, 2014 data from the USA collected by the National Science Foundation, National Center for Science and Engineering Statistics (NCSES), show that although the number of women earning degrees in engineering has increased in the 20 years from 1995 to 2014, women's participation remains well below that of men at all degree levels in Engineering, as well as in Computer Science and Physics. In 2014 women earned fewer than 23% doctorates in Engineering, 21% in Computer Science, 29% in Mathematics and Statistics and 19% in Physics

(NCSES, 2017). However, women earned more than 50% of the degrees awarded in Biosciences (58% bachelor, 57% master and 53% PhD). Studies ascertain that such gaps, are not the result of differences in intellectual ability.

Science education is compulsory for all at primary and lower secondary level in most education systems in the world. The gender gap in education at those levels also means a gender gap in science education. The 2015 Statistics from the UIS database show that except for tertiary education, the world taken as whole has achieved the target of gender parity at basic education levels (primary, lower secondary and upper secondary). World gender parity indices are: 1.00, 0.99, 0.98 and 1.12, respectively, for primary, lower secondary, upper secondary and tertiary education levels. However, gender disparity exists at regional and country levels. For SSA, the gender parity indices are 0.94, 0.90, 0.84 and 0.70, respectively, for primary, lower secondary, upper secondary and tertiary education levels. The 2015 UIS Statistics show the percentages of countries in the world which have reached gender parity to be: 66% in primary, 45% in lower secondary, 25% in upper secondary and 4% in tertiary education while 36% of SSA countries have achieved gender parity in primary education, 26% in lower secondary and 9% in upper secondary education (Global Education Monitoring (GEM) Report, 2018: p. 11). Gender disparity at tertiary level is very stark worldwide and in all regions. A very small percentage of countries in various regions have achieved gender parity in tertiary education where the World average is 4%. No country (0%) in four regions (Caucasus and Central Asia, Northern Africa and Western Asia, Pacific and SSA) has reached gender parity in higher education, but: in the regions of Europe and Northern America as well as Latin America and the Caribbean 5% of the countries have reached gender parity in tertiary education. While in the Eastern and South-eastern Asia region 7% countries have attained gender parity, in the Southern Asia region the percentage is 22%.

Based on household survey data in 2010–2015 (GEM Report, 2018, p. 15), the world completion rates were 83% for primary, 69% for lower secondary and 45% for upper secondary education. Globally, gender parity has been achieved in completion rates at the three education levels: primary, lower secondary and upper secondary, with gender parity indices of 1.01, 1.01 and 0.99 respectively. But disparities exist between regions. For example, 86 girls completed the lower secondary education level for every 100 boys in SSA, while in Latin America and the Caribbean, 93 boys completed the level for every 100 girls.

In tertiary education, only 4% of countries have achieved parity, with most countries reporting more female students than male. Overall, there are more women than men in tertiary education in five of the seven regions. The Southern Asia region is approaching gender parity where the index is 0.95. SSA is the only region where women still do not enrol in or graduate from tertiary education at the same rates as men (gender parity index in 0.70). However, in many countries, although women outnumber men as graduates, they lag behind men in completing STEM degrees. In Chile, Ghana and Switzerland, women account for less than 25% of all STEM graduates, while more women than men in Albania, Algeria and Tunisia earned a STEM degree. In Algeria, 63% of all tertiary graduates and 54% of all STEM graduates are women (GEM Report, 2018, p. 15, Figure 4).

The situation arising from the gap between men and women in STEM is not confined to SSA, being particularly acute in many high-income countries. In Australia, for example, women are under-represented among graduates from degrees in Engineering and Technology. In 2016, the share of women completing degrees in natural and physical sciences was 52.3%. However, only 17.0% and 15.6%, respectively, earned degrees in Information Technology and in Engineering and related technologies (Australian Government, 2016: p. 127, 137). In the same year, 2016, women accounted for only 12.4% engineers in Australia's labour force and as of 2017, women made up 20.7% of those employed in computer systems design and related services (Kaspura, 2017, p. 32; Australia Bureau of Statistics, 2017).

Caranci, Judge and Kobelak (2017) described the situation in STEM education for women as 'a weak pipeline'. Data from Statistics Canada (2015–2016) show that women are less likely to seek work in the higher paying STEM fields such as Engineering and Computer Science. The share of women enrolled in tertiary level institutions in 2015–2016 was 54.7% in Physical and Life Sciences and Technologies, 26.5% in Mathematics and Computer and Information Sciences and 20.3% in Architecture, Engineering and related technologies but in the same year, women accounted for 23.1% of Computer and Information Systems professionals and 13.7% of Civil, Mechanical, Electrical and Chemical engineers. Additionally, women who graduated with bachelor's degrees in STEM in Canada in 2015, earned only 82.1% of the salaries of their male counterparts (Statistics Canada, 2015–2016 cited in Frank, 2019).

According to Eurostat, there are still more male STEM graduates in higher education, although the gender gap is being closed. In the European Union (EU-28), in 2015 women made up 42.2% of the tertiary graduates in the Natural Sciences, Mathematics and Statistics and Information and Communication Technologies combined (Eurostat, 2017). However, the gap is wide in Engineering, Manufacturing and Construction, with women graduates in Engineering, Manufacturing and Construction making up 27.4% in EU-28, 22.3% in Finland, 26.2% in France and 23% in the United Kingdom. In the job market, according to EU She Figures, (2016) women made up 40.1% of scientists and engineers in the EU-28 in 2016, but they were only 32.2% of those employed in high-tech manufacturing and knowledge-intensive high-tech services (Eurostat).

The situation in Japan is worse, according to the Japanese Ministry of Education, Culture, Sports, Science and Technology data. Only 14% of undergraduate students majoring in Engineering in 2016 were women and women researchers in Science and Technology accounted for only 15.3%

in 2016 according to the Statistics Bureau, Ministry of Internal Affairs and Communication (Yoshikawa, Kokubo & Wu, 2018).

The same picture emerges in the USA, except in the Life Sciences, with fewer women earning degrees in other STEM fields than men. In 2015, in the USA, women made up 24% of those employed in STEM occupations (Noonan, 2017). In 2016, in Computer Science and Mathematical Occupations, the share of women was 25.5% while in Architecture and Engineering occupations, women accounted for 14.2% of the workforce. Even fewer women are found in the high-tech occupations. For example, they account for 20.0% as software developers, working on applications and systems software, 9.7% as computer network architects; and 7.8% aerospace engineers. Additionally, in the high-tech highly paid jobs women are less well-paid than men in the USA. For example, women in computer, engineering and science occupations were paid an estimated 79.2% of men's annual median earnings in 2016. Even though women earn less than their male counterparts in STEM jobs, they still earn 35% more than women in general and 40% more than men in non-STEM jobs (Noonan, 2017).

The global figures mask wide inter-country variations in women enrolled in STEM disciplines. For example, in 2015–2016, in India women were at or near parity among undergraduate degree earners in science (50.1%) and IT and computer (47.7%), but remain underrepresented in engineering and technology (31.9%) (Government of India, 2016: p.T-103). While 50% of engineering graduates are women in Cyprus, 38% in Denmark and 36% in the Russian Federation, for instance (UNESCO Science Report: towards 2030, 2017).

In some developing countries, the number of engineers is sizable, for instance, in Costa Rica, Viet Nam and the United Arab Emirates (31%), Algeria (32%), Mozambique (34%), Tunisia (41%) and Brunei Darussalam (42%); Malaysia and Oman, 50% and 53%, respectively. Of the 13 SSA countries reporting data, seven (Benin, Burundi, Eritrea, Ethiopia, Madagascar, Mozambique and Namibia) have observed over 5% increases in women engineers since 2000. Studies show that women in the tech industry constitute only 28% of professionals in the sector worldwide, and just 30% in SSA.

Implications for the Context of Sustainable Development

It is clear that girls and women are less represented in STEM education especially at tertiary level and consequently in STEM research and STEM careers. To achieve equality of educational opportunity, therefore, it is clear that more investment should go into female education in STEM fields. Given the importance of education, especially STEM to individuals and to society, it needs to be available equally to both women and men.

Indeed female education has a lot of positive effects, however, the main reason as to why girls and women should be educated should be foremost the rights of the girls and women themselves and not just the effect their education can have on their family, community and country's social economic development. As discussed above, gender disparities in STEM education still exist and they are even starker in rich, developed countries. It is thus not a phenomenon of poor countries only. The importance of women's and girls' education should be to create equality among the genders by removing discriminatory barriers. Equal educational opportunity and non-discrimination should be the main issues in need of a solution, and not merely because educating women and girls is valued when it has a positive effect on others.

As discussed above, women's and girls' education in STEM has preoccupied and continues to preoccupy various groups which seek to see the gender gap in STEM education opportunity removed. Women and feminist activists advocate for the opportunity for STEM education as a right for girls and women, for their personal success in life and for competitiveness in the labour market, moving beyond the expectations and demands inherent in the MDGs. The international community approves conventions and laws on women's rights to education and gender equality for countries to observe and it monitors progress on the extent to which countries are addressing the challenge of gender disparity in STEM education. Countries ratify the international conventions/laws, enact their own laws and create the environment to ensure goals and targets they set to bridge this gender gap are met by all institutions dealing with education, including schools, colleges and universities. Aid agencies support female education financially as a development tool, on the proposition that committing to women's and girls' education is a worthwhile investment which will lead poor countries to economic growth and wellbeing.

The efforts have borne positive results, much has been gained. Today more girls go to school, college and university, however, their share in STEM subjects and careers is still very low. Besides access to schools, colleges and universities, educational opportunities are also in apprenticeships, professional development and training and in many informal types such as public debates and lectures, time spent on reading, practicing, or thinking outside of a school context. There are numerous programmes such as Coding for Girls that are undertaking informal high-tech focused initiatives to increase the number of girls and women in STEM fields.

The commitment of the 2030 Agenda for Sustainable Development, i.e. the Sustainable Development Goals (SDGs), is to 'leave no one behind'. This has implications for STEM education for girls and women. This commitment is based on the premise that boys and girls, men and women should benefit equally from development on the presumption that all human potential is essential for achieving all the SDGs and that this cannot happen if one half of humanity continues to be denied its full human rights and opportunities.

The SDGs contend that progress toward gender equality in education can have important effects on equality in employment, health and nutrition. SDG 4 on education, (Ensure inclusive and equitable quality **education** and promote lifelong **learning** opportunities for all) explicitly recognises gender equality as a guiding principle linked to the realisation of the right to education. It states clearly that girls and boys, women and men, must be equally empowered 'in and through education'.

SDGs and Gender Parity

In the transition from the aspirations of the MDGs to the commitment of the SDGs, countries are moving from the focus on poverty reduction to a broader perspective combining socio-economic and environmental priorities, for example in areas such as food security, health, water and sanitation, energy, the management of ocean and terrestrial ecosystems and climate change. All the SDGs focus areas are very much gendered; but women and men are not affected the same way. Women are more affected and they are marginalised when it comes to decision making on these focus areas.

The focus in the MDGs on health and healthcare was on women's and girls' health needs as a consequence of their biology of reproduction. The SDGs, however, need also to be concerned with addressing socially related issues and conditions that promote inequality between men and women in relation to vulnerability to ill health and disadvantages in health systems that in turn lead to gender differentiated access to and use of health and health care services. Attaining food security requires sustainability and security of agriculture, forestry, aquaculture and fishing and thus natural resources management. These are very much gendered especially in SSA due to ownership issues (land, property, money and so on), gender stereotypes, differences in income levels by men and women and societal views, all of which put women in marginalised positions. Energy production and use is very much gendered, for example in access to energy technologies, in perception of technologies and their risks, energy needs and energy use. Environment, Climate Change and Disaster Management are gendered; men and women play different roles, they access natural resources differently and there are differences in how they use the natural resources and biodiversity. Having educated women working in these fields is essential and gender parity in STEM education must be seen as inevitable to ensure SDGs will achieve the objective of leaving no one behind.

References

Alexander, L 1985, 'Fair equality of opportunity: John Rawls' (best) forgotten principle', *Philosophy Research Archives*, vol. 11, pp. 197–208. Available at: https://doi.org/10.5840/pra19851111 [Accessed 03/32/20].

Australia Bureau of Statistics 2017, 6291.0.55.003 Labour Force, Australia, Detailed, Quarterly, August 2017, Time Series Spreadsheets, Table 6: Employed Persons by Industry Subdivision of Main Jobs (ANZSIC) and Sex.

Australia Office of the Chief Scientist 2016, Australia's STEM Workforce: Science, Technology, Engineering, and Mathematics, Australian Government, Canberra. Available at: https://www.chiefscientist.gov.au/sites/default/files/Australias-STEM-workforce_full-report.pdf [Accessed 03/31/20]

Bysiewicz, I 2018, Importance of Girls' Education around the World, the Bogen Project, July 14, 2018. https://borgenproject.org/importance-of-girls-education/. [Accessed 12th October 2018].

Caranci, B, Judge, K and Kobelak, O 2017, 'Women and STEM: bridging the divide', *TD Economics*, September 12, 2017. Available at: https://economics.td.com/women-and-stem-bridging-divide [Accessed 03/31/20].

Carnevale, A, Rose, S and Cheah, B 2011, *The College Payoff: Education, Occupations, Lifetime Earnings*, Washington, DC: Center on Education and the Workforce.

Convention against Discrimination in Education (CADE), UNESCO, December 1960. Available at: https://unesdoc.unesco.org/ark:/48223/pf0000132598 [Accessed 03/31/20].

Convention on the Elimination of All Forms of Discrimination against Women (CEDAW), UNESCO, December 1979. Available at: https://www.un.org/womenwatch/daw/cedaw/text/econvention.htm [Accessed 03/31/20].

Convention on the Rights of the Child (CRC), UNESCO, December 1989. https://unesdoc.unesco.org/ark:/48223/pf0000101215 [Accessed 03/31/20].

Duncan, G and Murnane, R (eds) 2011, *Whither Opportunity?: Rising Inequality, Schools, and Children's Life Chances*, Russell Sage Foundation, New York.

European Commission, Directorate-General for Research and Innovation, 2016, She Figures 2015, http://data.europa.eu/88u/dataset/she-figures-2015-gender-in-research-and-innovation. [Accessed 28 October 2018].

European Commission, Eurostat, 2017, Graduates by Education level, Programme Orientation, Sex and Field of Education, Eurostat Database (2017).

Frank, K 2019, 'A gender analysis of the Occupational Pathways of STEM Graduates in Canada', Analytical Studies Branch Research Paper Series, Statistics Canada. https://www150.statcan.gc.ca/n1/pub/11f0019m/11f0019m2019017-eng.htm

India, Ministry of Human Resources Development 2016, All India Survey on Higher Education (2015-16), Table 35: Out-Turn/ Pass-Out at Undergraduate level in Major Discipline/ Subject (Based on Actual Response". Available at: https://mhrd.gov.in/aishe-report-2015-16 [Accessed 03/31/20].

International Covenant on Economic, Social and Cultural Rights (ICESER), 1966, UNESCO https://www.right-to-education.org/sites/right-to-education.org/files/resource-attachments/ICESCR_1966_en.pdf. [Accessed 28th October 2018].

Institute for Higher Education, 1998, *Reaping the Benefits: Defining the Public and Private Value of Going to College*, Institute for Higher Education, Washington, DC. Available at: http://www.ihep.org/sites/default/files/uploads/docs/pubs/reapingthebenefits.pdf [Accessed 03/31/20].

Jacobs, L 2010, 'Equality, adequacy, and stakes fairness: Retrieving the equal opportunities in education approach', *Theory and Research in Education*, vol. 8, no. 3, pp. 249–268. doi:10.1177/1477878510381627 .

Kaspura, A 2017, *The Engineering Profession: Statistical Overview*, 13th ed. Engineers Australia, Barton, ACT. Available at: https://www.engineersaustralia.org.au/resource-centre/resource/engineering-profession-statistical-overview-13th-edition [Accessed 03/31/20].

Loury, Glenn C 1987, 'Why should we care about group inequality?' *Social Philosophy and Policy*, vol. 5, no. 1, pp. 249–271. https://doi.org/10.1017/S0265052500001345

Madu, C. 2013, 'Why we should support girls' education', July 12, 2013. Available at: https://www.voicesofyouth.org/blog/why-we-should-support-girls-education [Accessed 03/31/20].

Masanja, VG 2018, "What can be done at university level to bridge the gender gap in STEM in Africa", in Fernandez Polcuch, E, Brooks, A, Bello, A and Deslandes, K (eds) *Telling SAGA: Improving Measurements and Policies for Gender Equality in Science, Technology and Innovation Working Paper 5*, UNESCO, Paris, pp. 56–59. https://liseo.ciep.fr/index.php?lvl=notice_display&id=42998

National Science Foundation, National Center for Science and Engineering Statistics (NCSES), Women, Minorities, and Persons with Disabilities in Science and Engineering, 2017, Arlington, VA, NSF 17-310, January 2017. https://www.nsf.gov/statistics/2017/nsf17310/static/downloads/nsf17310-digest.pdf

Noonan, R 2017, Women in STEM, 2017 Update (USA Department of Commerce, Economics, and Statistics Administration, Office of the Chief Economist, November 13, 2017). https://www.commerce.gov/news/fact-sheets/2017/11/women-stem-2017-update

Nussbaum, M 1999, *Sex and Social Justice*, Oxford University Press, New York.

Protocol to the African Charter on Human and Peoples' Rights (ACHPR) on the Rights of Women in Africa 2003, Article 12. UNESCO. Available at: https://www.un.org/en/africa/osaa/pdf/au/protocol_rights_women_africa_2003.pdf [Accessed 03/31/20].

Reardon, S 2011, 'the widening academic achievement gap between the rich and the poor: new evidence and possible explanations', in Duncan, G and Murnane, R (eds) *Whither Opportunity? Rising Inequality, Schools, and Children's Life Chances*, New Russell Sage Foundation, New York, pp. 91–116.

Reardon, S, Robinson-Cimpian, J and Weathers, E 2015, 'Patterns and trends in racial/ethnic and socioeconomic academic achievement gaps', in Ladd, H and Goertz, M (eds) *Handbook of Research in Education Finance and Policy*, 2nd ed., Routledge, New York, pp. 497–516.

Reich, R 2013, 'Equality, adequacy, and K12 education', in Allen, D and Reich, R (eds) *Education, Justice, and Democracy*, University of Chicago Press, Chicago, IL, pp. 623–648.

Ryan, J 2008, 'Standards, testing, and school finance litigation', *Texas Law Review*, vol. 86, pp. 1223–1262.

Sahlberg, P 2011, *Finnish lessons*, Teachers College Press, New York.

Shields, L, Newman, A and Satz, D 2017, 'Equality of educational opportunity, in Zalta, E (ed.) *The Stanford Encyclopedia of Philosophy*. Available at: https://plato.stanford.edu/entries/equal-ed-opportunity/. [Accessed 03/31/20]. 2

Thousand Girls Initiative (n.d.), Cooperative Education, Why Girls?, https://www.thousandgirlsinitiative.org/about/why-girls/. [Accessed 10/12/18].

UNESCO 2017, Cracking the code: girls' education in science, technology, engineering and mathematics (STEM); report of the UNESCO International Symposium and Policy Forum. Available at: https://unesdoc.unesco.org/ark:/48223/pf0000253479 [Accessed 03/31/20].

UNESCO, Global Education Monitoring Report Gender Review, 2018, Meeting our commitments to gender equality in education, UNESCO and United Nations Girls Education Initiative (UNGEI). http://www.ungei.org/GEM_Report_Gender_Review_2018(1).pdf. [Accessed 03/31/20].

UNESCO Science Report: towards 2030. Is the gender gap narrowing in science and engineering? 2015, https://en.unesco.org/sites/default/files/usr15_is_the_gender_gap_narrowing_in_science_and_engineering.pdf [Accessed 28th October 2018].

Yoshikawa, K, Kokubo, A and Wu, C-H 2018, 'A cultural perspective on gender inequity in STEM: The Japanese context', *Industrial and Organizational Psychology*, vol.11, no. 2, pp. 301–309.

Contributor Biography

Verdiana Grace Masanja is a Professor of Mathematics at Nelson Mandela Institution of Science and Technology, Tanzania. She holds a Doctorate in Fluid Mechanics from the Technical University of Berlin (TUB), Germany attained in 1986. She has taught and held leadership positions in universities in Tanzania and Rwanda and on short-term assignments in Finland and several African countries. She has gathered wide experience in gender in Education, and Science, Technology, Engineering and Mathematics (STEM).

The Framing of Gender-Based Violence Discourses in Mainstream Development: From a Human Rights Violation to a Development Barrier

Astrid Escrig-Pinol

Abstract

This chapter discusses the emergence of gender-based violence (GBV) as a grassroots women's organisations' concern, and how it later became a human rights issue and a priority in the mainstream development agenda. The anti-GBV movement is deeply rooted in a human rights approach and in defending the right of women to a life free of violence. However, mainstream development and governmental initiatives have increasingly framed the fight against GBV in instrumental terms, situating GBV as an obstacle to development. The chapter uses a feminist lens to critically analyse mainstream discourses and their implications for policy and development programs aimed at reducing GBV rates.

Introduction

There is widespread agreement that gender-based violence (GBV) is a global pandemic of alarming proportions and one of the major obstacles to development. Worldwide, one in three women experience violence in their lifetime, with a majority of perpetrators being men (WHO et al., 2013). Although the global scope and magnitude of the problem is generally understood, it is often overlooked that it affects all women. While many women actually experience

---

How to cite this book chapter:
Escrig-Pinol, A. 2021 The Framing of Gender-Based Violence Discourses in Mainstream Development: From a Human Rights Violation to a Development Barrier. In: Randell, S., Yerbury, H. and Escrig-Pinol, A. (eds.) *Gender and Learning in Rwanda.* Pp. 93–106. Sydney: UTS ePRESS. DOI: https://doi.org/10.5130/aag.h. License: CC BY-NC-ND.

violence, the fear and threat of it is common to all, influencing women and girls' thoughts and actions at all levels: from the most intimate aspects of life at home, to participation in public, political, and economic activities (Pickup et al., 2001).

Rwanda is a global leader in gender equality. It was the first country in the world to enshrine gender equality in the constitution and to have over half of the seats in Parliament held by women (World Economic Forum, 2016). However, traditional patriarchal values and attitudes prevail and rates of domestic violence remain very high (ONE UN, 2014). The case of Rwanda illustrates how major gains towards gender equality in some spheres—while they ought to be celebrated and recognised—cannot be taken as indicators of the achievement of gender equality and the eradication of GBV at a societal level.

Discourse framing, a concept coined by Erving Goffman in the mid-1980s, explains the process by which discourses impact an audience or societies at large by selecting and disseminating specific frames or approaches through an agenda-setting exercise (Viladrich, 2012). The international development complex has set the global development agenda and framed mainstream development discourses for over half a century, with important implications for global issues ranging from agricultural practices to family relations.

This chapter looks at the emergence of GBV as a priority in the mainstream global development arena and examines the evolution and current framing of GBV discourses by development institutions. The chapter employs a post-colonial feminist (PCF) lens to critically examine the trajectory of the discourses guiding anti-GBV interventions. The analysis shows that the anti-GBV movement initially emerged as a grassroots claim for the right of women to a life free of violence, an approach that human rights advocacy groups kept but mainstream development institutions put aside in favour of another approach framing GBV as a brake to national development. Currently, the latter approach prevails, combined with a rhetoric of human rights as a supporting argument.

In the next section I define mainstream development and GBV for the purpose of this chapter, and briefly introduce the theories underpinning the analysis presented, namely, critical post-development and PCF. Then, I move onto the analysis of the human rights-based discourses underpinning the fight against GBV early on, and the macroeconomics discourse that mainstream institutions and organisations have taken up more recently. The analysis of each approach using a PCF lens includes a summary of how it became the dominant discourse, some past and recent applications, and the main critiques it received. Lastly, I summarise the arguments put forward in the chapter and present some of their implications for development policy and practice.

Theoretical Underpinnings and Conceptual Framework

Mainstream Development and Post-development Theories

Mainstream development in this chapter refers to the primary discursive framework underpinning policies and programs developed and implemented by multilateral institutions, bilateral donors, and large international NGOs. Development as a field originated after World War II with a clear focus on promoting economic growth through classic liberal economics. Soon after, the concept broadened up to include political and social modernisation. In the late 1960s, dependency theories marked the return to a narrow notion of development tightly controlled by nation states. The rising of alternative thinking mostly from the global South[1] challenged this understanding of development and introduced new themes such as human flourishing, participation, capacitation, and agency. Consequently, mainstream development broadened again to become an enabling instrument designed to increase people's choices. In a cyclical fashion, with the advent of neoliberalism in the 1980s, development theories re-focused on economic growth.[2]

In the 1990s, opposition to the hegemonic neoliberal principles sparked a quest for alternatives to the mainstream development paradigm. Critical approaches frame development as an apparatus sustaining unequal material relationships and processes which structure engagement between the global South and the global North (Wilson, 2015). Amongst them, post-development theories conceive international development as a failure and search for alternative answers. In the past three decades, post-development has deconstructed the dominant development model, and, more recently, post-development thinkers have focused on theorising viable alternative systems and articulated different strategies to contest the mainstream paradigm (Escrig-Pinol, 2012).

Post-Colonial Feminism

PCF emerged in the 1980s as a response to western-centred feminism, which failed to capture the experiences and knowledges of women from other cultures, and to post-colonial theory for not addressing issues of gender. PCF scholars introduced the concept of 'double colonisation' as the way to signal the double oppression endured by women over the centuries: from colonial powers and from patriarchy (Ashcroft et al., 2013; Mohanty, 1988). While simultaneously examining patriarchy and the consequences of colonialism, PCF underscores the importance of paying attention to the ethnic, cultural, and historical background of women from non-western culture[3] (Ashcroft et al., 2013).

Post-colonial feminists have contributed to the analysis of development by focusing on the deconstruction of the patriarchy embedded in mainstream development practices and have emerged as one of the multiple voices proposing alternative paradigms (see, for instance, Lind, 2003; McEwan, 2001; Mohanty, 1988; Mohanty, 2003; Narayan, 1989). PCF has the potential to contribute to the critical exploration of relationships between cultural and global economic powers. Moreover, it points towards a radical reclaiming of the political in both public and private spheres (Escrig-Pinol, 2012).

Defining Gender-Based Violence

There is no single definition agreed upon or term used by all concerned when discussing male-perpetrated violence against women (VAW). Given the ongoing debate around naming this issue, it is important to clarify the meaning for the purpose of this chapter. In mainstream development the two most commonly used terms are VAW and GBV. When examined, they both present strengths and drawbacks. GBV is a broad term that emphasises the importance of gendered identities to violence. However, it is not explicit about the disproportionate impact this violence has on women (Merry, 2009). While VAW explicitly recognises the impact on women but fails to capture the gendered power dynamics underpinning these acts of violence.

Violence is an expression of power. In most societies, social, economic, and political power remains largely in the hands of men, thus, power is socially gendered (Sen, 1998). Women-perpetrated violence against other women exists marginally, while the pervasiveness of male-perpetrated VAW responds to historically entrenched patterns of unequal power relations between men and women. In recognition of this gendered power imbalance at the root of widespread VAW, in this chapter we will speak of GBV. Moreover, some experts argue that framing the issue in terms of gender rather than women is an effective strategy for involving both women and men in resolving the societal issues that create gender inequalities (Vann, 2002).

GBV encompasses sexual violence, intimate partner or spouse abuse (i.e. domestic violence), emotional and psychological abuse, sex trafficking, forced prostitution, sexual exploitation, sexual harassment, harmful traditional practices (i.e. female genital mutilation, forced marriage, infanticide of girl children), and other discriminatory practices at the structural level based on gender (Vann, 2002). The term labels a wide range of acts of violence committed disproportionally against women and girls for being female, and based on how a particular society assigns gender roles and expectations to women.

Gender-Based Violence in the Mainstream Development Discourse

Development literature addressing GBV has explored the multiple effects it has on women, communities, societies, governments, and economies. An ever-growing body of research demonstrates that GBV denies women's most fundamental rights and impedes their human development; hinders women's participation in development; limits the efficiency of development projects; constitutes a public health threat; places a very high economic burden on governments, and has an impact on national productivity (Escrig-Pinol, 2012). While acknowledging the harmful impact of GBV on individuals, families and society at large, the focus of the anti-GBV discourse adopted by mainstream development to craft policy and programs has shifted over time. There have been two distinct approaches taken up by dominant development organisations and institutions: the women's rights discourse and the macroeconomics discourse. The rights-based approach appeals to the right of women to live a life free of violence (Sen, 1998), whereas the macroeconomics approach is an umbrella category for all discourses focusing on the economic cost of GBV, including the impact of GBV on national productivity, income generation, social services, and development funds (Buvinic & Morrison, 2004; Day et al., 2005). This section introduces these two approaches with applied examples, and brings forward critiques from a PCF stance that expose their limitations.

The Women's Rights Discourse: Gender-Based Violence as a Human Rights Violation

Emergence and Applications

The human rights approach to GBV is rooted in the belief that acts of violence against women and girls violate a number of principles enshrined in international and regional human rights instruments, including the right to life, equality, security of person, equal protection under the law, and freedom from torture and other cruel, inhumane, or degrading treatment (Vann, 2002). In the 1990s, international actors paid increasing attention to the GBV crisis. Sparked in part by the gaining momentum of the global feminist movement, the United Nations and numerous non-governmental organisations developed strategies to tackle VAW.

In the early 1990s, GBV was still largely a taboo and seen as a private matter, a family issue. Governments would not admit that widespread VAW took place within their borders, and even less acknowledge their responsibility for implementing policies or allocating funds to programs and services to address it (Spindel et al., 2000). The emergence of violence as a crucial concern for women occurred organically, arising from grassroots women's movements from the global South (see Carrillo, 1991). Women made alliances, lobbied states and municipal governments, and used international rights law and continental and regional organisations to draw attention and to seek redress from oppressive gendered social relations and practices (Manuh & Bekoe, 2010). In this way, GBV came to the forefront of national and global agendas thanks to grassroots women's movements and feminist organisations. Initially, approaches to GBV emphasised the impact of violence on the physical and psychological well-being of women (Yodanis et al., 2000), but soon it grew to become a matter of women's rights (Carrillo, 1991).

During the 1990s and 2000s, major developments in the field of human rights resulted in the recognition of VAW as a fundamental abuse of women's human rights. In 1993, the United Nations World Conference on Human Rights held in Vienna placed VAW on the human rights agenda. That same year, the UN General Assembly's adoption of the Declaration on the Elimination of Violence against Women added to the gains made in Vienna (Pickup et al., 2001). The Declaration condemns physical and emotional violence against women in the home, the community, and when condoned by the State, as an abuse of women's fundamental human rights (Declaration on the Elimination of Violence against Women, 1993). It frames VAW as a social mechanism by which women are forced into a subordinate position compared with men, and thus a manifestation of historically unequal power relations between men and women. The momentum created by the Vienna Conference led to calls for women's rights to be mainstreamed within the human rights discourse. Some scholars argue that the success of the human rights discourse to frame GBV as a global issue is partly due to the fact that it does not separate out the 'developing' from the 'developed' world, what led to an understanding of VAW as a worldwide problem (Sen, 1998).

Main Critiques

Of all development concepts and tools currently in fashion, human rights and their international legal articulations remain the most popular. Bilateral development agencies, multilateral organisations, and transnational NGOs have embraced the centrality of human rights in the development discourse and rely on their universality. They have permeated into all development discourses and agendas to the point of being implicitly assumed by most development actors. Human rights lay at the core of the leading global development instruments like the Millennium Development Goals (MDGs) and the Sustainable Development Goals (SDGs).

Post-colonial scholars have criticised the Western values underpinning human rights and critically examined the problems caused by the indiscriminate application of human rights-based development initiatives globally. Similarly, PCF warns that the principle of universality central to the human rights framework is problematic, as it assumes the applicability of Western-centric notions of rights to all societies (Man, 2018; Sen, 1998). PCF points at three key issues with the mainstream human rights-based discourse application to international development. First, the legal and professionalised nature of much of the rights work; second, its top-down approach; and third, a focus on civil and political rights, while sidelining social and economic rights (Yuval-Davis, 2006).

Within the human rights approach, strategies aimed at protecting all women from violence have focused on integrating gender issues into human rights instruments and on expanding the role of the state in protecting women. Organisations and institutions dealing with human rights tend to focus on enforcing women's civil rights and political freedoms, and have often overlooked the fact that women's ability to claim these rights and freedoms is constrained by poverty and the denial of their economic and social rights (Amnesty International, 2010; Pickup et al., 2001). Some PCF scholars argue that research focusing on the life experiences most common to women reveal principles of human rights that do not necessarily reflect the universe of such rights as they are commonly understood. While typical human rights cases involve issues like the political activist imprisoned for the expression of her views, other forms of oppression and GBV are not always recognised as human rights violations at the international and national levels. Widespread forms of violence relevant to women but commonly excluded from human rights-based approaches include issues related to marriage, procreation, labour, property ownership, sexuality, and other manifestations of unequal citizenship that are routinely viewed as private and reflective of cultural difference (Binion, 1995).

The Macroeconomics Discourse: Gender-Based Violence as a Brake to National Development

Emergence and Applications

During the late 1980s and the 1990s a new perspective on GBV emerged. Instead of focusing on women's rights, it highlighted the economic losses to individuals and societies resulting from women's suffering of violence. This approach examines how much it costs to individuals, governments, and the private sector when women are, for instance, injured or prevented from joining the labour market. Although researchers take different approaches to answer this question, they all aim at demonstrating the financial impact of VAW at different levels (Yodanis et al., 2000), and, ultimately, at linking it to the national economy. There is some evidence of the attention paid to the cost of VAW in early development research. For instance, although primarily framing GBV as a human rights issue, Carrillo (1991) contends that many work hours are lost as a result of violence, not to speak of the costs of providing services to the victims. The macroeconomics discourse rapidly gained weight among development actors during the 1990s—it was a good fit for the new emerging global economic system, neoliberal capitalism. Researchers and practitioners also adopted this view and engaged in all kinds of measurements. International Financial Institutions (IFIs) took the lead in introducing this approach in the mainstream development field. For instance, in 1993 the World Bank calculated that rape and domestic violence accounted for about 5% of the total burden of disease among women aged 15 to 44 in developing countries (Sen, 1998). Their argument was that for economic growth to be effective, women must enjoy good health, which may be jeopardised by violence. A technical report of the Inter-American Development Bank maintained that violence against women and children is an obstacle to economic development since it impacts on various education indicators (Buvinic & Morrison, 2004). For instance, it argued that abuse adversely affects a child's performance in school and, consequently, his or her future productivity, which in turn will also lower the government's return on investment in education. In a recent brief, the World Bank (2018) claimed that in some countries, VAW is estimated to cost up to 3.7% of their GDP—more than double what most governments spend on education. Another application of this discourse appears in an article published in the *UN Chronicle* arguing for the inclusion of direct expenses for services to treat and support abused women and their children and to bring perpetrators to justice to the already high costs of GBV for national economies (Manuh & Bekoe, 2010).

The UN MDGs guided the mainstream international development agenda for 15 years (2000–2015). This international instrument was criticised for omitting substantive issues, such as GBV (Fehling et al., 2013), and for applying a narrow definition of gender equality and women's empowerment (Mohindra & Nikiéma, 2010), leaving behind the broader vision promoted by the women's movement in the 1990s. Adopted in 2015, the SDGs for 2030 have become the guiding framework for international development policy and programming globally. The specific goal focusing on women and gender issues, Goal 5, incorporates targets related to GBV. The document's preamble states that 'ending all forms of discrimination against women and girls is not only a basic human right, but is also crucial to accelerating sustainable development. It has been proven time and again, that empowering women and girls has a multiplier effect, and helps drive up economic growth and development across the board' (United Nations Stats, 2017). This text reveals how despite the dominance of the macroeconomics approach in development discourses, there is still an accompanying rhetoric of GBV as an obstacle to women's enjoyment of their right to a life free of violence.

Main Critiques

Early PCF critiques of development interventions focused on deconstructing women's role in development as passive recipients of interventions and aid by highlighting women's agency (Mohanty, 1988). However, from the late 1990s onward, a neoliberal approach to gender gave way to an exaltation of the entrepreneurial, hard-working woman as the new ideal female subject, actively contributing to development and the economy (Wilson, 2015). This paradigm switch occurred across all globally dominant development institutions. In the 2000s, the World Bank's slogan 'Gender equality as smart economics' became a paradigmatic example of the turn in mainstream development towards neoliberal discourses on gender and GBV, which guided their interventions (Wilson, 2015). Thus, the macroeconomics approach can be seen as an alignment of discourses on GBV with this larger shift in framework on gender issues, and with the neoliberal paradigm more broadly.

Development programs focused on tackling GBV have become embedded in market dynamics and logic, and have increasingly taken an approach that argues for the eradication of GBV due to its high socio-economic costs. One strategy put forward for calculating the costs associated with GBV was to estimate the willingness of individuals and societies to pay for lives free of GBV. This has been used to measure the welfare loss occasioned by GBV, but the approach did not gain popularity because of the reticence to estimate the willingness to pay for what many still consider a human right—the right to live without violence (Morrison et al., 2007). This example illustrates why mainstream development has not let go of the rights-based discourse completely, and often supports the dominant framing of GBV as a break to development with a mention to human rights.

PCF argues that VAW is functional to the current unequal and exploitative global development and economic model, as it effectively excludes women from decision-making positions where they could contest it and begin to transform it (Pickup et al., 2001). A central criticism to the macroeconomics discourse currently guiding development initiatives is that, by focusing on the relationship between GBV and economic indicators, it fails at tackling the root causes of VAW, resulting in programs and policies largely ineffective at reducing gender inequality (Escrig-Pinol, 2012). For instance, targeting women in economic development initiatives such as income-generating or microfinance programs has not been linked to a reduction of VAW, and has in some instances sparked an increase of violence against them (Gibbs et al., 2017).

Conclusion

Mainstream development discourses have evolved from framing GBV as a threat to women's human rights to validating the fight against GBV in instrumental terms as an obstacle to national development. The chapter has examined this trajectory, which responds to an alignment of mainstream development discourses to the neoliberal turn driving the global economy. A critical analysis using a PCF lens reveals several distinct problems related to the two approaches discussed. I argue that while the human rights discourse ignores issues regarding the universality of the Western-centric human rights paradigm and focuses on civil rights and political freedoms, the macroeconomics discourse reduces women to productive and reproductive beings. Furthermore, a fight against GBV based on its detrimental effect on the current neoliberal exploitative global economic system, may suggest that VAW only matters as long as it impacts financial indicators.

This shift in rhetoric has had a material impact on the type of initiatives put forward by development institutions, and reduced their potential for effecting real change towards gender equality. In practice, the two leading approaches result in policies and programs that differ considerably, while human rights discourse led to interventions centred on physical violence and access to justice, the macroeconomics discourse led to interventions aiming at reducing the costs to communities and states by, for instance, promoting women's access to the formal labour market. Applying a PCF lens to critically review these mainstream discourses and their implications for development programs and policy may assist development actors in designing interventions more attuned and responsive to the nature of GBV, deeply rooted in power inequalities between women and men.

PCF understands GBV as a manifestation of the double oppression women suffer. From men to maintain their position of power in patriarchal households and societies, and from neocolonial systems and institutions to maintain a global order based on the exploitation and oppression of marginalised groups by hegemonic powers. The dominant macroeconomics discourse is based on the real concern that VAW limits the effectiveness and efficiency of national economic development initiatives. This chapter suggests the need for converging discourses so that the costs of GBV are known and taken into consideration, while interventions are mostly directed against the underlying causes of violence, i.e. a system of unequal gender relations, allowing women's interests to be addressed holistically.

The analysis of the two dominant narratives presented in this chapter has employed an interdisciplinary social science approach to examine GBV discourses in the context of global development initiatives and neoliberal globalisation. Although the specific orientation of the two discourses diverges, they both fit into an overarching neoliberal paradigm that rewards individual responsibility and self-sufficiency. I suggest that Goffman's framing theory is a fitting conceptual and methodological framework to examine mainstream discourses, and that it could also be a useful tool to generate alternative discourses more aligned with understanding GBV as an instrument of 'double oppression' for women.

Notes

[1] Global South broadly refers to low-income countries in the regions of Latin America, Asia, Africa, and Oceania, but also comprises low-income regions from mid- and high-income countries in Europe and North-America (Dados & Connell, 2012). The term was coined in the late 1960s but was popularised in the 2010s by post-colonial scholars as an alternative to expressions such as 'third world', 'developing', or 'underdeveloped' countries.
[2] For further information on the history of development, see, for instance, Pieterse (2010).
[3] Sometimes discussed as Third World Women in the post-colonial feminist literature.

References

Amnesty International 2010, *Uganda: 'I can't afford justice': Violence against women in Uganda continues unchecked and unpunished*. AFR 59/002/2010. https://www.amnesty.org/en/documents/AFR59/002/2010/en/

Ashcroft, B, Griffiths, G and Tiffin, H 2013, *Post-colonial Studies: The Key Concepts*. Routledge, London.

Binion, G 1995, 'Human rights: A feminist perspective', *Human Rights Quarterly*, vol. 17, no. 3, pp. 509–526.

Buvinic, M and Morrison, A 2004, *Violence as an Obstacle to Development* (Technical Note 4). Inter-American Development Bank. Retrieved from http://idbdocs.iadb.org/wsdocs/getdocument.aspx?docnum=362887

Carrillo, R 1991, *Gender violence: A development and human rights issue*. https://files.eric.ed.gov/fulltext/ED361235.pdf

Dados, N and Connell, R 2012, 'The global south', *Contexts*, vol. 11, no. 1, pp. 12–13.

Day, T, McKenna, K and Bowlus, A 2005, *The economic costs of violence against women: An evaluation of the literature*. United Nations. Retrieved from http://www.un.org/womenwatch/daw/vaw/expert%20brief%20costs.pdf

Escrig-Pinol, A 2012, *Preventing domestic violence in post-conflict: A multi-sectoral analysis in northern Uganda*. Unpublished master's thesis. York University, Toronto, Canada.

Fehling, M, Nelson, BD and Venkatapuram, S 2013, 'Limitations of the Millennium Development Goals: a literature review', *Global Public Health*, vol. 8, no. 10, pp. 1109–1122. https://doi.org/10.1080/17441692.2013.845676

Gibbs, A, Jacobson, J and Wilson, AK 2017, 'A global comprehensive review of economic interventions to prevent intimate partner violence and HIV risk behaviours', *Global Health Action, 10* (sup2), Article 1290427. https://doi.org/10.1080/16549716.2017.1290427

Lind, A 2003, 'Feminist post-development thought: "Women in Development" and the gendered paradoxes of survival in Bolivia', *Women's Studies Quarterly*, vol. 31, nos. 3/4, pp. 227–246.

Man, A de 2018, 'Critiques of the human rights framework as the foundation of a human rights-based approach to development', *Journal for Juridical Science*, vol. 43, no. 1, pp. 84–116. https://doi.org/10.18820/24150517/JJS43.v1.5

Manuh, T and Bekoe, A 2010, 'Confronting violence against women', *UN Chronicle*, vol. 47, no. 1, pp. 12-15. https://doi.org/10.18356/e9cb9eae-en.

McEwan, C 2001, 'Postcolonialism, feminism and development: Intersections and dilemmas', *Progress in Development Studies*, vol. 1, no. 2, pp. 93–111.

Merry, SE 2009, *Gender Violence: A Cultural Perspective*. John Wiley & Sons, Chichester.

Mohanty CT 2003, *Feminism Without Borders: Decolonizing Theory, Practicing Solidarity*, Duke University Press, Durham, NC.

Mohanty, CT 1988, 'Under Western eyes: feminist scholarship and colonial discourses', *Feminist Review*, vol. 30, pp. 61-88. https://doi.org/10.2307/1395054

Mohindra, KS and Nikiéma, B 2010, 'Women's health in developing countries: beyond an investment?' *International Journal of Health Services*, vol. 40, no. 3, pp. 543–567.

Morrison, A, Ellsberg, M and Bott, S 2007, 'Addressing gender-based violence: A critical review of interventions', *The World Bank Research Observer*, vol. 22, no. 1, pp. 25–51. https://doi.org/10.1093/wbro/lkm003

Narayan, U 1989, 'The project of feminist epistemology: Perspectives from a nonwestern feminist', In Bordo, S. & Jaggar, A. (eds.), *Gender/Body/Knowledge: Feminist Reconstructions of Being and Knowing*, Rutgers University Press, New Brunswick, pp. 256-69.

ONE UN Rwanda (2014, October 25), Gender Equality, Rwanda. Retrieved December 17, 2018, from http://www.rw.one.un.org/mdg/mdg3

Pickup, F, Williams, S and Sweetman, C 2001, *Ending Violence Against Women: A Challenge for Development and Humanitarian Work*, OXFAM GB, Oxford. https://oxfamilibrary.openrepository.com/bitstream/handle/10546/115387/bk-ending-violence-against-women-261000-en.pdf?sequence=5&isAllowed=y

Pieterse, JN 2010, *Development theory*, 2nd edn. Sage, Los Angeles.

Sen, P 1998, 'Development practice and violence against women', *Gender & Development*, vol. 6, no. 3, pp. 7-16. https://doi.org/10.1080/741922827

Spindel, C, Levy, E and Connor, M 2000, *With an end in sight: strategies from the UNIFEM Trust Fund to eliminate violence against women*. The United

Nations Development Fund for Women. Retrieved from: https://www.eldis.org/document/A29363

United Nations General Assembly 1993, Declaration on the Elimination of Violence against Women, A/RES/48/104 § 1993, Retrieved from http://www.unhchr.ch/huridocda/huridoca.nsf/%28symbol%29/a.res.48.104.en

United Nations Stats 2017, *Global indicator framework for the Sustainable Development Goals and targets of the 2030 Agenda for Sustainable Development* (No. A/RES/71/313; E/CN.3/2018/2). United Nations. Retrieved from https://unstats.un.org/sdgs/indicators/indicators-list/

Vann, B 2002, *Gender-Based Violence: Emerging Issues in Programs Serving Displaced Populations* (GBV Global Technical Support Project). JSI Research and Training Institute.

Viladrich, A 2012, 'Beyond welfare reform: reframing undocumented immigrants' entitlement to health care in the United States, a critical review', *Social Science & Medicine*, vol. 74, no. 6, pp. 822–829.

Wilson, K 2015, 'Towards a radical re-appropriation: Gender, development and neoliberal feminism', *Development and Change*, vol. 46, no. 4, pp. 803-832. Retrieved from https://onlinelibrary.wiley.com/doi/epdf/10.1111/dech.12176

World Bank 2018, *Gender-Based Violence (Violence Against Women and Girls)* Retrieved from http://www.worldbank.org/en/topic/socialdevelopment/brief/violence-against-women-and-girls

World Economic Forum 2016, *Global Gender Gap Report 2016*, World Economic Forum, Geneva. Retrieved from http://reports.weforum.org/global-gender-gap-report-2016/

World Health Organisation (WHO), London School of Hygiene and Tropical Medicine (LSHTM) & South African Medical Research Council (SAMRC) 2013, *Global and regional estimates of violence against women: Prevalence and health effects of intimate partner violence and non-partner sexual violence* (WHO Ref. No. 978 92 4 156462 5) Retrieved from http://www.who.int/reproductivehealth/publications/violence/9789241564625/en/

Yodanis, CL, Godenzi, A and Stanko, EA 2000, 'The benefits of studying costs: A review and agenda for studies on the economic costs of violence against women', *Policy Studies*, vol. 21, no. 3, pp. 263-276. https://doi.org/10.1080/01442870020019534

Yuval Davis, N 2006, 'Human/women's rights and feminist transversal politics', In Ferree, M and Tripp, *A Global Feminism: Transnational Women's Activism, Organizing, and Human Rights*, New York University Press, New York, pp. 275–95.

Contributor Biography

Astrid Escrig-Pinol is a professor and researcher. She holds a PhD in Public Health from the University of Toronto, with a specialisation in Global Health. Her research interests focus on the social determinants of health and health systems strengthening, using research as a tool to promote social justice and health equity. Astrid has an MA in Critical International Development Studies and a BA in Journalism. Professionally, she has extensive experience in qualitative research, teaching, non-profit program management, and knowledge mobilisation.

PART II

Graduate Stories

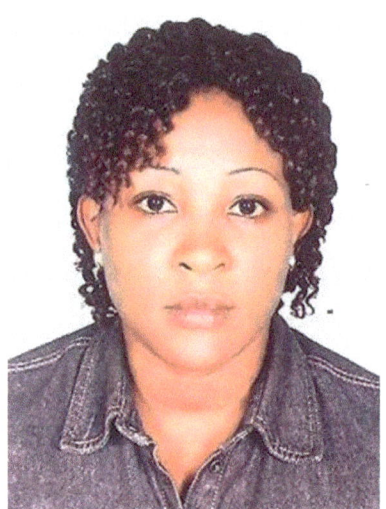

Image: Adeline Uwamahoro

Adeline Uwamahoro's story[1]

Thesis: 'Assessing the effects of a "women to women" entrepreneurship training/mentoring program in Rwanda: Rwanda Peace Through Business Program'.

Childhood and early education

I was born in Goma in the Democratic Republic of Congo in 1977, the first born in a family of seven children with three sisters and three brothers. I am Rwandese by nationality and my parents moved to Rwanda when I was four years old. I studied primary and secondary school in Kigali at Groupe Scolaire Notre Dame de Citeaux.

Career and higher education

I then taught at Gitega primary school, before going to the National University of Rwanda at Butare where I finished with a degree in Educational Psychology in 2005. I particularly feel privileged by doing the master's degree because it is intrinsically connected to the vocation that I chose of being a women's activist. It equipped me with necessary knowledge and skills in gender for my realisation and for my contribution to women's development in the world, and particularly in Rwanda. I have been CEO of a business Rwanda LinkCycle Company since 2006.

Personal life

I married in 2004 and have two children, a girl born in 2005 and a boy in 2006. In 2006, I began to work at the Kigali Health Institute and since then I have done much training on HIV/AIDS, social work and gender. I also completed a postgraduate diploma in counselling. I am a risk taker, optimistic and dynamic, but I am most happy when I take time to be quiet and explore nature. This helps me to listen to myself and feel peacefulness inside. During weekends and holidays, I love watching movies and reading non-fiction books.

I like handcrafts made by women, not just for seeing them as beautiful but also because they represent the hands of the empowered women who made them. I look at entrepreneurship as a catalyst to women's empowerment since many women didn't have the same opportunity to study as much as men, but I am sure that women are clever and could succeed if they were given a chance. They have inner potential which can be triggered for their empowerment.

Role models

I admire people who are passionate and with a strong sense of purpose. My personal unconventional hero is my Dad. I admire him so much for his strength. He made all of our challenges a lot lighter to bear because of his positivity and integrity. Ever since I was very young he used to encourage me, believe in me and show me that I have to think big and to go far. He created confidence in me and I really feel this confidence in every situation I have to face. It also motivates me to give each challenge my best shot, trusting that the future will be worth everything, as long as I don't give up on the current challenges I meet in everyday life.

Looking forward

All the colleagues I had in the Master of Gender and Development program inspired me. I believe that, as Rwandan gender experts, we will all work together and bring out the best in each other and I am looking forward to being part of a team with them to strengthen gender equality promotion in Rwanda.

Notes

[1] Autobiography written by Adeline Uwamahoro in 2011.

Image: Aline Mukantabana

Aline Mukantabana's story[1]

Thesis: 'Assessing the barriers faced by women export-oriented business owners in Rwanda'.

Childhood and early education

I was born in Burundi in 1970, the sixth of ten children, three boys and seven girls. My father was a very old man, who had not gone to school and had no work. He was much older than my mother, who was a teacher and at the same time a leader in the local community. The family left Rwanda as refugees in 1959 during the first conflict. They faced problems at first, but life was not so bad. My hardworking mum was teaching, and my sisters and brothers were all educated and started to help my parents. Mum died when I was seven, so my big sister looked after me, and she was like my mother. My primary and secondary school education was in Bujumbura, and I finished secondary school in 1989 while still in Burundi.

While I was growing up I used to ask my parents: 'Why am I here? Why are we Rwandans in Burundi?' They explained the stories of our history, and from my childhood I was thinking 'Let's go back'. When I finished my senior 6 in 1989, I moved to Kampala in Uganda to join the Rwanda Patriotic Front (RPF), I was still very young. I had met Aloisea Inyumba, who told me what was going on there. There were many women involved in the struggle, as cooks, nurses and fighters and in political and other roles. I was a fighter and Rose Kabuye was my boss. We women faced so many challenges and problems but the RPF leader, Paul Kagame, now president, really protected us in so many ways. We went back to Rwanda after the genocide and, by then, two brothers and many cousins had been killed.

Career and higher education

From 1994, I worked in the Ministry of Gender with Minister Inyumba, and then Minister Angelina Muganza. Both supported me going on to undertake a bachelor's degree. I received a scholarship from the Minister of Education and went to study gender at the University of Western Cape in South Africa, becoming the first person in Rwanda to get an undergraduate degree in gender.

In 1994, when I came back to Rwanda, I was appointed as Director for Good Governance and then Executive Secretary for the Eastern Province, 2008–2009. But all my life I wanted to work for myself, to have my own business. My idea is that, for women to be empowered, they need economic empowerment. I am doing business now and it is going well. I supply food and beverages to hotels, as well as office equipment and construction materials. I work in Bugesera. Starting a business is very difficult, so I wanted to conduct my master's research on women in entrepreneurship. The bank even had to ask my husband to sign for my loan as I could not get a loan as a woman. The bank manager asked me: 'How are you going to manage this money? Can you use this money? Ask your husband to sign'.

When I started the Master's in Gender and Development, because I already had a degree in gender, I thought that it would be easy for me. But the program has challenged me, every day I am learning something new.

Personal life

I married in 1996 to a man who had also been in the struggle with me in the RPF. By the time I was studying we had one son and my husband looked after him while I was away. I came back to Rwanda after my first year for holidays and again got pregnant. I went back to school in Western Cape and delivered my first daughter in South Africa, and immediately afterwards sat my exams. I now have three children, one boy and two girls.

Role models

My mother was my first role model. She was a very strong woman, really tough. Starting from my childhood my mum was a leader, supporting all the women in the village. She was a very respected leader, like a queen. I remember a story she told about a woman who had two babies and was pregnant and her husband came to beat her. My mum woke up and told the husband: 'I don't want you to beat your wife, I will put you in prison if you do it again'. Inyumba and Angelina were also role models to me.

Looking ahead

I loved the master's program and I want to go on to a PhD program. I want to be a role model for women and women's lives in Africa.

Notes

[1] Autobiography written by Aline Mukantabana in 2011.

Image: Allen Cyizanye

Allen Cyizanye's story[1]

Thesis: 'The role of higher education in achieving gender equality and women's empowerment'.

Childhood and early education

I was born in Uganda in December 1982. My family fled to Uganda before I was born. I am the third child in a family of six children, we are three girls and three boys. Among the girls, I am the oldest. I started primary school in 1988 when I was five and, in 1995, I started secondary school in Uganda. In 1997 I returned to Rwanda where I continued my studies after joining senior three. After, I joined the advanced level at Kayonza Modern Secondary School and was offered the combination of HED (History, Economics and Divinity). I finished my secondary school studies and joined the National University of Rwanda in 2002–2003 to study in the School of Languages. After, I joined the Faculty of Law, where I studied most of the courses in French while I had an English background.

Personal life

After finishing my third year of university, in December 2006, I got married. We are blessed with two beautiful daughters, the first one is almost finishing her primary six.

Career and higher education

After completing my first degree, I started doing family business, but later, in 2011, I started serving the Government in the Ministry of Justice, and I was privileged to contribute towards offering legal services, especially to victims of gender-based violence and child abuse. At the same time, I had started my master's degree in gender and development studies at the Centre for Gender, Culture and Development at the Kigali Institute of Education.

After four months on my first job, I got a job at the Gender Monitoring Office and I am still working at the same institution since then. I have occupied different positions and I am currently blessed to be serving as the Executive Secretary.

Role models

My career success is attributed to hard working, dedication and patriotism. My mother has been my role model ever since my childhood. I also pay tribute to my Chief Gender Monitor, who has supported my career and spiritual growth as I deliver my duties.

Looking ahead

My wish is to be in a community where both men and women are enjoying their full rights.

Notes

[1] Autobiography written by Allen Cyizanye in 2011, updated in 2019.

Image: Angelina Muganza

Angelina Muganza's story[1]

Thesis: 'The changing gender roles during refugee situations'.

Childhood and early education

I was born in Rwanda in 1958, the last of two sisters and two brothers. My mother was 40 when I was born. She was a housewife, a farmer who did everything, and my father was a trader. He came to Kigali to buy merchandise—salt, sugar, clothes and bicycles and take them to the Eastern province to sell. We left our home after my father was one of the first people to be killed in 1962, progressively moving until we reached Uganda in 1964. As she moved, my mother could see signposts, but she could not read them. I would hear her telling other women in Uganda that that was the reason she pledged to send her children to school—so they could learn to read. In the rural area, there were very few local schools and I regret that I never taught my mother to read when I was growing up. Later on, she became a small businesswoman. She counted her money and knew that she was making a profit. She then started owning property, cows and goats.

My uncle had left Rwanda in 1940 and still lives in Uganda. Uganda had some policies regarding coffee production, they used to whip people to force them to grow coffee. Some refugees went as labourers and others left, looking for something less coercive. We had lost all our cows but some of those Rwandans outside their homeland became cattle keepers for other Ugandan citizens. One of my aunties, my father's sister, advised my mother not to stay in the refugee camp because she thought I needed to drink milk. However, my mother stayed in the camp so that I could go to school, beginning primary school in 1966.

After finishing primary school in the refugee camp, I went to two different high schools attended by rich children I did not know. I always did well. I applied with eight others to what was considered a very good school and there was no discrimination if you had good marks. I completed high school in Uganda.

Career and higher education

I earned my tertiary education in agriculture in 1982. In 1995, I came back to Rwanda and worked in agriculture from 1997 to 1999, and then as Minister for Women and Gender Development from 1999 to 2002, to encourage women's political participation and change inheritance laws that favoured male heirs. In 2003 I was appointed Minister of State in the Ministry of Public Service and Labour (MIFOTRA) where I was responsible for labour relations, ensuring safety in the workplace so that people can work in comfortable, clean and safe places. In this role I led the Ministry's negotiations with public service unions before and during the large-scale public service retrenchment that took place in 2006. Rwanda's Public Service Commission (PSC) was established in 2007, and I was appointed its Executive Secretary in 2008, leading the process of staffing the commission, communicating its role to government agencies and assuring its independence. The PSC took over the supervision of the civil service from MIFOTRA, but whereas MIFOTRA had only supervised the recruitment process, the PSC standardised and centralised the process. Rwanda depends on its human capacity to grow the economy as we have no mineral resources. Before the genocide, recruitment was based on nepotism, connection and prejudice, but all these have stopped. The priority now is to find staff, with the entry year into public service at 18 and exit at 65. The recruitment process is done online.

In 2009, I was appointed President of the Rwanda Association of University Women (RAUW) and led it for three years, working to improve gender equity in the country. Gender roles changed during the refugee situation. Men lost their land and cattle, that which made them heads of families, and they were affected by it, going out looking for jobs. Women went out to look for jobs too. These factors had a negative effect on some men, who became idle as they didn't get to do what they used to. For my Master's in Gender and Development research I investigated this situation, to see how gender roles can change without it turning into a negative situation.

Personal life

I still had many relatives here in Rwanda when the 1994 genocide started: my father's sisters and cousins, their children and grandchildren. It was a huge family, 11 sons and a daughter, and only two, a deaf and dumb son and daughter stayed with the sister in Uganda. My mother's family too were in Gatete, on the same hill. It was a big family, of about 300, with wives and cousins. They had not left Rwanda as my mother's uncle had been in prison, and the women would not run away. So many were killed. But we have no choice other than reconciliation; it is a bitter one, but there is nothing sweeter than that.

I married in 1987 when I was almost 30 years old. We knew each other from across the border and he had had to move during the time of Idi Amin, when many professionals ran away from Uganda because of the war. I moved to where my husband was living in Kenya, and I worked in ActionAid Kenya from 1988 to 1994. My husband has been a professional language teacher for the last 15 years, teaching and translating English and French.

Role models

One of my first role models was Doreen Drake, a teacher at my high school in Uganda who particularly assisted Rwandan girls and boys to get scholarships from various benefactors. She handled this fund, which paid for our school fees. She was a career mistress at the school and she always guided us. Doreen was a very strong woman, very kind, who loved us and wanted us to be disciplined. I feared her and did not want her to hear me making a noise. She had chosen to be single because of her religious faith and was influenced by Pope Pius, who called people to teach children in Africa. I was surprised to find there were women like her in Africa.

My mother was such a strong woman and has been another role model. I knew her only as a widow, and I could see how hardworking she was with her brothers and brothers-in-law. She was more hardworking than the men and their wives. We children were never hungry and never deprived. We were so happy. We never lacked anything, and she always protected us. We never heard her complaining about anything. When we look back, there was no water and no electricity. People were very kind to each other and looked after each other. Rwandans were very industrious and very competitive, despite some hardships. When we saw poor families among Ugandans and in other places, we could see that in the refugee camp we were quite privileged. Some people managed to bring over their cows and harvest. We had access to schools, dispensaries and churches and led quite a dynamic life.

Another one of my role models was Dr Shirley Randell who I worked closely with in RAUW and who was the Director of the Centre for Gender and Development during my master's program.

Notes

[1] Autobiography written by Angelina Muganza in 2011.

Image: Anne Abakunzi

Anne Abakunzi's story[1]

Thesis: 'The contribution of the "Women Guarantee Fund" to the socio-economic development of women'.

Childhood and early education

I was born in 1964 in Uganda, the first of seven children, four girls and three boys. My parents were peasants working in agriculture and left Rwanda as refugees in 1961. Like almost everyone, in the first years they did not have cows, but after some time they did. I started primary school in Uganda, in a school mainly for refugees that started as a church school but later became a government school. I had to walk very many kilometres to reach the school, passing two other schools, just because they were protestant schools. I went to Maryhill High School for both O-levels and A-levels. My family was very religious. My grandfather was a catechist, and many people came to my home to teach and pray together. Even at the age of eight, I would be involved in teaching others.

Career and higher education

I started tertiary education at Nkumba University, a private university, and graduated with a bachelor's degree in Accounting and Business Studies.

We returned home in 1994, after the genocide. Together with other women friends, we started the Benishyaka Association as we wanted to help widows and orphans after the 1994 atrocities. Many of those orphans are university graduates now. I first worked at Concern Worldwide for two years as an administrator. Then I went to BCR, the Commercial Bank of Rwanda, as an accountant in the legal department at first, later, I requested to be put in the accounts department. Being at BCR encouraged me to continue studying finance. I became a branch manager at Novotel in 2002, then went back to head office in 2004 as a personal banking officer. In 2009, I moved to Bank Populaire, at the branch for the promotion of women, which was started by an association of women entrepreneurs. However, Bank Populaire is now a commercial bank with branches, giving no special consideration for women, but we hope this will change soon.

Personal life

I met my husband in Uganda and we had a son. I married him in 1999. Unfortunately, he had hepatitis C and went to South Africa for treatment. He came back when doctors suggested a transplant. He died when he was 50, in 2004. I have three children.

Role models

My most important role models are probably my mother and our President. In relation to my mother, it was the way she brought us up and her values of loving people. She used to encourage all of us. She did not think boys were better than girls. About our President, he loves his country and what he says is reflected in his actions. He lives by his word and I admire that. There are also many of my customers that I admire. Some of them are women who are not educated but they are just convinced that they can do something, so they have incredible stories. One woman was a primary teacher earning 30,000 RWF and she asked for an advance of 90,000 RWF which she used to buy items that she sold to her friends—she now goes to buy goods in Dubai and Tanzania. Some come to my office and say: 'This is my idea and I want you to put this into writing'. They really think about a project. They have not gone to school, but they have their own ideas. They are focused and inspiring and want to go on to higher levels even without education. That is why I think that women's empowerment is so important.

Looking ahead

I would like to go for a PhD and study the economic empowerment of women. I don't know why some women come to talk to me about experiencing gender-based violence, but they do. One woman told me about her problem the first time we met, so I called two of our fellow students for their advice. I want to study about this: how do people come to you, asking you to settle problems, and go on with their lives? I would like to leave banking and study the economic empowerment of women. My passion is to find the solution to all this violence against women, to end this war in their homes at night.

Notes

[1] Extract from an interview with Anne Abakunzi by A Escrig-Pinol and S Randell in 2011.

Image: Aquiline Niwemfura

Aquiline Niwemfura's story[1]

Thesis: 'Land Rights: Women's transformation in Rwanda'.

Childhood and early education

I was born in the Jari Sector, Gasabo District, Kigali, Rwanda, in 1952, the eighth child in a family of ten children, four boys and six girls. My father died when I was four years old. We grew up with the support of our brave mother's efforts, managing a big farm with the support of our brothers, who were adults. The oldest was working in the colonial public administration. In 1962, my family was forced to leave the country because of ethnic persecution and killing. At that time, my oldest brother was leading one of the districts, Kingogo, of former Gisenyi Province. He had friends in Goma in the Democratic Republic of Congo (DRC), and he advised my mother to go there, where he had relationships. After completing my secondary education in Lycée Amani in Goma, a well-recognised girls' school, I had to teach to help my mother. At this time, all my older brothers and sisters were married and had their own families to nourish.

Career and higher education

Two years after I finished school, I was offered an opportunity to pursue my studies in Kinshasa at the Higher Institute of Education. When I finished, I was lucky to be recruited in United Nations Development Program's (UNDP) local office, as administrative assistant to the Resident Representative, and, three years later, I was promoted to program officer. In 1989, I became a UN international staff member working in Guinea-Bissau, Zambia and Angola. In May 2000, I was requested by the Rwandan Government to set up and run the Beijing Follow-up Permanent Secretariat, of which I was appointed Executive

Secretary by Cabinet, so it was not possible for me to return to my UNDP international post. I do not regret this, compared to the modest contribution I have been able to make to the reconstruction of our country, especially in the area of women's promotion. To better advocate for women's rights, knowing Rwandan legislation was a must, so I decided to return to school and, in 2006, I completed my bachelor's degree in Law from the Independent University of Kigali.

In March 2009 I was appointed the Executive Secretary of the Gender Monitoring Office. In addition to studying for an advanced certificate from the Canadian International Development Agency (CIDA) in gender analysis, gender research and gender budgeting methods, I decided to update my skills in gender at a more specialised level. May God bless abundantly Professor Shirley Randell for her determination and active role in the setting up of the Master in Gender and Development degree. In my master's course I learned a lot about transitional justice, which was very new to me, and feminist research. I already knew something about masculinities and femininities and gender methods, but I learned a lot more. My thesis was about land rights and women's transformation in Rwanda, using the case of Gasabo district. Traditionally, women in Rwanda were not allowed to inherit property, and I wanted to see if, now, they really have equal rights with men. The law started only in 1999. I interviewed women who actually owned land, and discussed the size of their land.

Personal life

My mother passed away in Rwanda in 1995 at the University Central Hospital in Kigali (CHUK). In June 1997, I applied for a four-year temporary separation with the United Nations Development Program (UNDP) to settle in Kigali, where I had to organise and care for the four adopted orphans of my cousins killed during the 1994 genocide against the Tutsi. The youngest was one year old and the oldest was eight. Last year, the two youngest, Florence and Fabrice, finished their secondary school, the oldest, Christian, is already working, while Carine married after her secondary school and already has a son. In 2002, I adopted another orphan of the 1994 genocide, Françoise Byukusenge, with whom I have no family relationship. She is the only survivor of her parents and she stopped going to school because of lack of support. She was living with other orphans in a genocide survival Umudugudu [village settlement] in Kimirongo Sector. She returned to school and last year she also finished her secondary school. I am very proud of those children and I am very happy when I see them rejoicing, full of hope for the future. I praise God for having used me to re-give them hope and family.

Role models

When I was with UNDP my mentor was Robin Kinlock, the Chief of Staff in the New York Office. He used to be my boss in DRC. Once, when I was offered a good post in the United Nations Children Fund (UNICEF), Somalia, he recommended that I should not go there, but continue to gain what I was achieving and keep my life safe. He was keen for me to be an international staff member.

Looking ahead

My dreams for the future are to become a good writer and a publisher on gender matters and to participate through consultancies in regional and international fora on gender and development.

Notes

[1] Autobiography written by Aquiline Niwemfura in 2011. She was still studying for her master's degree when she contracted breast cancer in 2012 and travelled to India for surgery. She returned to complete her degree and continue to work in the Gender Monitoring Office. Sadly, she passed away in 2014.

Image: Claudine Murindahabi

Claudine Murindahabi's story[1]

Thesis: 'Women's role in fighting against domestic violence in Rwanda using the Participatory Action Research Model'.

Childhood and early education

I was born in a family of six people, including my parents and four children, one boy and three girls. Unfortunately, one son and one daughter passed away and, later, my father perished during the circumstances surrounding the 1994 horrible event: the genocide. I, my young sister and my mother were struggling to cope with the aftermath and consequences. My mother was a teacher in primary school and managed to do her best to get us educated up to university level. Later on, she retired, and it is now our turn to cater for her. Her advice and encouragement have made us who we are today. We are and will be forever grateful for her. Actually, her pushing lessons of life inspired me and rendered me full of hope.

Career and higher education

I and my young sister got bachelor's degrees in social sciences and vegetable protection (agronomy), respectively. Surprisingly, when I applied for a job, I was appointed in charge of social affairs at sector level in a rural area. This was really a good lesson of life due to the fact that it was a place where the issue of gender equality is yet to be understood. My position was not allowing me to react to the alarming situation of women in remote areas, but I had a dream of one day getting an opportunity to address the issue of gender inequality I observed that was exacerbated in one of the sectors under my jurisdiction in the Northern Province.

During my childhood, I was told that women are weak, but I did not believe it because my motto is: 'Known and positive weaknesses are more than strength'. Fortunately, after two years of bad experiences in a rural area, I got a job at one of local NGOs (HAGURUKA) which has the overall goal of defending women's and children's rights by assisting people in need of legal representation and providing psychosocial assistance. For the last three years, I have worked there as a counsellor. I help people with different problems to overcome them. Due to the fact that I was working in close relationship with women and children whose rights were denied, I had in mind that, once I got a chance, I would take a gender course. I managed to enrol in the master's gender programme in the Kigali Institute of Education. The knowledge that I am getting from KIE will allow me to be helpful for my country.

Personal life

I am married and have one son. My husband has two degrees, one in education (sports) and one in law. He likes studies and is always pushing me to go far in my studies because he tells me that my future is bright.

Looking ahead

I wish to now go up to a PhD in gender.

Notes

[1] Autobiography written by Claudine Murindahabi in 2011.

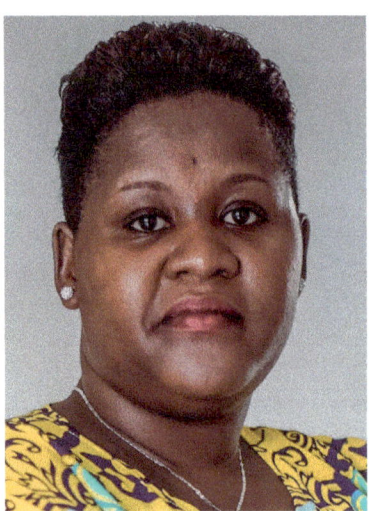

Image: Donatha Gihana

Donatha Gihana's story[1]

Thesis: 'Analysing impact of the nine years basic education policy on girls' education: A gender perspective'.

Childhood and early education

I was born in Kampala, Uganda, and I am the firstborn of six children. My parents were Rwandese refugees who had fled their motherland and joined other family members who had already exiled in Uganda due to political tensions. My father ran a small store for men's suits in Kampala and was part of the Rwandese community who had joined hands to own different stores in order to earn a living and take care of their families. Mama has been and will always be my role model. She initiated and ran small businesses including selling clothes and food for cash and was determined to educate all her six children, irrespective of their gender! Papa and Mama worked hard to pay school fees in time so that we do not miss any classes. Papa took a deep interest in our studies and at the beginning of each term he took extra time to meet with all our teachers. He kept a very strong relationship with our teachers and always checked in to see if any of us were weak in any subject and, where necessary, he paid for extra lessons. Papa's regular follow up at school gave me confidence as a young girl and my teachers regarded him as a very responsible man. I went to government-aided private missionary schools in Kampala for both my Primary and Secondary education. I was always a top student, Papa and Mama were proud of me.

When I became an adolescent girl in secondary school, my parents were very worried and protective at the same time. My mother provided me with what I thought was even unnecessary, things like perfumes and good lotions from her very little resources. She later mentioned to me that she did not want me to receive any of these things from men and did not want my studies to be interrupted at all. Mama always reminded me to take good care of myself but did not really explain to me her deeper fears. She always reminded me, using a Ikinyarwanda phrase '*Muko, ntuzankoze isoni mu mahanga*', which literally means 'My girl, never bring shame to me in a foreign land'. This phrase brought tears to my eyes, stuck in my head and I remembered it all the time. Mama was worried about her daughter seeing men at a young age and the most worrying thing, getting pregnant in a foreign land, would bring such a big shame to our family. I lived to Mama's statement because I wanted to make my parents proud!

My family's historical return to our motherland is a day we will never forget, 20th December 1996 is a day that Papa and Mama thought will never come. A day that marked the end of being called a refugee, a day of tears and joy—the day we returned back to a country we all call HOME. Papa's ancestral home is in Nyanza, former Butare Province, where most of his relatives were killed in the 1994 genocide against the Tutsi. Mama's relatives were killed too. The return to Rwanda was a new beginning—although I missed my old friends, neighbours and School, Papa and Mama were very happy to return home. They felt comfortable and easily interacted with our new neighbours, as we were somehow learning to cope up with a new environment. I grew up in a home where all siblings equally supported Mama with household chores, running her small businesses and in Rwanda, we continued to do the same. My young brother went to Kigali Institute of Science and Technology (KIST) and always helped Mama to run her business whenever he came back for holidays. I took care of the house and made sure it was always well organised. Papa and Mama supported each other so much in different business opportunities too. I thank God that I had both my parents as I was growing up. My biggest fear was becoming an orphan in a foreign country, that strong sense of family support, togetherness is fundamental for children.

My activism for girls and women's rights was more evident when I joined secondary school. I was part of the student leadership, actively engaged in different clubs and events. I always found myself among the few girls, if not the only one taking an active lead in different activities, especially when I joined a mixed school back home. The involvement of girls was even less when I joined University on a government scholarship, and this situation always made me very uncomfortable—I always asked myself, where are girls? Why are they missing out in different activities?

Career and higher education

Listening to the radio was one my hobbies, BBC World Service and Radio Rwanda were my favourites. One day, when I was listening to Radio Rwanda, I learnt about an organisation that empowers girls, the Forum for African Women Educationalists (FAWE Rwanda). I looked for FAWE Offices and, at the age of 18, I had an opportunity to be a young volunteer in this organisation as soon as I graduated from high school. This exposed me to a number of opportunities, I connected with Rwandan women leaders then and learnt a lot about gender equality especially in the education context. I experienced being in a workplace at a young age and had access to lots of gender resources. FAWE modelled me into a gender activist! Mentorship is such a great thing, very important in the lives of young girls and boys. Ms Anne Gahongayire, the National Coordinator of FAWE Rwanda then, was and will always be my great Mentor. Without this experience, I would have just stayed home to take care of my siblings and drown in household chores.

The activism I acquired from my volunteering experience helped me to champion gender issues when I joined university. In my 2nd year at the University, I was elected as the first Gender Commissioner in the Student Leadership Council. This leadership engagement built my activism even beyond the University campus. I worked so hard to address some of the major gender issues and negative stereotypes affecting female students, mobilised them to attend university events as well as organised specific gender trainings and, before I graduated, I was already one of the young women members of FAWE, an organisation that I later joined in a professional role, the National Coordinator.

I do not regret doing a bachelor's degree in education and then a master's degree in gender and development. My deep passion is gender, and I really wanted to be an expert in this field. Being passionate about something is not enough without the deeper knowledge, studying gender concepts and accessing different gender resources was very important.

After my master's degree, I was appointed as Deputy Country Director of Girl Hub Rwanda—an organisation that is championing girls' rights—and later its Country Director. Today I serve on the Rwanda Advisory Committee of the same organisation. In 2016, I was nominated in Africa's most Influential Women in Business and Government awards organised by CEO Global and later won two awards, Country and Great Lakes Regional Winner in the category of Welfare & Civil Society. I am currently a gender and development Consultant in Rwanda and Sub-Saharan Africa. I enjoy doing research on adolescent girls, youth and women's rights issues including sexual reproductive health, education, leadership, mentorship and civic engagement, and also serve on various NGO boards. I would like to empower as many young girls as I can and each year, I mentor two university young women whom I expose to different skills and opportunities.

Personal life

I have been married for over 10 years and I am a mother of two sons and one daughter. I have never viewed marriage as a time that would make me stop my activism. I knew marriage should not be a moment that makes me lose myself.

My husband is a very understanding person who truly supports my activism in all ways. When you are open with your partner and are friends, and as long as you are true to yourself, you truly enjoy your relationship.

Looking ahead

My dream is to pursue a PhD in Education or Gender studies.

Notes

[1] Interviewed by A Escrig-Pinol and S Randell in 2011, with Donatha Gihana's update in 2019.

Image: Edouard Munyamaliza

Edouard Munyamaliza's story[1]

Thesis: 'Improving cross-gender communication about sexuality to promote healthy families in Rwanda'.

Childhood and early education

I was born in the Democratic Republic of Congo (DRC) in 1970 and was second to an older girl in a family of nine, six girls and three boys. We were told we were not allowed to sit for primary examinations at age 11 and I had to change my birth date to put it back to 1969 to sit for a final exam as if I was 12. My family left Rwanda in 1959. My father told me our ancestors lived in Kibuye. They crossed the lake to Zaire (now DRC) and stayed for some time there. There were three main refugee camps at the time, one was Mokoto, not far from a monastery and it benefited from the support of some monks. The camp soon became a village situation. My father was a teacher at first, but then, those who were not qualified could not continue teaching, so he continued working as a religious teacher, a catechist, because he had only completed three years post-primary. My mother had not studied but she was good at taking care of livestock. After settling in Zaire, they started with one cow and soon they had many of them and a huge piece of land, but in the 1990s there was conflict and all their land was taken by a tribe, so the situation changed again. They lost their land and my father told me this small thing: 'In this country, Zaire, don't invest in anything material but only in your knowledge and skills because this can help you in tougher days'. I appreciated this advice. I finished primary and secondary school in DRC. My father died in 1992 and then my mother died too, and I had the six children to look after, so I had no means to get married early. When we came back to Rwanda we came with bare, empty hands because the soldiers in DRC would not allow us to carry anything.

Career and higher education

In 1994 I studied English in the faculty of arts, and humanities, literature, etc. After I graduated in 2001, I immediately worked with Trocaire, which means compassion in the Gaelic language, as a project officer, and then as a civil society and capacity building officer. The first job I started to do was to work in human rights organisations and strive to become an activist. I started to work as a field officer on human rights issues (Association des Volontaires de la Paix—AVP), then continued to create a youth human rights promotion and development (AJprodho) as a founder member and then President from 1999 to 2003. This organisation grew and with it my passion to see how I could help people to protect their rights. In 2004 I was one of the people who started the Junior Chamber of Young Entrepreneurs in Rwanda. I liked it there, but to do private business is not my passion. Then, in 2004, I joined USAID working as a conflict management adviser. Later that year I joined PACFA, Protection and Care for Families with AIDS, in the office of the First Lady as project supervisor, and then as acting coordinator for 8 months. In 2007, I went to the Canadian International Development Association, CIDA, as senior development officer.

It was really my choice to take a salary cut to go back to work with local civil society, and in 2010 I began to work for the Rwanda Men's Resource Centre (RWAMREC) as executive secretary, managing the day-to-day activities there. I found this much more challenging. In CIDA I was told what to do but in RWAMREC I was thinking, creating, and deciding on anything that can help. This was important for my autonomy in career development. We had started RWAMREC in 2006 with a board of directors and Fidéle Rutayisire as the chair. Because of my learning from others and contributing to other organisations' work I was elected chairperson of the Rwanda Civil Society Platform. I wanted to go as far as I could go in helping civil society in Rwanda to grow. I devoted 70 per cent of my time to that, and 30 per cent to RWAMREC, and they were happy about that. I was also appointed a Commissioner at the National Unity and Reconciliation Commission from 2013 for a term of three years, and in 2014 I was appointed a member of the National Labour Council for four years representing civil society interests at national level.

I am currently working as Gender Advisor to a humanitarian organisation called Nonviolent Peaceforce in South Sudan-Juba. The Master's in Gender and Development was very important for me. When we worked on the Economic Development and Poverty Reduction Strategy (EDPRS) I was with PACFA and had a particular interest in gender and women's issues as part of human rights activism in general. When we developed the gender checklist for priority gender objectives and indicators, I was active in the gender cluster. I had been trained for some 300 hours as a gender expert with CIDA and learned a lot. This provoked a thirst for more, so I said 'Yes' when I heard about the gender course at the Centre for Gender, Culture and Development, Kigali Institute of

Education. When you work in gender organisations you are just receiving part of it, only gaining the practical side but not the theoretical part. I wanted to gain both and to strengthen my skills and knowledge. I had a particular interest, as a founder member of RWAMREC, to try to promote positive forms of masculinities and work in partnership with women to promote gender equality and women's empowerment in general. For a long time, gender has been an agenda for donors, pushing gender on other development partners, especially local ones, and not so much of a home-grown initiative.

My master's research was looking into sexuality practices, a new trend of transactional sex where sexually dissatisfied women, or sugar-mummies, look for support from young men. These women would pay more than ten times the price for what men pay for transactional sex as a result of rigid traditional norms on sexuality. Women are doubly victimised as survivors of these norms that consider sex as a taboo. The word *Abunganizi/abapfubuzi* was forged for that purpose, meaning if you have done unfinished work, somebody else will finish or correct it—that is *umupfubuzi*. I wanted to look at the causes that push these dissatisfied women who are looking for something outside, and they have to pay a lot for that. The word is all about doing something halfway and then somebody else will continue to finish something you started and make the woman satisfied. Being done by women is seen as a shame, something extraordinary, in many newspapers it is portrayed as a strange and costly thing, while nothing is being said about some men who have concubines here and there and are paying almost nothing. So, my studies contributed a lot to my work in advancing positive forms of masculinities and femininities and gender equality in Rwanda through my organisation.

Personal life

I am married now with three children (two daughters and one son).

Role models

My role model is the late Minister of Gender and family Promotion, Aloisea Inyumba. The first time I came to know her was when she came to Butare as Rwanda's first Minister for Gender. At that time, she was talking of discrimination in households, things I saw with my own eyes and know are still there. When I Googled her and saw her entire life, I found her an extraordinary woman who worked very hard in liberating the country. She could walk from Uganda to Burundi, spending days and days doing the travel, and mobilising and sensitising people to join the Rwanda Patriotic Front (RPF) struggle. She was mobilising funds to support the struggle, and she did not use part of the funds for her own life, she was honest and dedicated. The ideals of the RPF that she was part of and working for might have disappeared with many people, but they are still in her. At the time I read in an article produced by CIDA where she was rightly portrayed as the mother of the Rwandan nation—I fully agree with that. It is true, we have good leadership, but we need the right people to translate that into work hard to uphold those values and to make them real in our country. I saw her real face when she was appointed again as Minister for Gender and Family Promotion and the first visit she made was to Profemmes. She is a feminist who does not have to be in a shell and she came out straight away to show what she is and what she is intending to do. Women and men can be proud of her—she wanted to do something to change the entire country for the better.

Looking forward

I want to continue my studies to do a PhD (when I get an opportunity) and go for more training so that I become knowledgeable and a great contributor to gender and development in my country. My ambition is to take more steps on what I have already started. I really want to see how I can be somebody who can achieve more in gender and development, continuing to do research and work to make a difference in people's lives. In 2002, while working as president of the youth human rights organisation, we helped around 2,400 workers at NUR who were expelled unlawfully. We advocated for them until they were re-established in their work. I was happy to see how people were thankful, we played a positive role helping them get their jobs back and earn a living. If my knowledge can help others I will be fulfilled.

To be behind a big organisation like Profemmes, that is my dream. However, there is a problem in Rwanda that most of the time we tend to work and already empower those already in a better position, rather than supporting those really in a status of marginalisation, powerless, and in the lowest positions in the community. I don't believe the country will develop unless we focus on the poorest segments of our population. Whenever they put in place a women's fund in Kigali, how do ordinary women up country make use of it? A member of Parliament can use that money for more activities for herself, but how does that translate into the welfare of other women in difficult situations in rural areas? The entire effort at national level must translate into something concrete and tangible for vulnerable segments of the population.

Notes

[1] Autobiography written by Edouard Munyamaliza in 2011 and updated in 2018.

Image: Egidia Rukundo

Egidia Rukundo's story[1]

Thesis: 'Gender, culture and sexuality: attitudes and considerations of labia minora elongation in Rwanda'.

Childhood and early education

I was born in Byimana Rwanda in 1981, the fourth in a family of six children, five girls and one boy. My father and mother were farmers. They did not have the opportunity to complete schooling because of political discrimination and suffered because of this, so were very motivated to make sure that all of their children had a very good education. My mother and other family relatives were killed in the 1994 genocide against the Tutsi. The rest of the family escaped because they were held in Kabgayi ghetto for Tutsis; it was like a concentration camp for the Jews. Every day, Interahamwe came to kill and rape women and girls. The young and still strong men were the first targeted by the killing, leaving the rest to die of starvation. The RPF arrived on 2nd of June 1994, before all of them were killed. I went to the Marist Brothers Schools for both primary and secondary and was one of few girls studying at the Byimana School of Science.

Career and higher education

I studied Sociology in Kigali Independent University and graduated with a bachelor's degree with first class honours. Later, I received a scholarship to go to Alexandria in Egypt from 2007 to 2009 to complete a two-year master's degree in development studies with a speciality in project management. All of my sisters and brother have gone to university, but I was the first to do a master's degree. Three of my siblings have now completed master's degrees. I started to become interested in gender issues when I was at university in 2003, working in a temporary job as a data collector on a project for fighting gender-based violence for the International Rescue Committee.

I worked as a trainer of trainers in gender with the Forum of Activists against Torture (FACT Rwanda), Africare International as Education Specialist and ActionAid International as the National Project Coordinator to fight GBV in and around schools. After graduating with a Master's in project management, I began work as the Gender Cluster Coordinator of the Ministry of Gender and Family Promotion. I developed the passion to work as an international staff in 2006 and, after applying for several positions, in 2013 I was appointed Senior Gender Specialist with the African Development Bank.

I joined the master's program so that I could have a theoretical understanding of my gender practice. My research thesis was on gender, culture and sexuality, particularly looking at attitudes and considerations of labia minora elongation. This work has been published. The master's degree qualified me to become Senior Gender Specialist at the African Development Bank (AfDB). I am now interested in conducting research on the role of women in decision-making positions in the organisation. As a senior gender specialist at the AfDB, I am responsible for gender mainstreaming in the bank's operations and participate in preparation and appraisal missions to conduct gender analyses and propose specific activities to promote gender equality and empower women. I also act as peer reviewer of project concept notes and project appraisal reports.

Personal life

I married in 2010 and my husband has been supportive of my studies. I was pregnant when studying for my MGD and I am now a mother of a three-year-old daughter.

Role models

From February 2015, I have had a mentor, Dr Victoria Chisala, the division manager at the AfDB. She coaches and guides me on career development and how to deal with the international work environment and family. I also have another role model, Mrs Geraldine J Fraser-Moleketi, the Special Envoy on gender at the AfDB. My other role models in the past have been: the Representative of Africare Rwanda in 2006, Mr Obura Willis, the first international staff I meet and who inspired me to be international staff and the late Aloisea Inyumba, Minister of Gender and Family Promotion, for her simplicity, tenacity and passion for gender and women's empowerment.

Looking forward

My goal is to work in management as a high-level representative of an international organisation or UN agency.

Notes

[1] Autobiography written by Egidia Rukundo in 2015.

Image: Egidie Murekatete

Egidie Murekatete's story[1]

Thesis: '"Suffering in silence": Sexual and gender-based violence victims at Muhima Hospital.'

Childhood and early education

I am the fifth born in a family of nine children, eight girls and one boy, who was born after me. From her second child, my mother was always expecting a baby boy, until her fifth. This time my mom was certainly expecting a boy and, surprisingly, I came out. When I asked my father the reason for my family name, he said that my mother was not happy to give birth to a baby girl again and I told her to let this girl be a favourable girl! Murekatete means 'everyone should cherish'. From my childhood I saw my mom was very close to us. She wanted every one of us to work hard so that each one would be able to survive when she would not be there. She is my role model, my inspiration. Because of this, from primary school every child wanted to be the first in her/his class, and I was used to being the first in my class. My father was formally educated; my mother had informal education, but she was always telling us: 'Even If I did not study much, you have to do so'.

Career and higher education

My mother loved me a lot because I was her first daughter to attend university. My older sisters got married after finishing their secondary schooling, but I am glad now that all completed their university courses. As a woman, being empowered and having my own financial means has been the aim of my life. I worked in HIV programs with a focus on sexual and gender-based violence and I have observed how difficult it is for women to disclose what happened to them. I decided to do my master's research on disclosing sexual abuse. In fact, I came across women who were abused by their bosses in order to keep their jobs. In countries where there is no sexual harassment policy at work, women are suffering. Indeed, whatever the circumstances, I work hard to meet my company's objectives.

I have always been ambitious to advance my career. As a matter of fact, after an international competitive recruitment I found a job at the International Criminal Court (ICC) in the Hague. Some of my women friends were so surprised because, in our culture, men are the ones who should travel outside the country and bring money while women stay behind taking care of the kids. I like my job and it has advanced my knowledge in gender programming, human rights and addressing sexual and gender-based violence in conflict. Supporting women and children who went through arduous experiences via the ICC Trust Fund for Victims assistance initiatives gives me professional satisfaction.

Personal life

I regret the death of both my parents, especially my mother, who died 10 months before my marriage. Since her death I am always committed to working hard so that my children will have a bright future. I have a feminist husband without knowing it before, because he is one of my supporters at home, during pregnancy and with childcare he showed he was different from other men in this patriarchal society. I am so glad to be doing gender studies that has helped me to look clearly at my vision and I am also happy to be a mother now. It is not easy to work, study and care for a child at the same time but I made it.

Role models

My mother has been a role model for me; she was a hard working person, I remember when the time came to go to school, our father gave us a little money, and I was surprised by the way my mother gave us supplementary money so that our needs were covered. I have never seen my father insult or argue with my mom. Looking at the way she gave birth to nine children and worked so hard, I said to myself: 'I will study until I get enough money to help my mother'. In the morning she was occupied by farming and agriculture and in the afternoon she sold drinks so that she could get more food and money to feed her children.

Notes

[1] Autobiography written by Egidie Murekatete in 2011 and updated in 2018.

Image: Emmanuel Bimenyimana

Emmanuel Bimenyimana's story[1]

Childhood and early education

I was born in 1968 in the Southern Province of Rwanda. I am the firstborn of a family of nine children: six boys and three girls. My father's education did not go beyond primary, and my mother is illiterate. My mother explained to us that, during her time, parents preferred to only send boys to school because, according to them, girls' education had no value. Now, I understand that my mother was a victim of gender discrimination supported by a patriarchal society. At some point, we encouraged her to join in an adult literacy program, but she withdrew after a short period. My parents are now in their 70s.

As far as my formal education is concerned, I completed my primary studies at Nsanga Primary School before joining High School at Collège St. André in Kigali. In 1989, I was granted a government scholarship to join the National University of Rwanda English Department of the Faculty of Arts. Like many other Rwandans, my education process was affected by the war and the 1994 genocide against the Tutsi. As a consequence of war, I was not able to complete my bachelor's degree program.

Career and higher education

In order to take care of my younger siblings' education, I searched for a job instead of going back to the university when it re-opened its doors after 1994. I worked as an interpreter for international journalists (NHK-Japan), then for NGOs, including the Avocats Sans Frontières (ASF) in their program 'Justice for All' which mainly focused on genocide trials in Rwanda. Finally, in October

2000, I was recruited by the United Nations International Criminal Tribunal for Rwanda (UN-ICTR) as a translator for the Office of the Prosecutor (OTP) in Kigali.

In January 2005, I enrolled in the Faculty of Law at the Kigali Independent University (ULK), in the evening program. I was motivated to study law because I was working with an institution of justice and wanted to grasp the necessary legal knowledge in order to be accurate in my translation services. I also wanted to practice as a lawyer to defend the oppressed and the voiceless. In 2008, I completed my bachelor's degree in Law, with distinction.

In 2010, I was excited to learn that KIE was launching a master's program in gender and development and decided to join since I consider gender to be part of human rights. For me, it was important that I could study while keeping my job.

In January 2011, when asked to draft a professional development learning plan, I wrote that my vision was to secure an international position with the United Nations system in three years' time where I could use the expertise acquired in the master's program.

However, I had to suspend my studies at the end of semester one when I was offered a promotion as an international civil servant within the ICTR in Arusha, Tanzania, where I was called to support the Appeals and Legal Advisory Division of the OTP.

From 2012 to 2015 I took a Graduate program in Translation Studies at Portsmouth University in the United Kingdom, to master my translation skills. From 2015 to 2017, I obtained a Master's degree in Criminal Justice (Law and Public Policy) at Walden University in the United States of America to enhance my capacity as a lawyer. From 2017 to date, I am still working hard to realise my dreams as a gender advocate. I am a part-time volunteer with the Department of Immigration Legal Services at the Catholic Charities of Dallas Diocese.

I am proud to have joined the master's program in gender and development at the KIE. The knowledge acquired concerning basic gender concepts and relations will surely guide my future career wherever I will be called to serve. I shall keep my commitment to promoting gender equality and women's empowerment globally. This is because I believe that there are so many women like my mother who are facing different types of discrimination and they definitely need a 'voice'.

Notes

[1] Autobiography written by Emmanuel Bimenyimana in 2011, updated in 2019. He started the MA in Gender and Development in 2010 but paused his studies due to a career conflict.

Image: Ernestine Narame

Ernestine Narame's story[1]

Thesis: 'Stressors, coping and social support among single mothers: case study of the mental health project of Handicap International Rwanda Program, Bushoki Sector'.

Childhood and early education

I was born in 1981 in Rwanda. I am the first born in a family of four; I have two brothers and a sister. My mother is a teacher in primary school and my father was a high school teacher and headmaster for many years and is now a pensioner. After primary school, I studied psychopedagogy in secondary school.

Career and higher education

In 2005 I completed a bachelor's in clinical psychology, and then in 2008, a master's degree in this domain at the National University of Rwanda. In 2010 I completed a Diploma in Child Care and Education from the Indira Gandhi National Open University, and in 2012 obtained the Master in Gender and Development at the Centre for Gender and Development Studies of the Kigali Institute of Education, now part of the amalgamated University of Rwanda. From 2005 to 2015 I worked as a clinical psychologist at Doctors without Borders (MSF/Bélgique) and Handicap International, and as a project officer in various community mental health and gender-based violence (GBV) projects. As well, I was involved in large research teams working on SGBV, child protection and mental health issues in Rwanda, Burundi and the Democratic Republic of Congo (DRC). Since 2015, I have been studying a PhD in Social Science, specialising in education at Lausanne University in Switzerland, that I successfully completed in 2019.

Personal life

I am married to Simon Nsabiyeze. Simon works in the humanitarian area and travels a lot. We have two children, a daughter of 12 and a boy of nine.

Role models

My first role model is my father: he loves and gets involved in his work to make the best of himself, whatever the circumstances. During my early childhood, he never stopped mobilising enough resources and 'motivation' to ensure the continuity and success of my studies. My second role model is Dr Naasson Munyandamutsa. He is the most prominent psychiatrist that Rwanda has had and has been a key player in the training of mental health professionals and dealing with the consequences of the genocide against the Tutsi. A human rights defender who has unwavering support for reconciliation, his interest and involvement in research is what pushed me to do my doctoral studies.

Looking forward

My research interests are to report on vulnerable populations, especially children and women. The livelihood and psychosocial programs I work in and the research I have undertaken about 'Rwandan children's school experience' during my doctoral studies have led me to discover that vulnerable children and single mothers are both categories that need attention to ensure sustainable development. I have had two articles on my research accepted for publication and am now working on an English one. After my studies I intend to work in education and continue research, especially with vulnerable children and women.

Notes

[1] Autobiography written by Ernestine Narame in 2011 and updated in 2019.

Image: Ernestine Uwimpeta

Ernestine Uwimpeta's story[1]

Thesis: 'Efficiency of microfinance loans in the economic development of women: the experience of beneficiaries of Duterimbere microfinance (COPEDU)'.

Childhood and early education

I was born the second child in a family of eight children: five daughters and three sons. My name, Uwimpeta, in Rwandan culture means 'the second child in the family'. My parents are Habiyakare Jean Berchmans and Bazarama Euphrasie. Both were born in Ngoma district, Eastern province, and were educated. My father studied Arts and was working as an Eastern province official agent, while my mother has knowledge of modern cooking. We did not have a chance to live for a long time with our beloved father; he died in 1975 when I was only five years old. A long time ago, Rwandan society did not recognise that women are able to guarantee education for their children. My mother used her skills and means to educate us alone. Every day we had to work hard in order to escape the negative stereotypes attributed to uneducated children when their mothers failed to do this after the death of their fathers. This situation that we grew up in incites me to think deeply about the extent of gender inequalities and their impact on women's lives; we were discriminated against as the children of a woman without a husband.

My mother couldn't tolerate any kind of mistakes; we had to execute all orders she recommended, such as good behaviour, and she encouraged us to study hard to sustain our life in the future. Those advocacies influenced my personality and guided my will in building my capacity. When I reflect on how much as a family we were consolidated, both economically and socially, after our studies because of our dear mother, I tell myself that there is no difference between the sexes to hinder your social and economic progress if there is good will, self-esteem and confidence in yourself. My mother supported our school fees without any help from our paternal family, who did not want her to stay with us on the family property. They wanted her to leave, but their wish was not successful as my mother was open and educated and it was not easy to practice gender-based violence against her. I now realise that she was a feminist without knowing the meaning of that ideology.

Career and higher education

The idea of continuing my studies became my dream after analysing the posts I occupied as a radio monitor and gender focal point in the Media High Council. I realised there is room to address challenges in order to enhance women's capacity through the principle of equal rights. I noticed that, even in the institution I worked in, there weren't any women among the decision makers because of their low level of education. I changed my post and continued to check on the extent to which women were employed in decision making positions as I moved to another job which did not give me the opportunities to be able to execute gender equality. I had enough of the image that women are not even able to deal with the simple responsibilities of a secretary or desk information officer. The new post of public relations and communication officer let me be open with the public and through that network I received the information that there is a master's program in gender and development at KIE. I decided to join, and I aim at being involved in gender economic development and promotion of equal rights for both sexes. Sincerely, the commitment to changing women's economic situation has marked me and I still reflect on gender inequality through our culture and have decided to double my efforts to improve the negative stereotype given to my mother and grandmother as ignored human beings and unvalued because they were not educated.

Personal life

After the Genocide, I married Habakuri Donat, and we have four children: two boys and two girls. Regarding the experiences I have had in my life, I am wondering to what extent our children will be gender sensitive. As far as I am concerned, I do my best to educate equally our children, but so far, society's norms and cultural practices remain the biggest challenges in gender mainstreaming.

Notes

[1] Autobiography written by Ernestine Uwimpeta in 2011.

Image: Fidèle Ndamyeyezu

Fidèle Ndamyeyezu's story[1]

Thesis: 'Reinforcement of women's participation in management of cooperatives (small-scale farming) as a way to promote gender equality and empowerment in Rwanda: A case study of Rutsiro District'.

Childhood and early education

I was born in Rwanda in 1974, the second born of seven children in a rural peasant family with four girls and three boys. My father completed primary school and my mother was illiterate. They worked together in agriculture. My family has a big coffee plantation and many cattle; my parents are still alive but are now old. We travelled to Burundi and Congo from time to time to visit friends, but we have always lived in Rwanda. I started primary school in 1981, when the educational language was Kinyarwanda only, and for eight years we learned French as a subject. I started secondary school in 1989 when French was the educational language, it was very hard for me to be with students who were used to French. I did secondary school from 1989 to 1995 in teaching practice school. I was good in mathematics in primary and secondary.

Career and higher education

I received training in accounting and banking, and then worked for three years as a bank manager for Banque Populaire. I went to university from 2000 to 2004 at the Kigali Institute of Education (KIE), and studied history, geography and education. After graduation in 2005, I worked as a civil servant at district level as a school inspector, a professional in charge of social welfare for vulnerable groups, like genocide survivors and historically marginalised groups. I then was employed by the Ministry of Public Service and Labour as a labour inspector.

When I read about the Master's in Gender and Development course it sounded good, so I applied. It was sometimes difficult to balance professional, academic and family responsibilities while studying. I had an office job in the Western Province, Rutsiro District, and I attended class every evening and Saturday in Kigali. I had to leave my office at 2.30 pm and it took me three hours to get to KIE on a little motorcycle to Kibuya and then 25 minutes to arrive. Otherwise, I either had to get a bus or travel with a friend, who was doing a master's degree at KIST, in his car for the next two hours to KIE. After class, I went back to my family which stayed in Gitarama, Muhanga District, Southern Province. Then, I left early in the morning at 5 am to go back to work. I was interested in doing this master's because I wanted to become a practitioner and specialist in this field. As a labour inspector I had to deal with gender equality and equity in the workplace, to prevent sexual abuse and harassment and to introduce child labour prevention mechanisms and fight discrimination.

My research was in the area of strategies for reinforcement of women's participation in the management of cooperatives. The cooperative business model is a major factor in realising economic and social development of women and men and achieving gender equality and equity. The UN Resolution of 18 December 2009 proclaimed 2012 the International Year of Cooperatives, and called on governments, international institutions, and other stakeholders to support the development and growth of cooperatives worldwide. I was motivated to pursue my master's thesis research in this field because I was very interested in the potential it has as a strategy to promote equality.

Personal life

I am married and have one child, a girl. I like to swim, if possible, every early morning and evening, listen to music and dance. I am a Roman Catholic and like to go to the church service every Sunday. My wife completed a bachelor's in law and worked as a secretary in prosecution. She is 40 and we grew up together.

Role models

When I was in primary school, I had five cousins who were priests in the Roman Catholic church, and it was a very beautiful period. As a younger child I saw them as role models to imitate: the way they spoke, smoothly, kindly, were well dressed, having a car, bringing gifts to our family, accompanying us to church, sharing food and Fanta—it was an enjoyable time. Also, in my bachelor's studies at KIE I met Professor Pierre Ilunga, who has taught me fundamental issues in life.

Looking ahead

In the future I would like to be integrated in the army. I have a neighbour in the army and he has inspired me.

Notes

[1] Autobiography written by Fidèle Ndamyeyezu in 2011 and updated in 2018.

Image: Fidèle Rutayisire

Fidèle Rutayisire's story[1]

Thesis: 'The gender socialization process of girls and boys and how it facilitates domestic violence in Rwanda'.

Career and higher education

I am the founder and executive director of the Rwanda Men's Resource Centre (RWAMREC), a leading Rwandan NGO that aims to promote gender equality and prevent gender-based violence through promotion of positive forms of masculinities in Rwanda. I am also a Researcher and Master trainer on Gender, Sexual and Gender based violence at the International Conference on the Great Lakes region (ICGLR), which is an intergovernmental organisation working on peace and governance in twelve countries of the Great Lakes region of Africa. I hold a master's degree in Gender and Development and a postgraduate degree in peacebuilding, and I am involved in many women's organisations in Rwanda.

After completing my master's in Gender and Development, I served as the Program Manager for a United States Agency for International Development (USAID) funded project named Human and Institutional Capacity Development. I also served as the National Director of Community Based Socio-therapy, which addresses psychosocial well-being issues including peace of mind and dignity, interpersonal reconciliation and social cohesion among people at grassroots level in Rwanda.

I am currently a board member of various national and international organisations including, Servas International, BENIMPUWE, Living Peace Rwanda, Rwanda Business Owner's Association, Community Based Sociotherapy Rwanda, Hope Assistance Foundation and Africa MenEngage Network. I have also been a board member of PROFEMMES TWESE HAMWE, an umbrella of 58 Women's organisations in Rwanda and the East African Civil Society Organization Forum (EACSOF). I also do consultation around gender equality, male engagement in different international organisations including Partners in Health, Catholic Organisation for Relief and Development Aid (CORDAID), United Nations Fund for Population Activities (UNFPA) West Africa, Johns Hopkins Program for International Education in Gynaecology and Obstetrics (JPHIEGO), For the World (PROMUNDO) US, UNDP Rwanda and many others.

Notes

[1] Autobiography written by Fidèle Rutayisire in 2011 and updated in 2019.

Image: Françoise Uwumukiza

Françoise Uwumukiza's story[1]

Thesis: 'Prevention of minor students' sexual abuse: Needs assessment approach. Case study of Rwamagana District'.

Childhood and early education

I was born on 25 March 1973 in Rwamagana Hospital, Rwamagana District (the former Commune Rutonde) in Eastern Province in Rwanda. I am the fourth of nine children, two boys and seven girls, from a military father and a farmer and handcrafter mother. I grew up in a military camp, and I attended nursery school in Gabiro and Muhima Military camps until the age of six. Then, I pursued primary school with success at Nyarusange Cell, Muhazi Sector, in Rwamagana District from P1 to P8. My mother instilled in me morals and values and taught me to stand on my own. I was the most trusted and loved child of my family from the day I was born in such a way that I was named Françoise, almost the same name as my father, François. My late sisters Uwamariya Christine and Uwimana Claudine used to be jealous of me because of that. I refused to imitate them as we were growing up, since they opted for a life of luxury during their adolescent age and after, even though they belonged to a family with limited means of subsistence (given that five of us were attending high schools without any other financial support except from my father's job and my mother's handcrafts).

I have the wonderful privilege of still having parents in a country where most people are orphans. At the age of 12, I began to realise the importance for a young girl of being trusted in and feeling loved by her parents. The fact that I did not want to disappoint my parents' love, shaped my educational life and my behaviour in the community. I was obedient to God and was tirelessly praying for my eldest sisters' behaviour to improve and for my siblings in general. It was the beginning of a new life that I had in mind: to become a nun. This idea gave me a future as I faced temptations successfully, in particular, those related to sexual relations, but more importantly, it gave me hope. I always strongly said No to those who wanted to corrupt me and to have sex with me during my early age. In particular, God helped me to strategically overcome the incident of one married man who tried in vain to rape me in 1998 when I was studying at the National University of Rwanda (NUR). During 1997–1998, two men fell in love with me and I was wise enough and strong to manage this very uncertain situation.

Career and higher education

After getting my Diploma of Arts with Education with Distinction in 1999, I joined the convent where I stayed for five years in training, praying and service. One of the men who had fallen in love with me came once to visit me at the convent in 1999. He was so disappointed that one of my superior spiritual Godmothers could not leave me alone with him, but rather kept her eye on his face. The year 1999 was also the year I sadly lost my first elder sister Uwamariya Christine who was suffering from HIV/AIDS, leaving a five-year-old boy child, Harerimana Patrick, under my family's responsibility after disclosing that he was born from a Congolese father who never came to see his child. I thank God for having allowed me strength, time and willingness to accompany her until her last breath at Rwamagana hospital. During my religious trainings and while a nun, I worked as a deputy head teacher in charge of discipline in Kiruhura Secondary School from 2001 to 2002 and in College Sainte Marie-Kibuye from 2003 to 2005. In the meantime, in 2000, I sadly once again lost a sister, this time my second elder sister Uwimana Claudine, leaving a boy child, Banamwana Jean Claude of nine years. I got a short time to assist her in the very last days of her life. One day before her death, my sister Claudine left a legacy to my little sisters to always observe my advice as their remaining elder and wise sister. I was proud to hear that, thanked God and committed myself to observe that legacy of being a role model to my young sisters and to the departed one, even though she realised that when it was too late for her to survive. At that time, no vaccine and no treatment for HIV/AIDs sufferers were easily accessible; I'm not sure if HIV medicine was not available in Rwanda at that time, what I know is that we could not have access to it.

While a nun, I was a school-based mentor in terms of girls' education in charge of discipline. I was trained by ARCT-RUHUKA: Association Rwandaise des Conseillers en Traumatisme, where I learnt best practices about guidance and counselling for two years and was practising active listening to deal with the consequences of the genocide against the Tutsi in 1994 in Rwanda, such as trauma and self-isolation among students. I was very innovative in making sure girls were well managed and supported to improve their academic performance, as well as their behaviour on a daily basis.

In December 2005, I was no longer a nun. Through a non-religious movement called Focolari founded by Chiara Lubich that I had already joined while a nun, I had the opportunity to be hosted by a family of Ugandans, Paul and Edith Magimbi, who generously accommodated me during the entire month in Kampala, Bugolobi City, improving my English skills before I was reintegrated into the University for my Bachelor's degree studies. I took this decision after a lot of thought because, within the same period, I was offered a job to work for the National Commission of Reconciliation through the good leadership of its former Chairperson at that time, currently Honourable Ambassador Fatuma Ndangiza. In December 2006, I graduated and was awarded a bachelor's degree of Arts with Education with Distinction from the former NUR.

Afterwards, I worked as a Deputy Head teacher in charge of discipline with Lycée de Kigali. After three months, I had to leave the school for a higher position as District Education Officer in the whole District of Rwamagana from April 2007 to February 2008. Meanwhile, in 2007, I got a contract to work with Amici dei Popoli (as a consultant), an Italian Project working in Rwanda to support the young generation, where I trained teachers at Gatenga Youth Centre on Psychology and new Pedagogy (active methods of teaching/learning). I worked for five years (2008–2012) with the former General Inspectorate of Education (GIE), covering seven Districts of Eastern Province, Bugesera, Rwamagana, Kayonza, Gatsibo, Nyagatare, Ngoma and Kirehe. Under the GIE, I received training in many educational domains, such as Early Childhood Development, Adult Education, Girls' Promotion and Inclusive Education.

In July 2009, I was appointed the Vice-President of the Board of Directors of the former National Curriculum Development Centre (NCDC), today CPMD (Curricula and Pedagogical Materials Department of the Rwanda Education Board—REB) by the Cabinet of Rwanda.

The year 2011 was the year of great achievements for me. Firstly, I worked as an REB Focal Point with a USAID funded project of the Education Development Centre in its Literacy, Language and Learning (L3) Initiative in Kigali City. Secondly, I won a NORAD partial scholarship with the top marks out of 25 successful candidates to attend the Kigali Institute of Education's Centre for Gender, Culture and Development (CGCD), in the first cohort of students to obtain my master's degree in Gender and Development. Without the scholarship, this hope would not have existed because my family could not have afforded the full school fees. I was attending evening classes, and at the time my home was based in the Eastern Province, Rwamagana District and my job was across the Province, comprising seven Districts. I used to come to the Centre in Kigali after work, sometimes from 200 kilometres (Nyagatare and Kirehe Districts for instance) and go back home after class at around 10 pm because I had to wait for a UNILAK (Université Laic de Kigali) student van to transport me from the University to Rwamagana District. From 2012, I coordinated Duterimbere activities (a local women's network) in Rwamagana Region until 2016. In August 2013, I joined RWAMREC (Rwanda Men's Resource Centre), a local NGO aimed at men and women working together for gender equality where I worked as a Community Trainer for a Project called 'MenCare': 'Bandebereho' in Kinyarwanda meaning 'I'm a role model man' supported by Promundo-US. In December 2013, I founded a Club at Rwamagana District for an organisation called Soroptimist International and coordinated its activities up to March 2015, advocating for girls and young women with unwanted pregnancies, involving boys in family planning and gender equality in close partnership with nurses who were members of this club.

In March 2015 I was engaged as an independent consultant with RWAMREC, and Concern World Wide, where I successfully applied my experience and competences in leading the group trainings at Huye District. In December 2015, managers in Promundo-US in Rwanda and in the United States also engaged me in an assessment for two weeks to evaluate the impact of MenCare Project activities in Rwanda. From March 2014 up to 2016 I was employed by EDC-L3, a USAID funded Project, as a Provincial Coordinator, Eastern Province, with a variety of coordinating, management, training and reporting tasks. During this period, I focused on gender equality among boy and girl pupils and I always had an opportunity to support girls as well as boys from isolated areas to have access to school resources. In 2016, women from the village to national level voted for me to represent them as the President of the National Women's Council (NWC). This Forum aims at building women's capacity and ensuring their participation in national development through advocacy and social mobilisation under the guidance and supervision of the Ministry of Gender and Family Promotion (MIGEPROF). NWC is composed of all women and girls aged from 18 and above. It also engages in consultation with foreign organisations with similar mandates. I did this voluntary work to serve the women of Rwanda for two years, motivated by the high political will of the Rwanda top leaders lead by His Excellency Paul Kagame, the President of Rwanda and Champion of Gender Equality, who backed gender equality movements such as the He for She campaign, leading to his recognition through honours such as the Gender Champion Award by the African Women's Movement. I was also appointed a Member of the Consultative Committee for the Gender Monitoring Office (GMO) by the Cabinet of Rwanda, where I contributed to advising the Institution on how efficient they can oversee and monitor gender equality accountability for all Rwanda Institutions. Cabinet also appointed me as a Member of the Chancellery for Heroes, National Orders and Decorations of Honour (CHENO) to contribute to the promotion of good values and recognition of Rwanda citizens ready to act as heroes and heroines. In 2017, I was elected by the National Parliamentarians to represent Rwanda as a Member of Parliament in the East African Legislative Assembly (EALA), an Organ of the East African Community (EAC). Before the swearing ceremony, I had the opportunity to travel to China in November 2017, nominated by RPF-Inkotanyi, to participate in the third China-Africa Political Parties Theoretical Seminar held in Beijing with the theme: 'Building a China-Africa Community with A Shared Future'. The Government of China gave opportunities for representatives of African English-speaking Political Parties to participate in a workshop and field visits and to attend various lectures at Guilin, Yangshuo County, Baise Leadership Academy, Tianyang County and Nanning.

In March 2018, I was nominated by EALA Speaker to participate in the 138th Inter-Parliamentary Union (IPU) Conference in Geneva, Switzerland. Some of the conference resolutions were supporting gender-responsive legislation, policies and budgets aimed at ensuring equal access of youth, women and men to science and technology, education and training, capacity-building programs for women, especially in rural areas, and equal opportunities to engage in all stages of the renewable energy value chain.

Personal life

I met my husband Banzubaze Evariste at the university in 2006. The hard work, the team spirit and goal-setting principles put us closer without knowing that God was preparing a surprise for the two of us, getting married on 14 July 2007 for our legal civil marriage and 29 December 2007 for our religious wedding. In June 2009, we were blessed to welcome our first girl child, Neza Kelia. My family was happy to welcome our second child, a son Mihigo Ganza Angel in 2012, the year I graduated with a master's degree in Gender and Development with First Class Honours. In 2015, we were blessed to receive our third and last born, our daughter, Hirwa Lisa.

Currently, I am living with my husband, who works as a Headteacher of a Twelve-Year Basic Education school in Gasabo District, Kigali City. My husband and my children are the most important part of my life, as well as the engine of my successes. My husband is a supportive man, cultivating in me strength that I never want to lose, and with his blessings, encouragement and our shared faith in the Almighty God, I am becoming the woman I always wanted to be. It is the influence that I have from my family as well as my personal goals that have driven me to want to excel in all I do and try to be a good role model for my family

Looking forward

I am now a mature wife, a mother, an educationalist, a gender practitioner, a legislator and a master's degree holder aspiring to a PhD within three years from now. As a professional, I hope to become continuously an important member of the Rwandan community throughout the institutions I will work with in the future. I am practising what I learnt, and I am realising at a daily basis that education is vital to my life, if associated with hard work and decision-making capacity, I will always successfully accomplish all my dreams and goals. To conclude, I am committed to keep advocating for the poor, especially girls and women in need and other underprivileged populations.

Notes

[1] Autobiography written by Françoise Uwumukiza in 2011 and updated in 2019.

Image: Grace Igiraneza

Grace Igiraneza's story[1]

Thesis: 'Sexual and reproductive health: The challenge for women living with HIV-AIDS in Rwanda'.

Childhood and early education

I was born in Gikondo, Kigali on September 22 1983, the second of four children with two younger sisters and an older brother. Born and raised in a Christian family, I always had a passion for service and social justice. Understanding the role of education to acquire the skills that I needed to accomplish my dreams, I studied biology and chemistry as major courses, among others, in Groupe Scolaire Saint André secondary school.

Career and higher education

I went to medical school at the National University of Rwanda in 2002. During my university training, my extra-curricular activities included community outreach activities, where we organised and conducted educational activities to raise awareness about sexual and reproductive health issues among secondary school students and uneducated youth in the Southern Province of Rwanda.

After graduating from medical school, I worked in the Police Hospital in Kacyiru as a general practitioner, during which period I served as the coordinator of Isange One-Stop Centre, an organisation that offers holistic care to victims of gender-based violence. The job offered me the opportunity to realise my dream: I practiced as a clinician but was also able to participate in women and child rights advocacy. Beyond this practical experience, and in order to better understand the concepts of gender inequalities and their consequences on individuals and society at large, I enrolled in the 18-month Master in Gender and Development program at the Kigali Institute of Education and graduated in 2012. As part of my dissertation, I worked with women living with Human Immunodeficiency Virus (HIV), and through focus group discussions I learned about their reproductive and sexual health challenges. These interactions allowed and empowered them to understand opportunities and advocate for their reproductive rights.

I then enrolled in a residency program and four years later graduated as a specialist in Internal Medicine, after which I worked at Kigali University Teaching Hospital with a career focus in Nephrology. I then pursued a clinical subspecialty with a fellowship, training in Nephrology at Yale University School of Medicine, USA. I am also engaged actively in clinical research and with interests and focus on acute kidney injury, noncommunicable diseases in resource-limited settings, as well as women's reproductive and sexual health issues, including sexually transmitted infections such as HIV. I have published many papers on my work.

Personal life

I am married and blessed with two sons.

Looking ahead

I will be excited to return to Rwanda upon completion of my training with two major goals in mind: to institute programs and protocols in collaboration with other nephrologists to prevent kidney disease, and also to improve the care of patients who have already developed the disease in Rwanda. I share my personal philosophy to encourage others who are like minded, encouraging young women and men to pursue their dreams, whatever the obstacles may be. I believe that there is always a way forward if you truly believe in your dreams and they can come true.

Notes

[1] Autobiography written by Grace Igiraneza in 2011 and updated in 2018.

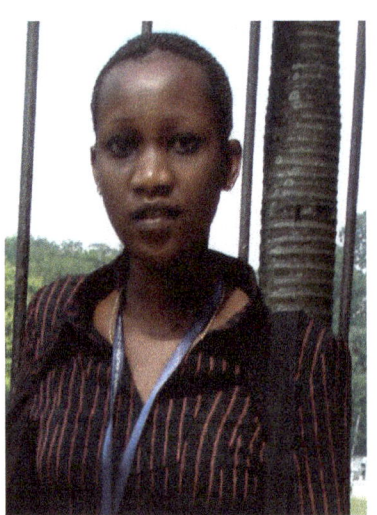

Image: Irenée Umulisa

Irenée Umulisa's story[1]

Thesis: 'Male involvement in family planning decision-making: a qualitative case study in Kagugu health center, Kigali city.'

Childhood and early education

I have five sisters, but neither parents nor brothers as all of them died. After the 1994 genocide, even though I was young, I decided to live a better life to honour my parents and brothers. That is why I always do my best in everything I do. This has allowed me to realise achievements in medicine, in my career and in my social life.

Career and higher education

I studied at the National University of Rwanda (NUR) to be a medical doctor. Since I entered university, I have been an active advocate for gender equality as I consider gender as a pillar for sustainable development. I believe that promotion of gender equality implies explicit attention to women's needs and perspectives. In the early 2000s, while I was a student, I was a member of the NUR University Women Students' Association (UWSA) and led the Association as its President for two years. I continued as a gender advisor and trainer for UWSA for another two years after leaving NUR. I have been a mentor and counsellor for the Forum for African Women Educationalists (FAWE) girls' school for five years. I like encouraging young girls to fight to be examples in all the things they do and everywhere they are.

After my graduation as a doctor, I worked at the NUR Teaching Hospital of Butare in charge of the antiretroviral clinic. I then worked with the Ministry of Health in the Rwinkwavu district hospital in Kayonza district as the head of the Department of Internal Medicine and in charge of antiretroviral and tuberculosis treatment for some health centres of the program. I am currently the Senior Programme Officer at African Leaders Malaria Alliance. Prior to that, I worked with the Rwanda Biomedical Center and the World Health Organization. Through these positions, I have gained extensive experience coordinating, developing and implementing programs, and overseeing clinical studies and operations research, including recruiting subjects, conducting follow-up surveys and collecting data. I have published extensively in medical academic journals. Education is important to me and I now have three master's degrees, the first one in Gender, Culture and Development, the second in Public Health and the third from the Field Epidemiology and Laboratory Training Program.

Personal life

I am a Christian. In 2009, I married Alex Hakuzimana and we have now three children.

Role models

Among the people who inspired me are both my parents, Dr. Kathy Kantengwa, the former FAWE coordinator, and Prof. Shirley Randell.

Looking forward

My wish is to work towards achieving my objectives and to offer care to families and individuals of the community with a preferential option for the poor. Something which makes me happy is to see how our beloved Rwanda is developing so fast and I am happy to work hard to be among the contributors to its sustainable development.

Notes

[1] Autobiography written by Irenée Umulisa in 2011, with 2020 updates.

Image: Jane Umutoni

Jane Umutoni's story[1]

Thesis: 'Nurturing women entrepreneurship and promoting reconciliation in post-conflict Rwanda: A case study of Buranga Women's Cooperative'.

Childhood and early education

Prior to relocating to my country, Rwanda, my family and I lived in Uganda and Kenya. It is in these two countries that I had part of my education. I have very fond memories of this part of my life in these countries. Despite the fact that we were living away from our motherland, it felt like home away from home and I will forever cherish these memories.

I moved to Rwanda in 2001. Just like many fellow country folk, I must say this was one of the most wonderful feelings in my life. It was like finally coming home where I truly belonged, no more words like refugee, stateless, foreigner, etc. Sadly, my country had just gone through the worst period in its history, the 1994 genocide. However, despite the horrible tragedy that had befallen my country, it made me happy that at least I had come home to be part of the efforts to rebuild our beloved country. We are still doing the same and by all indications our joint efforts are paying off amazingly. I am very proud to be called a Rwandan.

Career and higher education

I acquired my initial working experience in Kenya, in the private sector, first as an intern and later as an employee in the same company. By qualification, I hold a Bachelor of Business Studies (BBS). Currently, I am an employee in a public institution of higher learning. Working in an institution of higher learning has a way of inspiring one to upgrade their qualifications. Through observing colleagues growing academically and then finding yourself still in the same status year in, year out; you then begin to question yourself, 'What about me, why not me?' This is partly what happened to me; a motivation to grow professionally and academically. My first thought was to try a master's programme that was in line with my business studies background.

At just about the time I was thinking of enrolling in a Master of Business Administration (MBA) programme, a new Master of Social Sciences in Gender and Development was introduced at the Kigali Institute of Education (KIE), the first of its kind in the whole country. In Rwanda, as widely acknowledged, promotion of gender equality is a top priority, I thus said to myself, 'Wow, this is a God-sent gift to me and many other Rwandans'. While growing up, the issue of gender inequality never really crossed my mind. This was because in my family setting all children were treated equally. However, as I became older, I would notice issues of gender inequalities around me, but they were just accepted as normal. In a way, I must have known it wasn't right, but then who was I to change or say anything, besides, I grew up in the same society and most of it appeared normal to me too. Little did I know that, at a much later stage I would begin to see gender inequalities through different lenses and could actually have a say on such issues.

So, I grabbed the opportunity of the new master's programme with both hands, dropped the MBA idea and registered for the Gender and Development Master's programme. I was so lucky to be selected among the fifty pioneers and later qualified as one of the 25 beneficiaries of the NORAD partial sponsorship. I have never regretted the decision; I am so happy I made this choice. In fact, I feel so privileged, honoured and dignified to be part of the pioneer group thanks to Professor Shirley Randell and her team for this noble initiative. For my master's thesis I chose to research saving cooperatives as a tool for promoting women's entrepreneurship as well as reconciliation in Rwanda after the 1994 genocide. This is my small contribution to an area that has always been of personal interest, women's socio-economic empowerment and the building peace after conflict. With regards to women's entrepreneurship, the business sector in Rwanda is currently buzzing with women involved in all sorts of businesses, both at small and large scale, and I must say this brings joy to my heart.

Personal life

I am blessed with a wonderful daughter; she is my joy, my treasure and my best friend. I am also an aunty to delightful nieces, nephews and a sister to loving siblings.

Role models

While growing up, the eldest sister in my family was my mentor. She actually tripled as a big sister, mother and friend. She watched me grow, taught me much of what I know and this has pretty much determined who I am today. There are many qualities that I borrowed from her that have positively steered me through life. She went to be with the Lord years ago but still remains my role model and will always be in my heart.

Looking forward

I am using the valuable knowledge acquired so far in the best way I can in a continued joint effort to promote women's empowerment. I look forward to doing even better and bigger things upon graduation from the master's programme.

Notes

[1] Autobiography written by Jane Umutoni in 2011 and updated in 2019.

Janvière Mukantwali's story[1]

Thesis: 'Community perceptions of women workers in reproductive health/HIV-Aids programs: A case study of Kimironko Health Centre'.

Childhood and early education

I was born in 1960, the first born in a family of four children, two boys and two girls. My mother and father are farmers. My father had P4 schooling and my mother P2, and both were able to read. My family was not rich, but we were together. We shared what we had, and I enjoyed it. I finished public primary school but did not pass the national exam. My father transferred me to an Adventist primary school and when I completed that year successfully and passed the exam for the Adventists, I went on to their secondary school, Collège Des Adventistes, finishing in 1980.

Career and higher education

I started university in education and science at the NUR and completed my degree in 1985. I began to teach then and taught for two years. In 1987, I became a professional in charge of training in the Ministry of Health (MoH). In 1991, I passed a test and became a director of the centre on the intervention, counselling and taking care of people living with HIV/AIDS. I worked in that position for seven years and left in 1997. Then I did a test for an American NGO, Africare, and worked there for six months on a project on local governments. Then I was offered a job in a regional organisation, the NGO PREFED, which focuses on capacity building within Rwanda, Burundi and the Democratic Republic of Congo (DRC). From 1997 to 2004, I was Coordinator for the Kigali branch of the organisation, and after that I was the regional coordinator. From 2005 until now I am in the unit support program of the Canadian Cooperation.

At first, I was coordinator of a project on technical and vocational education and training (TVET), then I was in charge of the education sector and now I am mainly their gender advisor.

I enrolled in the master's program because it is linked with my professional occupation as I am in charge of gender, and secondly, I would like to learn in the real academic world, beyond professional training. At a personal level I was looking for a team with gender professionals, just to be connected to and to learn from them, and perhaps to develop more my understanding of gender interventions. I also thought that studying in English would help improve my English proficiency. I had not previously had time to practise writing, reading and so on.

Personal life

My interest in gender in general began as a first born. When I failed the national exam, my father paid for a private school education for me and this was very difficult for my whole family. He had to sell all his cattle to take care of my school fees. When I was in P4, his capacity was really down, and the people said 'Why are you investing in a woman? Perhaps she will get pregnant from someone and you will lose all your investment'. He really struggled to give me an education. I never studied with girls only, we were only two girls in a class of 25 students. That helped me to understand how all human beings have weaknesses and strengths. Being with men and with women doesn't give me trouble but helps me to really look at men as people and human beings who have weaknesses. Because I was always in the top ten of my class, there were boys who needed my help to learn.

I married in 1987 but my husband died in 2009 of a heart attack, at 62. He was a good man, seven years older than me, and was a public professional in transport engineering. I lost a lot of weight and still have difficulty sleeping. My daughters studied maths, physics, anatomy and physiology at FAWE school, and now my first born is at KIST studying electronics. The second is in Canada studying civil engineering and the last is in France studying information technology.

Role models

My best role model was my father. He was the one who influenced me a lot in my life. I liked my family in general, but my father was the best and I liked him a lot. My other role model was the wife of our Director when I was in college. She was an American, with a strong character, and had a heart for looking for people who are in need. She would not only look at a needy person but gave them the values to become a woman or a man. She influenced me with her approach, her principles and as a human being. You try to understand people to be empathetic, but you have to have principles. I am a hard worker, even if I have to go to sleep at 2 am in the morning. My work every time is hard, but I never have problems with my bosses. The first influence to improve myself came from my husband.

Looking ahead

When I graduate from the Master's in Gender and Development, I will work with community workers, because I have worked with them in eight programs and I want to perform better in this area. I want to see how the community perceives them and how the message they deliver changes according to their gender. Women are able to do things but they need an environment that is really supportive. I work with widows and have seen how they can improve their lives, but they need an enabling environment and support, and sometimes that environment is not there.

Notes

[1] Autobiography written by Janvière Mukantwali in 2011. There is no image with this contribution.

Image: Jean Damascène Gasasira

Jean Damascène Gasasira's story[1]

Thesis: 'The Rwandan Government Family planning policy: Muhima sector study'.

Childhood and early education

I was born in Rutsiro District, Western Province on 1 July 1968, and I am the seventh of nine children in my family. In 1991 I went with my young brother to Democratic Republic of Congo to study in secondary school and we stayed there as refugees until 1994 as Rwanda had not yet achieved peace and security. My wife also studied in DRC. The chance for Tutsis to get places in secondary school in Rwanda was limited.

Personal life

All of the members of my family who stayed in Rwanda were killed in the genocide against the Tutsi. My mother survived—she was 90 years old and was living with me before her death in 2013. My mother was helped during the genocide to cross Lake Kivu to Ijwi island, where Congolese came to take some refugees from there. She stayed with Congolese families and when they knew that she had a child who was studying in Goma, they started to look for me and found me. I was very happy to see my mother. My sister who was pregnant and too tired to flee quickly during the genocide was killed while running away with my mother.

I am married to Donatha Tuyishimire and we have six children, four girls and two boys. The first was born in 1994 and the last in 2003. After the genocide it was necessary to rebuild my family that had been completely destroyed. My brother is also married and has four children, two girls and two boys.

Career and higher education

I studied in the Paramedic School until 1994. I returned to Rwanda after the genocide and war, and I continued my paramedic courses in Anaesthesia at Kigali Health Institute (KHI) and graduated with an advanced diploma, A1 level, in 2000. I started work providing anaesthesia in the University Central Hospital of Kigali (CHUK) as a non-physician specialising in anaesthesia. Since 2007 I have held a bachelor's degree in demography (Population Studies), and work as an Executive Secretary/Secretary General of the Anaesthetics Association and continue also to provide anaesthesia in CHUK.

I wanted to empower my children by continuing to study for a master's degree. In my work on a peace-keeping mission in Sudan in 2009–2010, I saw in conferences that the United Nations gave much importance to gender. When I returned to Rwanda, I saw in the newspaper that there was a masters' course in gender, and I applied. My work at the hospital was very hard during the period of my master's. It is still the same today, because I am still working in the anaesthesia domain with additional responsibilities in the Quality Assurance unit, where I am in charge of the Resuscitation system of continuous quality improvement and at the level of an advanced diploma. I represented Rwanda at the World Congress on Anaesthesia and Resuscitation in Hungary. After my master's I did a six-month voluntary internship in the Gender Monitoring Office.

Role models

My older brother who was killed in the genocide was my first role model. He fled to Burundi and Congo in 1973. He studied at university and returned in 1986 to teach mathematics and physics at a secondary school in the Eastern province. I was happy to see him and knew that studying was good. I could see that one day I would be in secondary school like him, and get a job and be a good man, respected by others and who respected others. He was very serious and treated me very well. Unfortunately, he was killed during the genocide against the Tutsi in 1994.

My second role model is the current President of the Republic of Rwanda, Paul Kagame. I have not seen such a good leader in Rwanda. He is developing a country destroyed by genocide in a little time. I follow his example in order to achieve many valuable projects in my life and help people to develop themselves. That is still my aim with my master's degree, to help people, those who are not empowered to empower them socially and economically, working for maintaining security and sustaining development as certain goals.

Looking ahead

During my studies for the Master in Gender and Development I learnt theories, insight and skills that have influenced my life and my work, and I expected to be able to do a lot of things. Some have been done but a number of them are still pending. I am still interested in projects in gender, culture and development. However, starting in a new field is still difficult. I wish to get a national or international job to stand strong in this field.

Notes

[1] Autobiography written by Jean-Damascène Gasasira in 2011 and updated in 2019.

Image: Josephine Kobusingye

Josephine Kobusingye's story[1]

Thesis: 'The factors that affect sexuality among secondary school girls in Rwanda'.

Childhood and early education

I was born in 1969 in Uganda, the youngest of ten children, six boys and four girls. The family moved to Uganda in 1962 due to the turmoil in Rwanda. My father was an administrator then. I saw my mum crying for the first time when they burnt our house and took the cows. My dad went to stop them, but they had a huge stick with nails in it. My mum was behind, and she came rushing to help him. She was cut in the head, but a neighbour came to her rescue. My father was wounded, they had crushed his head, so he had to stop working. The effect was long lasting, and he died. I do not remember him much. All of the people in the same area in the east with us were wounded. They collected money at the church and decided to go to Uganda. Mum had to get ready very quickly. My older brothers and sisters helped.

Although I was the baby, I did not have time to be spoilt. My mother was very strict and very kind at the same time. She was clever, though she did not go to school, but she insisted on us all going to school and taught me how to read and write. She looked at things with a sharp eye. For example, earlier on she was saying people should not have only a few children: 'What if I had stopped at three children, then seven of you would not be there'. Later, when things got tougher and tougher, she realised how difficult it was to send them all to school. Now she is saying, 'I hope this pregnancy is the last, what are you doing with all these children? I could not understand this in 1995, after so many people had died. If we were to replace those who had died, we had to give birth to 20 or 15 children'. But she said, 'The land is small'. She mixed modern and traditional positions and the way she did that was very interesting to me. My mother worked in agriculture for what the family could consume at home and others paid the school fees, so we could all go to school. I completed primary in Uganda but when there were problems during Idi Amin's regime, the whole family went to Kenya, in 1979. I went to secondary school in Kenya until S5 and S6 when I went back to Uganda. In 1987–1988 I went to Nabingo High School.

Career and higher education

I attended the College of Commerce to learn secretarial work. I worked first as a secretary in Uganda. My first important job was as a functionary in a private company. Then I went to Rwanda to the Minister of Health. From 1995 to 1997 I was secretary to the Minister in the Ministry of Education. After that, from 2004 to 2006, I went to South Africa to do gender studies at the University of Western Cape and completed a bachelor's degree in Women and Gender studies.

I still wanted to know more. I know that gender is dynamic, things keep changing and there are specific books available as more information is being generated every now and then. I found that there was a lot I did not know that I still have to learn. I am glad I completed the Master of Gender and Development. I learned many things about what I really believe in. Gender is a social construction. This is the same in America and in Russia as well, even in Australia, where the men feel they have the right to chastise women. They are wrong. Who gave men that authority worldwide? There are a few islands where women have power over men. I want to know more about that, and why is it like this? The more I learn the more worried I get, I am disappointed. When I was growing up, I had a nephew who was the same age, but I was more responsible than he was. He would say: 'Do not forget that you are a girl, come and clean this'. When my brothers would come home for holidays it would be me who had to wash their clothes. They liked me so much, but it was still the fact that it was me who had to do this. I had to wash the plates, and my nephew was there with the others, playing together.

I work as a Program Manager in the African Women Educationalists (FAWE) in charge of gender-responsive schools, two centres of excellence and mentoring. My master's study was on sexual and reproductive health, the sexual activity of young girls. I wanted to know their attitudes, knowledge and practice. In culture and Christianity, people know that having sex is bad, but they still have unprotected sex and can get a disease. They know that if they go out, they can have an early pregnancy, but with all that knowledge, they still go ahead and get diseases. They still jump barriers and go out. I am intrigued by this.

Personal life

I got married in 1999, and when I was going for my degree I had to go to Cape Town and leave my husband behind. He wanted me to get what I wanted but to stay here on his own was a big problem. People would say, 'When she comes home, will she be a husband or still be a wife?' My husband is a veterinary doctor and he understands about education. I had to ask myself several times if I had made the wrong decision. When I arrived in South Africa, I spent three months crying every day because I was not sure I was doing the right thing. After the first year I got an award, a golden key because I had performed very well. There was a celebration with the certificate and I had a photo taken with the rector. My husband put this photo on the table and in the car. He said, 'You see what my wife is doing?' That did a lot to make me feel relieved. He did a consultancy to pay for my fees.

Then I did my master's degree. When we first discussed it there were no funds, and he was not working because he was sick at home for some time. At first, I was scared to tell him, but when I told him, he told me to go ahead and do it. People told me that, when I came back, I would rule over him. I was scared to be as educated as him as he is no longer employed. For me, working in a non-government organisation like FAWE is better than being in the government. When I got the job, things were fine. Now my contribution to the welfare of the home is much better. Now, we are living and staying ok, at home. My husband says, 'I think you did well by going to school. If you had not gone, we would not be surviving now'. We are considering taking a loan. We had started to build a house, and now I think I can get another loan. Now my husband is so proud of me. He says, 'My wife is well educated'.

Role models

My sister, Christine, is my role model, and then my mother. My grandad had three sons, all of them with wives. My mum brought up two of them and she was admired by the whole family and had good relationships with the in-laws and the women in the village. When I saw how the rest of the women in charge looked at her, I knew she was a good woman with her energy, her way of doing things, not being proud but very approachable.

Looking ahead

I want to do another master's degree to reinforce the field I am in and to add on to my gender knowledge.

Notes

[1] Autobiography written by Josephine Kobusingye in 2011.

Image: Josephine Mukakalisa

Josephine Mukakalisa's story[1]

Thesis: 'Consequences of lack of male involvement in the women's reproductive health: The case of selected women in Mageragere, a rural sector of Kigali City.'

Childhood and early education

I am 54 years old, the fifth born in a family of eight children, five girls and three boys in Rusizi district in the Western Province of Rwanda. Although my mother never went to school, she was very intelligent, hardworking and lived peacefully with neighbours and family members. My father was a teacher and inspired me. I was among the best in primary and secondary school and dreamt of becoming a teacher like my father. I completed secondary school at Nyamasheke, Institut Sainte Famille.

Career and higher education

I liked to play volleyball at secondary school, which constituted one of the motivations for me to pursue university studies, where it was possible to develop my sport talents by participating in competitions and tournaments. That was achieved when I had the opportunity to be part of the first Rwandan national female volleyball team in 1989. After secondary school, I started working as a teacher at Murehe primary school in a remote rural area. Although this was the achievement of my childhood dream, it was not sufficient. My objective was to teach at secondary school. French and Physical Education were my favourite subjects and I wanted to do further studies and teach in French in secondary school. After only one year of teaching at primary school, in 1985 I won a scholarship to go to the National University of Rwanda. In 1990, I graduated with a Distinction in the Faculty of Education Sciences, majoring in School Psychology. Late in 2010, I had the chance to join the Centre for Gender,

Culture and Development (CGCD) to study for my master's degree in Gender and Development.

I have worked in different organisations, both national and international non-government organisations (NGOs). This has been mostly in the area of reproductive health where I began in 1991 with the National Population Office after the completion of my university studies. I was responsible for the integration of population and development content, including sexual and reproductive health, in the national education curriculum for primary and secondary education.

From 1998, I worked with Association Rwandaise pour le Bien-Être Familial (ARBEF), the Rwandese Family Welfare Association, a specialised national NGO for sexual and reproductive health and a member of the International Planned Parenthood Federation. In ARBEF I occupied the positions of Responsible for Information, Education and Communication, Director of Programs, and Director of Advocacy and Partnership. In 2005, I joined IntraHealth International with responsibility for supporting the development of the curriculum of A1 nurses and midwives being established for the first time in Rwanda. In 2007, I was appointed National Program Manager for the Right To Play Rwanda Country Office, and after excellent performance was promoted to Country Manager for Right To Play Tanzania. With the team I lead, we have done a great job in terms of growing the country program and positioning the organisation as an important stakeholder in education. We successfully scaled up our program at national and district levels. Right To Play Tanzania has one of the program models of the Integration of Play Based Learning approach in the national education curriculum materials for the pre-primary stage, with a plan to extend it to primary level and pre-service teachers training in collaboration with teacher's colleges.

I have facilitated various trainings, workshops and conferences for staff and partners of many organisations. Combining managing programs with managing people has not been an easy task but with patience, hard work and determination, it became possible for me, and led to the position of country leader in an international organisation in Tanzania. There are not many challenges with the job except the responsibilities related to a leadership position and workload within NGOs but we are used to it, and during this time—it is about seven years in the position—I learned the importance of investing in building the capacity of team members, in order to be able to delegate and build a strong country program. I learned about how to motivate team members and retain good talents. I believe that my personal empowerment has come from different capacity-building opportunities, through trainings, experience sharing, travelling to different countries and learning from other women's successes. Inspiration, good coaching from supervisors who provided me with opportunities to take initiatives and make decisions have contributed to my growth, and I feel responsible for passing this on with the people I am coaching now. I will be pleased when a successor arises from the people I supervise at this moment. Participating in sport has also played a big impact in my life. The skills I learned through sporting activities—teamwork, discipline, resiliency, respect for the rules, confidence, striving to reach goals—have contributed to my personal development and the leader I am today. This has also led to me liking the philosophy of my organisation, Right To Play, which is using sport and play to educate and empower children and youth.

During all these years of experience, I have been inspired by the need for promoting the wellbeing of families, most specifically children and youth. During my professional life, I was appointed to the board of the National Information Office of Rwanda (ORINFOR) from 1999 to 2009 and have also been board member and president of the Women Cooperative for Family Economic Development from 2007 for many years. I have continued to learn and have completed an online course on leadership in Global Development with edX.

Personal life

I married in 1991 and have one child, a boy of 24 years, who has graduated as a Medical Assistant at Baker College, Michigan, USA. He is working as an intern at Henry Ford Hospital, while waiting to continue his master's degree. I have joy and am satisfied any time I achieve my goals and when I am with my son and my husband, taking care of them, and when I visit my mother and see how she is still hard working despite being 89 years old.

Role models

My mother has been my source of inspiration in terms of hard work and patience. Dr. Shirley Randell has been my mentor and I learned from her to always have objectives and strive to achieve them as hard as that can be. My Supervisor at Right To Play Rwanda, Massamba Gningue, has also played an important role in my leadership skills by supporting me and coaching me for high performance.

Looking ahead

My dream of becoming a university teacher is still alive and I am still watching for any opportunity to join a PhD program that will allow me to occupy confidently the position of university lecturer when I leave my work with NGOs. Our organisation is promoting active learning and competence-based learning and my dream is one day to share a model of teaching that prepares students for the development of their competencies and for self-reliance.

Notes

[1] Autobiography written by Josephine Mukakalisa in 2018.

Image: Jovia Kayirangwa

Jovia Kayirangwa's story[1]

Childhood and early education

In 1959 my family was exiled from Rwanda. I was born in Kampala, Uganda, in 1975 and was the third born and the first girl in a family of five children, I have three brothers and one sister. I completed my primary and secondary schools in Uganda. My parents were teachers, my father in secondary and my mother in primary. They were very strict; all their children are now university graduates. They helped us and forced us to complete school. Being urban refugees in Uganda had a big impact on us and helped us in a way. Most of our close relatives were outside of Rwanda during the genocide, in Tanzania, Burundi and the Democratic Republic of Congo, but many cousins died, and our friends lost many relatives too. That created a bond between us and we became like family.

Career and higher education

We came back to Rwanda in 1995, and I studied law at the newly opened law faculty at the National University of Rwanda in Butare. I graduated in 2000 and worked with the Minister for Justice for three years. I was doing mostly family cases. In my work as a Public Prosecutor, abused women would come to me as the only woman in the prosecution department. I helped them with legal challenges, learning from them and interacting with them—and this inspired me to work as a leader towards the empowerment of women in society. I was among the first lawyers to review and pilot the Gacaca courts structure in Rwanda.

The way I was able to help women appealed to me. Then I worked at ActionAid Rwanda for two years in human resources and logistics.

I worked for three years on the UNHCR GBV (Gender Based Violence) committee that sorted GBV and all other protection issues for urban refugees and was able to help reintegrate many Rwandan returnee families, mainly female-headed households, to resettle back into their country. The biggest achievement of the team was to repatriate 4,000 Burundians and resettle over 80 families in other countries like Canada, Australia and others, and to finally close the Burundian refugee camp. On a daily basis, I supported refugees to organise their lives, supervised distribution of food and non-food items, ensured children were enrolled in temporary schools and organised refugee committees and governing bodies. My inspiration during that time was women refugee leaders who managed crosscutting issues around their complicated lives, working hard to uphold their families when their husbands had given up because of displacement and the loss of their livelihoods. These women took advantage of the Rwandan system and laws, which were fair and empowered them, and 80 couples who understood the benefits of living in a legal union had their marriages legalised.

After, I worked with Imbuto Foundation for three years, leading the GBV project funded by USAID—PEPFAR that focused on enabling HIV positive mothers to be mentor mothers at health centres. This project concentrated on the prevention of transmission of HIV from mother to child to prevent HIV negative babies. I worked in 50 health centres across the country and closely supervised 80 HIV+ empowered women who gave testimonies to encourage expectant women to test for HIV and enrol into the PMTCT (Prevention of Mother to Child Transmission) program. These women's stories had a big impact on my life—coming to know that empowered women, despite HIV stigma, can change the world. In my next job with Girl Hub I entered a new world by focusing especially on adolescent girls—with the motto 'educate the girl and you will have educated the world. Empower the girl and you will have empowered the woman of tomorrow'. It is joyful to see adolescent girls becoming empowered, making right choices around education, job opportunities, reproductive rights and marriage, knowing that later this will have a positive impact on their lives, families and society as a whole. With my gender expertise I was in the position to continue to provide leadership in advising how gender can be mainstreamed to ensure equality and equity are attained.

Personal life

I have a girl and a boy, and I have raised my children in a similar way to the way my mother raised us. My mother was strict with me but tried to help us as well. My growing up was influenced by her in the same way as my children's growing up has been influenced by me.

My husband studied political science, which he finished in 2004 at Makerere University, and went straight to work in the Ministry of Foreign Affairs. His first political appointment was First Counsellor in Rwanda's High Commission in South Africa. He is very supportive and said maybe I should stay and complete the Master's in Gender and Development course I had enrolled in at the Centre for Gender, Culture and Development, but he is very hard-working and I knew he needed me as a diplomatic wife. This master's course came as a big opportunity for me. I dealt with sexual and GBV cases in the refugee camps but did not have enough knowledge, and I have learned so much since then. Not only definitions, but the course really opened me up to many things. I looked forward to the South Africa appointment but was sad to leave Rwanda. When I had my last farewell with Imbuto, people praised me and appreciated my work. I am also an Anglican, and active in the mothers' union, so had farewells at the church as well. I have been told I am a role model and I have worked with women in most of my jobs.

In Pretoria, I did voluntary work with the Mothers to Mothers peer group to support HIV women, who are very courageous. Testimonies say they still suffer stigma, but drugs are free and things are changing. As a diplomatic wife I would have liked to use this time for study as well, because I was not allowed to work. I wanted to take up as many courses as I could and go on to do my PhD. While in South Africa, I came to learn more about women issues, which were more alarming—women faced rape, murder and other forms of violence—and this made me realise that I needed to complete my studies in gender to find out why there was so much violence against women in different societies. I enrolled in an online master's course in Human Rights at the University of South Africa, which unfortunately I did not complete because relations between South Africa and Rwanda deteriorated and we had to relocate back to Rwanda.

This was a blessing in disguise because I was able to re-apply at the Centre for Gender Studies in Rwanda after being away for three years and have completed all modules of the Master's in Gender and Development. I have learnt to analyse all aspects of my life using a gender lens, including my own family, realising that change needs to start from the smallest unit of society, which is the home. My thesis will highlight the challenges faced by the Batwa women who live in Kigali because they have many disadvantages; first their identity as Batwa people, then being women, then living in the urban area and being exposed to GBV both from their families and community.

Role models

My mother was my biggest mentor and role model and had a major impact on my life. My mother pushed me to achieve my best, taught me how to work hard and to relate with everybody and how to love God above all. During my time at Imbuto, I met my other role models, the First Couple of Rwanda. The

First Lady of Rwanda, Jeanette Kagame is so zealous about her work in helping the most vulnerable families in the Rwandan community to have a better life. She is humble and loves excellence in all her work. She taught me how to work with the local community—she always mentioned, 'be humble and the most vulnerable will reach out to you'. Her husband, H.E. Paul Kagame, the President of Rwanda, loves his country and his people with so much passion—African leaders should borrow a leaf from his life. They both always inspire me, and I will always look up to them. At Girl Hub Rwanda, my role model was the then Country Director, Kate Wedgwood, she was very passionate to ensure that the girl effect happened in Rwanda.

Looking ahead

Unfortunately, I have not yet been able to complete my thesis because of the demands of my work. I'm now based in the biggest refugee camp in Rwanda, hosting more than 57,000 Burundian refugees (Mahama Refugee camp in Kirehe District). I am with UNHCR as a Protection Associate and deal on a daily basis with children and women survivors facing different sexual and GBV issues. The camp is located in the Eastern province, 15 minutes from the Tanzania boarder. I leave home, Kigali, early Monday morning (4 am) for Kirehe and I return to Kigali on Friday at 6 pm. During the weekend I concentrate on my family plus my weekly reports, it is very hectic, but I guess if I push hard enough, I can still do it.

Notes

[1] Autobiography written by Jovia Kayirangwa in 2011 and updated in 2019. She paused her master's degree studies due to increasing job demands.

Image: Jules Sebahizi

Jules Sebahizi's story[1]

Thesis: 'Educated women as social and economic agents of change within households in Rwanda'.

Childhood and early education

I was born in the Central-Eastern Africa region. Growing up in a country with multiple tribal conflicts, poor governance, and inequalities among men and women, insecurity and disturbances were features of normal life. As a member of a minority tribe in eastern Democratic Republic of Congo (DRC), born the fourth child in a family of eight boys, I was raised with a strong sense of culture and solidarity in the community where we lived. This strong community existed despite experiencing years of conflict due to absence of government, being robbed of our national identity, and being accused by all neighbouring tribes as foreigners who did not belong there. Although we lived in the richest part of the DRC, with an abundance of minerals, forests, water, and development aid, our community has been plagued by conflict for over half a century.

After primary school I went to high school for my secondary education and started suffering from the taunts of peers and teachers who called me 'Rwandese', meaning that I am not Congolese like them. One day a teacher said to me, 'We, as Congolese, we are going to take you back where you came from'. I asked him where that was, and he said, 'Rwanda'. I was very frustrated and confused. I wanted to know why this happened. Is there something wrong with me? My parents always taught me to love and live in peace with all people, and yet people here did not seem to feel that way.

In 1991, President Mubutu attacked the University of Lubumbashi and I was forced into exile in Burundi through Zambia. Several fellow students were killed; our sisters were sexually abused, and many of them were raped. From that experience, I started thinking and questioning about what my contribution should be to change the situation. What could I do to make people think more positively and believe in peaceably sharing the land together? When I imagine how the women students were threatened, violated, and sexually abused, I thought maybe I should just move away from that part of the world. I spent the following years exiled in Burundi and then the same situation occurred in 1993 with the assassination of the first elected president, Melchior Ndadaye. People—even children—were killed, women raped, and families displaced. People went into exile in the neighbouring countries of Tanzania, Rwanda, and DRC (Zaire at that time). I went into exile with a family friend in a place called Ruyigi in eastern Burundi. I spent three months in fear of being killed, but my faith (trust in God as a Christian) and good friendship helped me through those difficulties, and I survived.

Career and higher education

In 1989, I went to the University of Lubumbashi and found the same taunts and discrimination. Getting admission to university was a privilege, not a right to me or those from my tribe. We were forced to pay extra money while other students were admitted with no unusual fees. I endured those frustrations throughout my education and constantly questioned why this discrimination continued. Often people of my tribe were beaten, verbally abused, and qualified as foreigners—this kept them from getting higher education like other Congolese.

Because of insecurity in the eastern DRC where my family was living, I was not able to travel to that part of the country. So I remained exiled in Burundi and had to look for job. As a refugee, the only job I was permitted to do was teach. I taught at Nyankanda College for almost one and a half years. During that time, Burundian colleagues called me Rwandan, while others called me Congolese Munyamulenge—the real name of my ethnic group of Congolese Tutsi living in the Southern Kivu province of eastern DRC. The same situation happened again and again. I used to visit displaced people in different camps and see the pain they endured. Women and children suffered the most. The same question came up again for me: why doesn't anyone—the government of Burundi, international organisations including the United Nations, and strong powers like the United States and European countries—take action to pursue peace?

In 1994, after the genocide in Rwanda, I decided to move to Rwanda for two reasons: firstly, I was interested in witnessing Rwanda's reconstruction and the peace-building process after such a violent national tragedy, and secondly, to explore the possibility of continuing my education there. I was admitted to the National University of Rwanda to pursue my undergraduate studies. In 1996, the first war started in DRC by the Alliance of Democratic Forces for the Liberation of Congo (AFDL) with its former leader Laurent Desiré Kabila.

During that period, people in my home village were killed and others took refuge in Rwanda and Burundi. Women and girls were raped, forced to marry former soldiers and authorities of the former Zaire, and then brought with them to refugee camps in Tanzania. In 1997, Kabila took power in Kinshasa with help of the Rwanda Patriotic Army. In 1999, I finished my bachelor's degree in Public Administration and decided to look for a job.

My interest all through my undergraduate studies, professional career, and master's level degree was to know why people, despite international assistance, continue to kill and rape, and why women are the first target of all wars but are excluded in peace talks and negotiations. It is in that framework, when I finished my Master's in Gender and Development, that I decided I must search for a recognised doctoral program in international relations to explore more and understand the theories and practices of international affairs, conflicts, human rights, and humanitarian and international interventions. I am interested in studying how these factors affect peace negotiations to end conflicts, with a focus in the Great Lakes region of Africa where I was born and lived most of my life.

In 2000, I was recruited into the public sector as a Junior Trainer under a UNDP project supporting capacity building in Rwanda. From 2001 to 2006 I joined the Ministry of Public Service and Labour as the head of the division in charge of training, director in charge of Human Resources and Capacity Building, manager of the reconversion program for civil servants from the public sector, and coordinator of redeployment of civil servants of the provincial decentralisation process to restructure local government in collaboration with the Ministry of Local Government.

In 2007, I decided to leave the government and join the private sector. I started my own consulting company, which I still manage today, but also work as senior consultant with international firms in developing countries in Africa. My 18 years of professional experience, as well as personal history of growing up in a conflict region, contribute extensively to my current work and build strong sense for peacebuilding wherever I go. In addition to my consultancy business, we decided together with my wife to start charitable activities in 2011 helping the poorest widowers and teenage pregnant girls without means. Since that time, some other people have joined us in that precious responsibility. From 2016, as activities grew, we created a non-government organisation called Youth and Women Drivers of Peace (YWDP), a national non-governmental organisation which aims to empower vulnerable (the poorest) widows and youth who drop out to find or create job opportunities through income generating activities and hands-on skills and advisory services. Currently we are supporting more than 50 families in the Ndera Sector in Gasabo District.

Personal life

I married in 2004 and have four children, three boys and one girl. The way I do things and live with my wife and four kids follows the model of my family and I am proud to have that harmony in my family. I married my wife when she was at the level of Senior 6 and helped her get to master's level.

Role models

My father is and will remain my central role model. He lived with honesty, integrity, morality, and love for all people. He was also loved by people. I think all the time about my father, who taught us to be always seeking to be the first. He told us 'don't be satisfied with second place at school, seek always to be the first in whatever you do', and added, 'don't fear challenges; they will make you stronger'. So, when I faced those challenges, I thought about his words and that made me what I am today. Thank you, my Dad.

In my career, one person who inspired me by the way he works and his career path is Ambassador Vincent Karega, my former Secretary General at the Ministry of Public Service. He coached me in my career—he was my supervisor, with a very frank, open mind who openly discussed things with me and showed me how things should be done. I learnt more from him and this helped to understand the world of the public sector. Thank you, H.E Ambassador.

Looking forward

From the situations I have lived and experienced, my central research question is to understand the role of gender in civil and international conflicts, particularly the use of rape as a strategy of war and the exclusion of women in peace talks. In war there is often no victory for women, no matter which side wins. Women are the often disproportionately affected by war, and are hence the highest stakeholders for peace, says Noeleen Heyzer. The ultimate goal is to pursue my doctorate in this area. Further doctoral research will help me understand and contribute actively at global, academic and individual level as scholar in peace making and contributing to equal gender representation at peace negotiations. It will also emphasise the centrality of the role of women during negotiation among parties in conflict in the respective countries. The research will also enhance further international focus on making effective peace through mediation processes. The research will help us to understand more deeply the continuing discrimination against women in peace talks despite international legal frameworks that, in theory, respect the principles of non-discrimination of any form. Additionally, I would like to explore the existing international legal frameworks in post-conflict countries to assess how political peace talks contributed to reducing rape and increase the role of women throughout the conflict, as well as in the post-conflict period in the Great Lakes Region.

Notes

[1] Autobiography written by Jules Sebahizi in 2011 and updated in 2019.

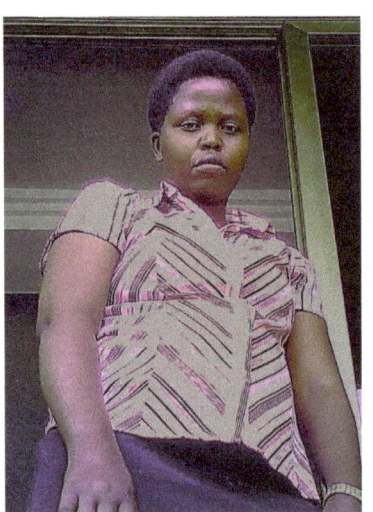

Image: Landrade Umuraza

Landrade Umuraza's story[1]

Thesis: 'An analysis of women and poverty in rural areas of Rwanda: Case study in Karongi District'.

Childhood and early education

I am Rwandan and was born in September 1972. My father was Twagirayezu Antoine and my mother was N. Ngororano Vénantie. I completed primary school in 1986 and my secondary school in arts in 1992. After finishing secondary school, my aspirations changed and I wanted to become a teacher.

Career and higher education

I undertook studies in higher education from 1995 to 2000 with an option for public administration in the Faculty of Social Sciences, Economy and Management at the National University of Rwanda, and completed a bachelor's degree. I have undertaken a number of training opportunities: Public administration, Decentralization and Management of the Changes; Conflicts Resolution, Human and Stock management, Organization of Work; Circulation, Treatment, Information management and Files; Administrative and Decision-making Methods and Techniques of Training of the Adults; and Training on Public Procurement Procedures. I travelled overseas in 2004 to do a 3-month training course in Belgium at the Institute of Public Affairs on 'The Management of the Administrative Acts, Finances and Human Resources of Decentralized Entities for local development'. My next course on 'Leadership, Management and Training of Trainers Skills Development' in 2005 was organised by the Eastern and Southern African Management Institute in Tanzania.

I have had several management and political experiences in my employment. I was elected Commissioner in National Electoral Commission during the elections for District Mayors in 2000, and then in 2001 was appointed Executive Secretary of Maraba District in charge of governance and management of the district's assets. In 2003–2004, I became staff-in-charge of civil servants in the Ministry of Public Service, then Director-in-charge of planning and finance in Kibuye province. From 2005 I moved to Director in charge of public relations and human resource management in the former Kibuye Prefecture, then Executive Secretary of Rubengera Sector in Karongi District and Director of administration and good governance in Karongi District. After my appointment as Director of Human Resource Management I was appointed Deputy Mayor in charge of social affairs in Karongi District. Since my appointment in October 2008 I have been a Member of the Parliament representing the Western Province in the Rwanda National Assembly.

In 2011 I began the Master's in Gender and Development. For the thesis, I undertook research on poverty of women in rural areas. By analysing this, I presented recommendations to different stakeholders who played a role in social transformation, including the government. In 2013 I was appointed Commissioner at the National Itorero Commission, a platform for educating and training Rwandans on shared values and taboos in coexistence and contribution to national development. Previously, Itorero, borrowed from traditional Rwandan culture, which was launched in 2008, was a task force that operated under the National Unity and Reconciliation Commission. The Itorero was a cultural school and it was the channel through which the nation could convey messages to the people regarding national culture in areas such as language, patriotism, social relations, sports, dances and songs and defence of the nation. Different groups of people get a chance to attend Itorero and get training which usually lasts two weeks. Every intake is given a different Kinyarwandan name and a self-praising slogan which resonates with that particular group—university students, women, youth, artists, journalists, teachers, medical practitioners, bishops, judges, members of cooperatives, district and city council members and committees, health workers and public servants. By 2018, over 1.5 million people have passed through Itorero, and the target is that all Rwandans undergo the same training to promote patriotism, unity and fraternity.

Personal life

I am married to Muligande R. Augustin and we have two children. The role I play in my family is not different to other women. I am a sister, a wife and a mother, but I am fighting for gender equality, especially with the education I give to my children.

Role models

When growing up, my role models were nuns in a parish near our home.

Looking forward

I hope I will continue my management and political career and work for projects which aim at the transformation of our people, especially for poverty reduction.

Notes

[1] Autobiography written by Landrade Umuraza in 2011 and updated in 2018.

Image: Laurence Uwera

Laurence Uwera's story[1]

Thesis: '"Child Friendly Schools" as a way to improve retention rate of primary school girls: Four case studies'.

Childhood and early education

I was born in 1980 in Butare City, Rwanda, the second of four sisters. My mother was a nurse. She returned to study at the Kigali Health Institute and finished her first professional degree in nursing with distinction at the age of 55 years. My father was a judge. He has now retired. My mother has been my role model. She was very intelligent in her studies and was always the first one in her class. From primary school, I was also the first in the class and ended both my primary and secondary schools as the first in the school. In my secondary education, I studied how to teach, so after finishing school, I was a teacher for one year in a secondary school in Southern Province.

Career and higher education

I won a government scholarship to continue my studies at the Kigali Institute of Education where I studied for a Bachelor of Arts: geography, history and education. I passed every exam without a supplementary and finally I graduated with a distinction—upper second-class honours. My family encouraged me to continue studying and I wanted but had no opportunity to do this immediately after graduating, because it was hard to get a scholarship. I was trying to apply to go study abroad, but we thought it would be hard with two small children. When I saw the advertisement about the master's degree in Gender and Development with a scholarship in Rwanda I immediately applied and was selected. We were happy in the family because we were all able to stay together in Rwanda while I was doing my master's studies. I graduated in 2012.

When I graduated from KIE, I gained a job in an American non-government organisation, WE-ACT (Women's Equity, Access to Care and Treatment). I began as a Program Coordinator, working on a program to educate people on the prevention of HIV and AIDS and later was promoted to be Project Manager for a project funded by USAID, supporting Orphans and Vulnerable Children. I then moved to World Vision International as Education Specialist and later I worked for SOS Children's Villages International as the Program Development Director/Deputy National Director in Rwanda. In 2016 I began an international position in Guinea Conakry where I worked as Program Director for Child Fund International and I played an important role in fighting against Female Genital Mutilation (FGM). I participated as a speaker in the European Development Day's event of 2017 to advocate for the abolition of FGM in Guinea. Currently, I am representing FHI 360 (formerly Family Health International) in Guinea and managing a USAID funded $12 million project, Citizen Involvement in Health Governance, where I am leading a team of 20 staff in Guinea Conakry. It is challenging to be a woman leader in Guinea because the country is male dominated. I am involved in different women's networks in Guinea to promote women's empowerment. I aspire to continue my career at the international level and to continue the advocacy for women's empowerment in Africa.

Personal life

I married in 2005 and we have two children; a boy named Yvan born in 2006 and a girl named Ketia born in 2008. My husband is supportive, he is a consultant in accounting with a Bachelor of Accounting degree. We both want to go further with our education.

Role models

My mentor and role model is Professor Shirley Randell, my thesis and research supervisor when I was a research mentee in a project on Child Friendly Schools (CFSs) for the Forum of African Women Educationalists, evaluating the impact of CFSs on the dropout rate of girls at primary school level.

Notes

[1] Autobiography written by Laurence Uwera in 2011 and updated in 2019.

Image: Leonie Mujawayezu

Leonie Mujawayezu's story[1]

Thesis: 'The analysis of factors influencing girl pregnancy in nine years basic education in Rwanda: case of Burera district'.

Childhood and early education

I was born in 1975. I did my primary education at Mucaca Primary School from 1982 to 1990 and completed my secondary education at Groupe Scolaire Notre Dame des Apôtres de Rwaza (Normale Primaire) in 1998.

Career and higher education

In 2006, I obtained a bachelor's degree in education at the National University of Rwanda (NUR), and in 2014 I graduated from the Master of Social Sciences in Gender and Development. I have been a teacher since 1999 and in 2009 I became the head teacher at the G. S. Kigeyo. From 2011 to 2016 I was a representative of the National Women's Council at the Burera District, and since 2017 I am the president of the economic commission of the District Council.

Personal life

I am married and currently live in Rwanda, in the Northern province.

Notes

[1] Information obtained from a CV provided from Leonie Mujawayezu in 2018.

Image: Marie Odette Kansanga Ndahiro

Marie Odette Kansanga Ndahiro's story[1]

Thesis: '1994 Genocide Memories: Genocide raped women's relationship with their rape conceived children, Study on "SEVOTA"'.

Childhood and early education

I was born in Rwanda, the first born in a family of three girls and four boys. My family is Christian in the Catholic Church. My parents were both educators in primary schools in Gatsibo District, Eastern Province. They were also the elders of their families, so my entire life has been surrounded by young loving people of whom I am the eldest. I believe this situation shaped my leadership skills from a young age. Furthermore, my early life was influenced by three very important old people who formed my character and made me believe that 'a woman can do'. Those were my paternal great grandmother, paternal grandfather and maternal grandmother, whom we called Mama. My grandfather could not tolerate any abusive attitude towards women. My grandmother was the one taking us to and from school. The three were coordinated in a way to always be present in all stages of their grandchildren's lives. I believed they were my own parents as I considered my father and mother my older siblings then.

When my father was two months old, he lost his mother, so his great grandmother raised him until he married. She remained with the family as she was too old to stay alone. She was older than 110 when I was born. She was very strong and would not allow any house worker to care for her children. She liked to tell stories and she told me she had left her husband when she was young, in her early 20s, because she gave birth to only two girls and was subsequently harassed by her in-laws, so she left with her children. She assured me she was proud of her two daughters and their offspring when they married.

My grandfather lived seven kilometres away but travelled once a week to check on us. He made it clear that he had zero tolerance for any contemptuous attitude toward women in his family. From the age of five, I became my grandfather's informant on my dad's and brothers' behaviour. This forced everyone in the family to grow without gender differences and with fewer stereotypes. The controversy was outside the family. My favourite games were dancing, poetry, football and spear throwing, the latter not deemed to be girls' games. My father was my personal trainer and wanted me to be sufficiently strong both spiritually and physically to defend myself. He specifically mentioned that he did not want anybody to be able to hurt me just because I was a girl.

From the age of 14 I pursued studies in economics in the secondary school, usually the choice of students from socially highly ranked families, of which I was not. I was a high achiever at school. I became interested in the analysis of power relationships in society, the politics, beliefs behind them, and the strength this power has to be able to shape and construct inequalities between social classes, race, religions, men and women. I joined, and soon headed, a cultural research group, focusing on history, culture, kingship and leadership, politics, epic poetries, writing and dance and other entertainment clubs. The 1994 Rwanda Genocide against Tutsis disrupted my education, which I stopped in order to support my younger siblings. I was fortunate to survive the killings, although with many narrow escapes.

Career and higher education

In 1995, I married and now have three children. Although I had a record of good jobs and great experiences in international organisations, the private sector and public institutions, I had not finished my studies. Therefore, I decided to enrol with the Association of Chartered Certified Accountants as a professional accountant, graduating in 2007.

Late in 2009, after many attempts to get admission to universities, I won a scholarship to join the first group of Masters' students in Gender and Development students at the Kigali Institute of Education (now the College of Arts and Social Sciences at the University of Rwanda). The study confirmed my vocation: to study society. I had a strong interest in the relationships between the minority versus the majority, the powerful versus the vulnerable and men and women. Perhaps because I was a genocide survivor and until then could not face my traumatic memories, this served as the genesis of my master's thesis on the Rwanda 1994 Genocide Against the Tutsis and the lives of raped women. The objective of this research was to allow the flow of victims' memories to be told and known, and to facilitate them to discover similar groups to identify with. This revolutionary work raised both theoretical and methodological innovations. At the same time, the study allowed a deep analysis of rape, children born of rape and war and its consequences, in an attempt to change Rwandan society's view of women and children victims of war rapes and community exclusion. Additionally, the thesis addressed a long-standing deficit in Rwandan women academic writers on the causes and consequences of genocide rape; a perspective that was missing from the literature largely debated by international researchers. It became my first cornerstone, my healing process as one of many members of the genocide survivors' community. As well, it constituted a platform for advocacy to the leadership, law and policy makers in the country.

Ever since my studies, I have taken positions in the community and participated in positive small changes. African and Rwandan universities have invited me for public speeches, women's mentoring and role modelling. I was given an important presidential appointment to head the National Electoral Commission as the Vice Chairperson. I was nominated 'Champion for Reproductive Health Rights' by the Rwanda Women's Network Organization for fighting and enforcing these family rights. I was then elected Senator. I won a position in the body of Rwandan academic researchers, mainly university professors, academics, researchers and media journalists in the National Centre for the Fight against Genocide and Conflict Resolution. We regularly participate in debates on research papers on genocide, transitional justice, international law, governance and corruption.

Since graduating with my Masters in Gender and Development studies where I learnt about and internalised feminist methodologies and ethnographic methods of research, I have gone deep into the knowledge and practice of them as pillars of my academic and research work. As a feminist ethnographer, since 2012 I have acquired important skills and tools. I usually handle a large volume of data and allocate enough time and effort, with a reflexive analytical approach, to ensure proper analysis. Participants who are survivors of atrocities require a sensitive and special approach. I personally have developed a rich experience running qualitative ethnographic research in East African countries. I use ethical guidelines of research in post-conflict countries, emphasising eight ethical value guidelines to guide the qualitative field work: beneficence, minimising harms and maximising benefit, informed consent, right to withdraw, culture, context, respect and confidentiality.

Looking ahead

Given that academic research has been my focus since I was a teen, my next step is to do a PhD. It will provide me with precious opportunities to gain academic maturity and profound professionalism, to learn about other academics' culture and practices and develop a global research perspective.

Notes

[1] Autobiography written by Marie Odette Kansanga in 2011 and updated in 2018.

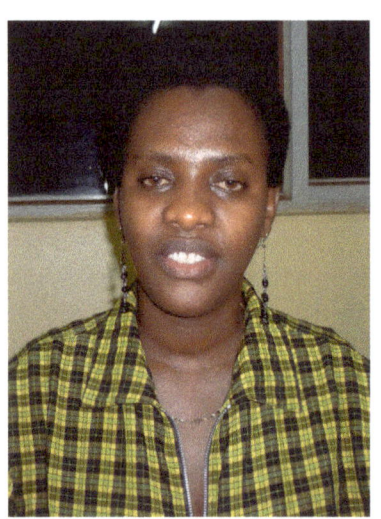

Image: Mediatrice Mukeshimana

Mediatrice Mukeshimana's story[1]

Thesis: 'The socio-economic conditions of households headed by girl children in Rwanda: Experiences in the Niboyi Peace Village'.

Childhood and early education

I was born in 1978 in Bugesera District, Eastern Province. My parents are Wenceslas Runyambo and Costasie Icyitegetse. I was the third in the family of six children; three boys and three girls. In our village, many neighbours are relatives; grandparents, aunts, uncles and cousins. I studied at a primary school three kilometres from our home. I was very competitive because our teachers sometimes said to our boy classmates, 'You should be the first rather than the girls'. When I finished my primary school in 1991, I had the chance to go to a public secondary school at Groupe Scolaire, Remera, Rukoma, now Southern Province. While I was in Secondary 3 in 1994, the tragedy of the genocide against the Tutsi occurred and my parents and many relatives and friends in my peer group died. Only three of us children survived. In 1996, I continued my study at Groupe Scolaire, Zaza, now Ngoma, Eastern province.

Career and higher education

When I finished Secondary 6 in 1998, I got a job in a supermarket, where I worked for one year, and after, I continued my study in Kigali Independent University, in the Social Sciences department of sociology in an evening class. When I finished my studies, I got a job and worked for five years in an international non-government organisation called Africare, in the COPE project, in charge of psychosocial support to Orphans and Vulnerable Children (OVC), especially those who are infected and/or affected by HIV/AIDS. In this project, I realised that, in general, all OVC are psychologically affected by the consequences of HIV/AIDS in the family, but girls are more affected than boys due to their tasks at home, like taking care of their siblings and their parents when they are in the depths of sickness. From 2010, I worked in the Ministry of Family Promotion (MIGEPROF) as OVC Technical Assistant in charge of the implementation of the National OVC strategic plan.

With my experience, since 2005, I have worked in the OVC area, where I saw the different vulnerabilities of children and how the Child Heads of Household (CHH) try to fight for the survivors themselves and their siblings. I also saw how the support provided by stakeholders for the common needs of education, health and insurance for OVC is very limited compared with the needs of children who are at the same time the heads of households. My master's research was about the responsibility of family management and development in female-headed households. The objective was to explore the social, psychosocial and economic challenges faced by the female children-headed households, how they are considered and how they try to change that situation.

Personal life

In 2003, I married Jean Claude Bariruka.

Looking ahead

My vision is to continue to help and to advocate for OVC, especially girls, in order to help them to access to their basic needs.

Notes

[1] Autobiography written by Mediatrice Mukeshimana in 2011.

Image: Monica Kirabo

Monica Kirabo's story[1]

Thesis: 'Analysing the role of women in peace-keeping missions: Rwanda National Police as a case study'.

Childhood and early education

Both of my parents are peasant farmers who became Rwandan refugees after they escaped Rwanda in 1959. A large number of Rwandans had to seek refuge in neighbouring countries. I was born in 1979 in Uganda, the third to last in a family of seven girls and one boy. I was always good friends with my brother and always asked God why I was not born a boy, so I grew up with a longing to be a boy. However, when I realised that it was God's wish, I thanked him for what I am and the way he created me with a unique character and personality. During my teenage time, I came to appreciate myself as a woman and became proud of it. I have a zeal to explore my potential as a woman, to use it to bring change to my people and the entire world. I have come to learn that the tools, skills and potential to achieve my dreams are within me.

Career and higher education

I am glad that after attaining my first degree in education and pursuing my masters' degree, I know the sky is the limit.

Personal life

I am married with two sons.

Role models

My role model from early childhood was my father; regardless of the challenges he went through as a refugee he tirelessly did his best to make sure all his children were educated. He was always proud of us because most of us performed well in class. He always stressed that the best gift you can ever give your child is education.

Notes

[1] Autobiography written by Monica Kirabo in 2011.

Image: Natacha Kaneza

Natacha Kaneza's story[1]

Thesis: 'Women entrepreneurs and access to finance: Challenges faced by rural women in Bugesera District, Rwanda'.

Childhood and early education

I was born in 1980. I am the second child in a family of five children, four girls and a boy. I did my primary and secondary education in schools managed by Catholic sisters. My mother was an assistant in a public company and had a secondary level education, and my dad was an engineer and a manager of a national institute in charge of protecting the environment. Even though my father knew that women had no role in determining the sex of the future child, he blamed my mother, saying that it was her fault that they had mostly girls. It was my father who decided everything: management of family properties, school of the children, etc. According to him, my mother had nothing to say even though most of the time it was her ideas that were practical. However, due to our culture, she had to be submissive and try to correct the consequences of the wrong decisions made by my dad without my father knowing it. Even if my dad was so patriarchal, he pushed me and my sisters to study hard and we were all performing well at school.

Until now, the majority of my family members are still in Burundi. There is no political will for gender equality there. When I was doing my studies, I tried to explain to my father the gender concepts, but for him, women have nothing to say. He thought that gender equality will bring women to disobey their husbands. However, I promised myself that one day I will go there to explain to my father and other family members that gender equality is a good policy for the development of the family and the country.

Career and higher education

In university, I studied Economics and finished with distinction. From my life and work experience, I knew that women have problems with access to formal credit. That's why I took a decision to do my thesis in the Master's in Gender and Development on challenges faced by women, especially women entrepreneurs, while accessing formal credit in the banks and the extent to which credit can empower them and change their lives once they access to it. I also identified strategies women use to overcome those challenges. My thesis ended by giving recommendations to enhance women's accessibility to formal credit in order to empower them economically.

Personal life

In 2007, I married a classmate. We have three kids, one girl and two boys. When I was doing my Master's degree in Gender and Development in 2011, my first born was one and a half years' old. It was so difficult for me to manage the work, parenthood and my studies. In the first three months it was not easy to balance all the important things. The church, social life and sport and leisure were forgotten. At that time, I was new in my workplace and had to perform well during my probation period. My husband has been patient and so supportive, encouraging me to continue and perform well at work and at school. He was caring for our kids and other home needs.

I remember that it was my husband that had to take our boy to the doctor whenever he got sick during that period. At that moment, his job was asking him to work more often in the field than in the office, which gave him the possibility to come home and see our boy during lunch time and also to come home early from work. Therefore, our boy was closer to his dad than me and it was difficult for him to pronounce the word Mama. It affected me and made me feel guilty for abandoning him. My husband has been so present, and it gave me strengthen to work and study He used to tell me that he was proud of me and that he is ready whenever possibly to help me and reduce my stress. His support was vital to the success of my studies and work.

Role models

When I met Mrs Shirley Randell and knew that she has four children and also grandchildren and that it did not prevent her from studying to the PhD level, it gave me the courage to go far in life, to continue my professional development. She has been a role model for me. Her capacity for balancing work, social, sport and family life is so incredible. She used to push students to be serious and meet deadlines given by professors, but also added that we should relax and do sport.

She made me know that if you have a plan in life, you can achieve regardless of the present challenges.

Notes

[1] Autobiography written by Natacha Kaneza in 2011 and updated in 2018.

Image: Oda Gasinzigwa

Oda Gasinzigwa's story[1]

Thesis: 'Women in political leadership positions: challenges and barriers in Rwanda'.

Childhood and early education

Born in Tanzania on 1 August 1966 to refugee parents who fled to Tanzania in 1959, my father was a teacher and my mother a nurse, may their souls rest in eternal peace. I was second among eight children, four girls and four boys. I completed primary, secondary and University education in Tanzania. Thanks to my parents who relentlessly supported and encouraged me and my siblings to excel and succeed in our studies regardless of life hardships they were facing as refugees. I remember how it used to be exciting whenever I received gifts from my parents in appreciation of my good performance in my studies.

I joined different youth groups such as Girl Guides, Young Women's Christian Association, basket and netball teams, etc. The exposure in co-existing with my fellow students from different backgrounds, cultural and gender diversity, family upbringing and religious beliefs was a life experience that prepared me for the challenges ahead in life and also my contribution to society.

Career and higher education

At the university I pursued Local Government Administration. Successful graduates were to be given jobs immediately after graduation in districts. This standing offer for employment motivated most young students like me to join the program. After graduation, I was offered a job. However, at the same time I was lucky to be offered another employment opportunity at the National Bank of Commerce in Dar es Salaam. At the time, the bank had a program to promote young professionals where I was hired as an administrator. With other fresh employees we underwent different on-the-job special training courses in bank operations. I worked with the bank for eight years through which I received several promotions.

When RPF (Rwanda Patriotic Front) stopped the genocide against the Tutsi in 1994 and started rebuilding the country, most refugees including my family returned. Back in Rwanda people were filled with mixed feelings, excitement, diverse expectations but also tears and sorrow for the tragedy that left the country in ashes and agony. Life had to continue and everyone was trying to contribute in building a new Rwanda. Gender stereotypes were also still in existence in some sectors, especially the private sector, hence a hindrance to young mothers and girls in the process of searching for jobs. I am grateful to my president H.E Paul Kagame for championing the promotion of gender equality and eliminating discriminatory laws and policies in Rwanda. Strong political commitment in Rwanda has resulted in significant positive strides in the promotion of gender equality and women's empowerment in Rwanda.

Fortunately, I came across a job offer and I was employed at the Ministry of Family and Social Affairs, responsible for gender, family, children and social promotion. This was a new and challenging sector especially in the aftermath of genocide. Gender equality was identified as one of the pillars and a priority in the new constitution; I was happy for the opportunity to serve my country and work with others in strategising, putting in place policies and laws and supporting communities especially at the family level. My main task was to support women in preparing viable projects and link them with banks for credits hence improving their well-being, with the support of a guarantee fund established by the Government of Rwanda. My eight years' experience in bank operations was of great value to my new assignment.

In 2001 I joined a UNDP project working in partnership with the Ministry of Environment under the department charged with resettlement of newly returning refugees and displaced people. The objective of the project was to promote for their welfare. This enabled me another opportunity of working closely with communities at the grassroots level and enhance my better understanding of the challenges being faced then by both women and men and their endeavours in building a new Rwanda. I later joined the Ministry of Agriculture, working in the crop intensification program, designed to promote large scale farming in Rwanda.

Gender equality and women's promotion became my passion and I joined women's associations inside and outside the country. I became a member of Profemmes Twese Hamwe, an umbrella for women's associations in Rwanda. I also became a member of the National Women's Council, a forum for women and girls in Rwanda. In 2001 the first election for the National Women's Council was conducted and I was elected to be a secretary at the cell (grassroots) level, and in 2004 I was elected at the National level as the National Women Council Chairperson.

It is important to encourage and support women and girls during elections. When people tell you that you can do it, you build confidence and move forward. Through these forums, women continue to be empowered socially, economically and politically. I am humbled and thank the leadership for the opportunity.

Appointed as the first Chief Gender Monitor in 2008, the establishment of the Gender Monitoring Office was in fulfilment of article 185 of the constitution which provides for the independent public institution as a reference point on matters relating to gender equality. The office is an icon observatory for gender equality that promotes accountability for sustainable development.

I enrolled for the Master's Program at the Centre for Gender, Culture and Development studies at Kigali Institute of Education in 2011 in the first cohort and graduated in 2012 with a Master of Social Sciences in Gender and Development. I thank Professor Shirley Randell who was the first director of the Centre. My appreciation also to the Government of Rwanda for establishing and supporting the Centre.

In 2013 I was appointed Minister of Gender and Family Promotion, the central government institution mandated to ensure strategic coordination of policy implementation in the area of gender, family, women's empowerment and children issues.

I was then elected by the Rwanda Parliament in 2016 to join the East African Legislative Assembly (EALA) as Rwanda's flag-bearer. Article 49 of the EAC Treaty established EALA as the legislative organ of the community, its core functions being legislating, oversight, and representation.

Personal life

I am married to a civil engineer and blessed with four children. My husband is a loving and supporting, wonderful man; my lovely boys are my treasure in life and they have also been supportive in my family life and career development.

Role models

My father and my mother; they were loving, hardworking and more importantly believed in me, I learned many different things from them. They supported our family and all who were needy during difficult times. All believed in educating their children as a first priority.

Looking ahead

Our country has registered tremendous success in empowering women and making sure women participate fully in all sectors for national development. However, this has been a journey and is a work in progress. My research findings on women in leadership I believe will inform policy makers and other researchers to continue searching for solutions for existing gaps in giving equal opportunity for women. I aspire to pursue a PhD Program in Gender Sector in the near future to continue researching on the still pending challenges.

Notes

[1] Autobiography written by Oda Gasinzigwa in 2011 and revised 2020.

Image: Odette Bagitengire

Odette Bagitengire's story[1]

Thesis: 'Legal analysis of informal marriage and its impact on women: Gicumbi case study'.

I am from Rwanda, married and the mother of two children. I earned a bachelor's degree in Political and Administrative Sciences at the National University of Rwanda. In 2011, I obtained a Maîtrise, Gestion des Resources Humaines at the Université Mercure International with grande distinction. I served for more than five years in the public sector, especially in the administrative area. I have also worked for the UN and NGOs: four years with the United Nations High Commission for Refugees, three years with United Nations Population Fund and two years with Danish Centre for Human Rights.

Notes

[1] Biographical note written by Odette Bagitengire in 2011.

Image: Odile Muhayimana

Odile Muhayimana's story[1]

Thesis: 'Gender-based economic violence in Rwanda: a case study of the Bugesera District'.

Childhood and early education

I was born in 1984, the only daughter among three boys. I am very proud of my brothers, the eldest is a doctor of medicine, the next is a computer scientist, and the last one, who is the youngest in our family, is finishing his studies for a bachelor's degree in project planning and grant management in Uganda. My parents are Gakwandi Jean Baptiste and Mukantaganda Madeleine, who are a civil engineer and a civil servant, respectively. They encouraged me to become an intellectual person and be a respectable woman. They always taught me to avoid a life of dependency. I acknowledge that my parents were really gender sensitive, because they always considered me in the same way as my brothers and gave us all the same rights. I remember that several times I was the first to have everything I wanted, even before my brothers.

Career and higher education

I studied for a bachelor's degree in economics. I always remember my first job. I was 22 years old, and I applied for the first time in my life for a position. I was appointed a branch manager of Réseau Intérdiocésain de Microfinance. It is from that time that I came to believe that to be a woman for me is not a simple thing. I worked also as statistician for three years. Fortunately, in 2010, I got a job in Gender Monitoring Office and my dreams have become a reality, because I'm now in the field that I really like. In addition to this, I have a master's in gender studies.

Personal life

My husband, Rukundo Olivier, is a lawyer and has a master's degree in business law. His advice reminds me of my childhood and my parents because he really likes education, to the extent that he always encourages me to go ahead with my studies.

Looking ahead

I will have at least two master's degrees, the first one in gender and development and the second one in economics. As I have built in me the spirit of competition, I aspire to a PhD in gender studies. Finally, let me say that, in my life, I really enjoy being a wife, mother and advocate for other women through my work. I really wish to be a good gender analyst in order to handle gender inequality, and to prevent and fight against all forms of gender-based injustice and violence.

Notes

[1] Autobiography written by Odile Muhayimana in 2011.

Image: Patrick Mico Ntunga

Patrick Mico Ntunga's story[1]

Thesis: 'Rwandan men's perception of positive discrimination for women: the case of the 'constitutional clause'—at least 30% women's participation in political decision making'.

Childhood and early education

I was born in the Democratic Republic of Congo (DRC) in October 1973, the fifth in a family of nine, five sisters and four brothers. Two of my sisters are married to Burundians. In the Rwanda crisis of 1959, my father was a teacher and he became a refugee in DRC. When he arrived, there was no job but then he became the head of a primary school. My mother was caring for the children and in the agriculture business. They were married at the time and their first child was born in Burundi on the way to DRC.

We came back to Rwanda after the genocide, but my mother stayed in the DRC until 2005. Two of my brothers and two sisters were in the Rwanda Patriotic Front. My father died in 1985 when I was in primary school and we had problems because DRC took our property. I was starting secondary school with limited means, but my mother did everything to help me to continue my studies. She inspired me and I stayed very close to her and took responsibility for the other children. 'What can you do for those young sisters and brothers?' my mum would ask. She told me to consider them as my sons and daughters.

Career and higher education

I was accepted at the National University of Rwanda (NUR) in 1995, but the first thing I did was to look for a job to see how I could help my mother. I worked for the Red Cross for a year in Butare and was well paid. Life in DRC is cheaper than in Rwanda. When I finished secondary school in 1993, I became a teacher for two years. I bought a lot of cows in DRC, gave them to my mother and hired someone to look after the cows. I studied education and science at NUR. One of my cousins was there with me. My father was the last born of the family and they all stayed in Rwanda. All the children were killed as well as my mother's father. Only some of my cousins were alive after the genocide.

I started working with MIGEPROF in 2001, in charge of gender advocacy. In 2003 I became head of the division of gender mainstreaming and advocacy and, in 2005, acting director of administration and human resources (HR). In August 2007, MIGEPROF became part of the Prime Minister's office and they took over the administration and HR. In 2006–2007 I worked in the Beijing Secretariat and in 2007 became coordinator for the UNFPA gender mainstreaming and women's empowerment project. I moved to the Gender Monitoring Office (GMO) in 2009 as coordinator of the pool of experts. The GMO is now developing tools for auditing and monitoring in partnership with MIGEPROF.

My education background was in another field than gender, and I learnt gender by experience, so I came to the master's program to build my theoretical knowledge and academic background. In all assignments given to us in this program I see the direct relationship with my daily job. I chose to write my master's thesis on the contribution of men to gender. I was a man born in a family with a powerful dad. He worked in another area without learning about gender, so how can he contribute to gender? Because of the patriarchal system, some men have problems if their wife is a leader somewhere, like a mayor. If women don't have value in the society, they become an obstacle to the development of the family. If I wanted to become a minister, my wife would be the first to help me to accomplish my duty. If I have a problem, my wife would help me. This is not the same for men. Men need to change their behaviour, to help their wives to do work in the home. Women have a problem if this is not the case, we need social transformation.

Personal life

I am married and have two boys. My wife was the Executive Secretary of the Unity Club and is an independent consultant in HR. My wife is Catholic and I am Protestant, and we are inspired by religion. We wanted a religious marriage, so we asked a Catholic priest. In this patriarchal system it is not so easy to go into the wife's church. Other people queried this, so we analysed it. My pastor had no problem. For special events we go together to our churches and we share what we learn. The Catholic religion wants the children to be in their church.

Role models

My role models include Ghandi, Mandela and Nyerere for their promotion of peace building. My mother was also a very interesting person and my relationship with her changed me. I remember what my mom did in a difficult situation and how she found a solution. I am what I am now because of my mother. She took the trouble to help me to be what I am now. At that time my mother was a widow. There were other families who lost their mother and stayed with their father. I saw a very big difference if the family was headed by a woman or a man. The men married again and gave birth to other children. These families are often a problem because of conflict between the children. We have a patriarchal system, but I don't accept that women don't have capacities. My mother was strong and had integrity. She facilitated love between the kids. She was responsible for women at the church and had time to pray. In the rural areas people started the day at 4 am with prayer and my mum led that session. When I was 10 to 12, I would go with her to pray.

When I started work and it was new to it, John Mutamba helped me by coaching me. He encouraged me and appreciated me, and that made me do better in order to be more appreciated. It was my first time meeting with him and we became good friends. Even now, if I have any problem, he is like my dad. If he has to do something on gender, he asks me to help him and we discuss it. So now I have this moral responsibility to do the same with others. I learned from him how to analyse everything in a positive light. Every person has good things and bad things and I learned that we should try to analyse the good things in others, without only considering the negative things.

Notes

[1] Autobiography written by Patrick Mico Ntunga in 2011.

Image: Radegonde Bayisenge

Radegonde Bayisenge's story[1]

Thesis: 'Factors affecting girls' performance in rural primary schools: Gikomero primary schools'.

Childhood and early education

I am the third born in a family of four girls and three boys. My father was a public worker and my mother was an educator. At the age of 16 I lost my parents, my two brothers, and one sister. We remained as orphans, two sisters and one brother, and our elder sister had to stop her studies and head the family. We continued our studies, but it was very difficult. We faced many problems like school fees, school materials, uniforms, notebooks, and so on. It was a struggle to be a teenager without parental protection. That situation pushed me to get married at an early age, and other constraints forced me to stop my studies for two years.

Personal life

I am 45 years old, married, and I have three children, a son and two daughters. After having my first boy, I returned to school when he turned one. My husband encouraged me to continue my studies as soon as possible. He was very supportive. Even my little brothers and sisters are assisted by my family. I completed high school in human sciences. At that time, I had one goal: to be among the best and receive a university bursary. I achieved my dream and registered in social work at the Faculty of Social Sciences, National University of Rwanda. However, before starting university I had my second child. It was difficult to study with a baby, but I had a vision to be among intellectual Rwandan women, to have a good job, to help my husband to support our family, and to also help my elder sister to return to school. Now my sister is an educator in primary school.

Career and higher education

Before starting my master's studies, I worked for a local non-governmental organisation called the Women's Promotion Initiative, in Nyamagabe District, a rural area where women are facing problems of poverty and different kinds of violence. In this association women received training, like modern agriculture, entrepreneurship, project management, etc. They also received information about family law, land law, and gender-based violence law, and were able to share their life experiences. They manage to stand for their rights. I loved working with women, but I looked for a higher paying job so I could support my family.

I joined the Ministry for Gender and Family Promotion and was in charge of orphans and vulnerable children, based at Gasabo District. I am interested in working with children, to identify children in need, to assist them, to hear them, and to share my life experiences with them. It was God's will and a joyful time to work with those to whom I can compare my past life. During holiday meetings as a facilitator, I introduced some gender issues for discussion. I realise that boys have the same thoughts as their fathers and girls as their mothers. Girls must stay at home helping their mother in home chores and helping them to look after their little ones, while their brothers are at school. Starting there, I try to show them the truth, that sustainable development requires efforts from both men and women, boys and girls, and that education is the pillar for all.

I decided then to study a Master's in Gender, Culture and Development to learn what gender really is, what gender issues are, the ways to handle them, and to become an expert in gender issues. My master's research was about girls' performance in rural secondary schools in Rwanda. I found that socio-cultural factors and school-related factors affected girls' performance. After that, I decided to change the way I raise my own children, to let both the boys and the girls explore their potential. It helped me visualise the potential of both boys and girls in different life aspects in Rwanda. In my village, I helped with the creation of Urukundo Family, a women's association. We meet once a month, we exchange life experiences, we teach each other, and we explore different laws and policies to protect women, children, and families. This is a good opportunity to decrease violence against girls and women in our village. All in all, my master's degree had a big impact in my life since the knowledge and skills I acquired have helped me to relate positively with my family, friends, community, and in my workplace as well.

After the master's studies, I changed my position at the same institution, and I am part of the team in charge of reintegration of all children from orphanages to their families or foster families. That is to help children to be raised in families instead of institutions, to be loved, and to benefit from the family's warmth.

Notes

[1] Autobiography written by Radegonde Bayisenge in 2011 and updated in 2019.

Image: Regine Abanyuze

Regine Abanyuze's story[1]

Thesis: 'Analysing the effect of the "one cow per poor family" Program on women's economic development in Rwanda: A case study in the Rulindo district of Northern Province'.

Childhood and early education

I was born in Uganda in a family of eight children, five girls and three boys, and we lived there for about 30 years. At that time, very few girls would go to school because of their culture. I thank my parents who thought wisely to put us in school and supported us all throughout. My childhood was influenced by my brothers who made me believe that girls can also compete in science subjects. I studied science up to high school level.

Role models

An important person who contributed a lot to my character is my daddy who always reminded me that life is not a straight line, especially for girls, putting more emphasis on working very hard to obtain a bright and independent future. Another very important person I will never forget is my cousin, the late Dismas Rutayisire, who loved me so much, encouraged me in all angles of life by always saying that nothing is impossible if one is determined to do it in a wise manner. He always encouraged me to be courageous by being a good example to others in order to become a lady of integrity. He was the same person who paid my school fees from primary three to senior four; unfortunately, he died when I had just joined senior five. I will never forget his kind heart and determination to make me a model to the girls and boys of those days.

Career and higher education

I joined the Institute of Teachers' Education Kyambogo in Uganda and later became a teacher of chemistry and biology. Due to the advice, wisdom and words of encouragement from the above-mentioned people, I have been given the chance to look ahead. When I left teaching, I joined the National Unity and Reconciliation Commission in 2000. For the first five years I was challenged by my lack of managerial skills, so I decided to do a bachelor's degree in management, which I successfully completed in 2007.

Personal life

I am married to a civil servant and we are blessed to have six children, three girls and three boys. I no longer have children at home during school time, and this has facilitated me in doing the master's degree in gender and development, a field I appreciate and longed for. I am sincerely happy about this. Indeed, I am very grateful to my husband who contributes to all the family needs in order to allow me to manage to pay my tuition, and I also appreciate the way he encourages me always to succeed in life.

Looking ahead

From the time I was still very young, I felt bad about gender inequalities of any kind found in different societies, especially in Rwanda, which I know most. One day I thought of contributing to the fight against inequalities, but I realised that I must first understand them well so that I have the knowledge and practical skills to find a solution to these inequalities. I am really very grateful to be among the few people who were selected to be pioneers in the Master's in Gender and Development at KIE. When I complete this program, I am determined to work in a network with other feminists to fight against all discrimination and oppression against women worldwide.

Notes

[1] Autobiography written by Regine Abanyuze in 2011.

Image: Shamsi Kazimbaya

Shamsi Kazimbaya's story[1]

Thesis: 'Impact of polygamy on the lives of Muslims in Rwanda: Kigali women's experience'.

Childhood and early education

I am Rwandan, born in 1975 in the Democratic Republic of Congo (DRC). I am the first born of a big family of one boy and seven girls, this being, I believe, the reason behind my passion and interest in the field of gender. My parents left Rwanda in 1959, when hundreds of Tutsis were killed, and millions displaced and forced to flee to neighbouring countries. Since then, my parents, like many other Rwandans, became refugees in DRC (then Zaire), navigating in the Great Lakes region in order to survive. They lived a relatively good life in DRC, well integrated with all the rights of a Congolese citizen. By the end of 1980, when Rwandan refugees in different countries started to organise themselves to return to their homeland, things started to become very bad in DRC. Locals started feeling animosity towards them, categorising them as intruders.

In 1992, as the tensions became so high in DRC, my family decided to move to Tanzania where they thought the climate was better for Rwandan refugees. They struggled there for two to three years. My young sister and I were left in a family in DRC because our parents thought it would be difficult for us to reintegrate in new schools, given the difference between the educational systems in the two countries. They decided to take the younger ones only, so I pursued my secondary school in DRC and finished in 1994. Life in Tanzania was not that easy for my parents, this being the worst of all periods of the Rwandan wars and killings that were marked by the 1994 tragedy of the genocide against the Tutsis. In late 1994, after the Rwandan Patriotic Force stopped the genocide, my family returned to their homeland, my sister and I also returned from DRC and the family was reunified again. This was the beginning of a new and bright life and future.

In all that struggle, my parents made sure they gave us a good education, teaching us to be responsible, smart, love our country and practice our religion. They always gave us equal education as far as gender is concerned, until today, we have never felt or seen them preferring or favouring our brother because he is a boy, regardless of the common 'son- preference practice' in most societies in Africa. As Africans say, first born children are deputy parents and this is how my siblings proudly call me and I like it because I feel I deserve it—I have developed the sense of responsibility from an early age and this both at home (responsible of all household tasks and caring for my siblings) and at school (working hard to always perform very well). In fact, I can't remember myself being a child. This became then a real challenge for my siblings, with my parents telling them they should be like me, and indeed I was and still am their role model in many ways. This makes me feel very happy and proud and continues to inspire me to work even harder. I also feel very blessed to be a role model and inspiration for many other women and girls.

Career and higher education

I went to university in Rwanda and studied public administration, receiving my Bachelor of Public Administration in 2000. Right after I graduated in 2001, as a young woman without any experience, I was fortunate to start my professional life in a senior position. I was the first, among very few women, executive secretary of Nyamyumba District in the Western Province (then Prefecture de Gisenyi). I was struggling and it was very challenging, but I made it, and this was a very good experience for me, which I think has been a very strong foundation for my career success later on. In 2003, as I felt that I wanted to grow professionally, I competed for the position of 'in charge of good governance, and decentralisation' at provincial level and got the job. I was not happy with that position and only stayed there for a few months, then left to work with the National Unity and Reconciliation Commission. At first, I was coordinating the Southern Province and then was promoted to the position of Director of Planning and Programs based in Kigali at the Commission's headquarters.

During my entire career I always had in mind my wish to work in gender-related projects. Luckily, one day I saw an advertisement for the position of Executive Secretary of SWAA (Society for Women and AIDS in Africa), and I applied and got the job. I stayed there from 2006 to 2012 and this experience allowed me to love my work more and think big about how to grow, to do better and to achieve more. I started dreaming of working with bigger organisations such as the UN in the field of gender. As I started looking for such jobs, I realised that I needed a master's degree in gender, which I managed to do with Dr Randell's support. Regarding my Master's in Gender and Development, after

I submitted my research proposal, I realised it was too broad. At that time, I was lucky as a young woman to start early to be seen in the public sphere, in decision-making positions, especially as a member of the Rwandan Muslim Council. It was a challenge to be the only Muslim in my class and that pushed me to do my own research, to be able to explain my belief.

After graduation, from 2012 to 2015, I worked as the MenCare+ National Coordinator for the Rwanda Men's Resources Centre. As a senior manager I was responsible for the day to day implementation and coordination of all project activities, particularly those aiming at promoting men as positive fathers in maternal and child health, and as caregiving partners in sexual and reproductive health. I was also responsible for promoting good working relationships and networking with the donors, government and civil society organisations for effective implementation and ownership by other stakeholders. From 2016 to 2017 I was a Gender Advisor with JHPIEGO, an affiliate of John Hopkins University. In this role I worked to reduce child and maternal mortality through increased coverage and utilisation of high-impact low-cost reproductive, maternal, newborn and child health interventions and innovative new approaches, and to strengthen the capacity of the Ministry of Health to manage and scale up these interventions. The position was focused on developing, integrating and documenting strategies to address gender issues related to the uptake of health services, especially respectful care, gender-based violence, male norms and involvement and fees.

I then joined Promundo in the position of Program Officer for Promundo in DRC and soon after was promoted to Senior Program Officer, leading Promundo-US technical assistance to projects in East, West and Central Africa. Since its founding in Brazil in 1997, Promundo has worked to advance gender equality around the world through formative research and rigorous evaluation, implementing evidence-based educational and community-wide programs and partnering with women's rights groups. Our advocacy campaigns, community mobilisation, group education and group therapy create safe spaces for men and women in post-conflict and high-violence settings to heal from trauma. Youth in over 22 countries are involved, and encouraged to question harmful gender norms, and for men around the world to discuss the benefits of involved in fatherhood and shared decision making, and the costs of violence and exploitation. My work with Promundo expanded when I was sent back to be based in Rwanda as Senior Program Officer, involving extensive overseas travel. Our research, programs and advocacy efforts show that promoting healthy masculinity (or positive notions of 'what it means to be a man') and femininity (or 'what is means to be a woman') leads to improvements in men's own lives, and in the lives of women and girls. Our programs strive to create change at multiple levels: in addition to working with individual men and women, we use campaigns and local activism to build community support, and advocate with institutions and governments to adopt policies and scale up programs that reinforce personal and social change.

I am very grateful to all my lecturers at the master's program in gender and development who provided me with the necessary quality knowledge and skills, which allowed me to progress so quickly in my career and make my dream a reality. I owe them a lot in my international position today with Promundo US, as a very highly qualified trainer and researcher in gender and masculinities. The most important skills and methodologies that helped me most to do my work are those related to feminist/qualitative research since these are the core of my work; the various gender analysis frameworks are very helpful to me during my gender transformative trainings. As a gender activist I am a member of various women and feminist organisations at national, regional and international levels, and regularly speak at international conferences like Women Deliver and the United Nations Commission on the Status of Women.

Personal life

In addition to all this, I was able to build a family. I married in 2008—relatively late in an African and Rwandan context and expectations of a woman. In fact, there is a certain age when a woman should get married otherwise it becomes an issue and you start being pressured and even given names. I am happy to have two beautiful girls today, six and nine years old. However, my marriage, like any other, has had some challenges, first because of our different backgrounds as far as the Rwandan history is concerned: me with my whole journey that I described above and my husband with his own, born and raised in Rwanda then survived from the 1994 genocide against the Tutsis. When it comes to gender, being a gender expert who has strongly improved her understanding, knowledge and skills, it is very challenging for us to deal with the persistent unequal gender norms and negative masculinities in our own relationship and turns out to be source of conflict and frustration sometimes.

Looking ahead

I know that the victims at the end of the day are women—although some women, sometimes, are the ones reinforcing gender inequalities, unfortunately—and would like to continue advocating and working to increase their knowledge and awareness, alongside men. I know that is a process that will take a long time, but I believe it is possible.

Notes

[1] Autobiography written by Shamsi Kazimbaya in 2011 and updated in 2019.

Image: Sidonie Uwimpuhwe

Sidonie Uwimpuhwe's story[1]

Thesis: 'Effects of Rwandan culture on female commercial sex work'.

Childhood and early education

I was born in Southern Province, Huye District, in 1979, the fourth of six children, three boys and three girls. My parents have always worked in the education sector; my father as a secondary school teacher and my mother as a primary school teacher first, and later as a public officer in charge of teachers' affairs in the ministry of Education (MINEDUC). Two of my older brothers and my father were all killed during the 1994 Tutsi genocide. This was the case for many Rwandan survivors of the genocide; life was not easy. I completed primary school at Byimana, and secondary at Nyamirambo St André College.

Career and higher education

I studied a bachelor's degree in Sociology at ULK (Kigali Independent University). I hold a master's degree in public health (MPH) from the National University of Rwanda and a second master's degree in social science in Gender and Development from KIE (Kigali Institute of Education). My research for the gender and development degree sought to understand and unpack the interconnections between sexuality, gender and the agency of practicing commercial sex for women and girls in the Rwandan society. Our assumption is that they are not doing this because they want to. I considered whether this was the product of a patriarchal society, whether it was that they have been denied access to basic services to meet their basic and strategic needs and whether commercial sex work was a radical alternative for a desperate woman to face life.

I have extensive professional experience of 15 years; i.e., in the public sector (8 years), especially in the health sector in Rwanda where I played various key roles in tailoring the national HIV response in planning, coordination, monitoring and evaluation in the area of integrating HIV/AIDS services within the general health care system while working as a technical expert in the Ministry of Health. I was responsible for mainstreaming HIV in the poverty reduction strategies and processes while working as an expert in the National AIDS Control Commission. I ensured gender equality in the national HIV/AIDS response when I was appointed as a senior advisor to the Head of the Institute of HIV disease prevention and control of the Rwanda Biomedical Centre (RBC-IHDPC). I was also project manager of a UNWOMEN funded project in RBC-IHDPC entitled 'Supporting gender equality in national HIV/AIDS response'.

In International Development (7 years), I have worked for two major international organisations. First, at CARE International, where I was heading all gender equality and women empowerment programs, focusing on: women's economic empowerment; prevention and response of violence against women and girls; women's leadership and political participation; engaging men and boys for gender equality; sexual reproductive health and rights; grassroots activism, and women's collective action, advocacy, national civil society strengthening. I am currently serving as a Country Director for Clinton Health Access Initiative (CHAI) Rwanda.

Personal life

I am a proud mother of two children, a boy and a girl.

Role models

I have two special role models. In the academic world, Dr Paulin Basinga was the director for my MPH dissertation and has been mentoring me for my master's studies. He is still young and has pushed very far with his academic studies, doing amazing work and publishing. He is very inspiring, helping me to publish too and I am currently preparing an article for publication in a peer-reviewed journal. In relation to family, my role model is my mum. She has been a perfect mother to me and my siblings. She had to struggle to look after us alone after the genocide, and she gave the same opportunities to all her children, both boys and girls. We got the essentials of life and now are all able to look after ourselves. My mum has been always there for me and my children. What I love on her side is that she used to pray a lot; in so doing, this helps us, her children, to stay in God's boundaries and so make us feel God's presence and favour in our lives. Her passing away, back in 2015 (may her soul rest in eternal peace), triggered a revelation to me that led me to dedicate my life to Jesus Christ, following my mum's path. Even dead, she continues to be my source of inspiration like no one has ever done.

I particularly recognise and I am forever thankful to the Government of Rwanda, under the leadership of President Paul Kagame. I am a product of Rwanda's development and girls and women's empowerment programs. Right from my earlier years of the orphanage back in 1994, the government has been there to provide me scholarships through my education, and has given me employment opportunities, that I earned, at times competing with others who studied in the world class universities. And here I am, heading one of the most reputable international organisations. I encourage the youth, especially the girls, to take up the opportunities that are presented to them, and seize them to uplift their lives and those of their families and communities.

Looking forward

I am motivated to give back to the community. I have been doing it in the framework of the various positions I have occupied, focused on the most vulnerable segment of the Rwandan population. I always seek various opportunities to volunteer in restoring social justice and giving back to the community. I have plans to create my own organisation that would be using its own resources and others from like-minded partners to empower girls. In the future, I would also like to pursue my studies for a PhD in an area that combines public health issues and gender equality, which are at the core of my career development goals.

Notes

[1] Autobiography written by Sidonie Uwimpuhwe in 2011 and updated in 2019. Sadly, she passed away suddenly in 2021, just before this publication went to press.

Image: Sifa Bayingana

Sifa Bayingana's story[1]

Thesis: 'Causes and consequences of domestic violence among couples: Perceptions of Women and Men of Kacyiru in Gasabo District-Rwanda'.

Childhood and early education

I was born in Uganda in 1969, the second in a family of seven children, four boys and three girls. My parents were refugees from Rwanda. I studied primary and secondary school at a time when the education of the girl child was not given due value in most societies. Some families, especially those which did not have sufficient means to support the education of all their children, preferred supporting boys because they believed that girls would be married off to other families and contribute to the wellbeing of their husbands' families.

Career and higher education

After completing secondary school, I joined Makerere University to study social sciences (political science, sociology, and French), and then, Education as a Postgraduate Diploma.

My first job was with the National Insurance Company, and after, I worked with different government institutions including the National Population Office, the National AIDS Control Commission, and the Ministry of Local Government. I also worked with the United Nations High Commission for Refugees, World Food Program, and the UN Population Fund in Rwanda, as a consultant in the areas of HIV and Gender. Currently, I am working with Rwanda Governance Board as a Governance Specialist and expert on gender aspects.

In 2011, I joined the master's course in Gender and Development Studies (MGD), which I found very interesting. Before joining the MGD program, I had studied the tools for gender analysis and gender mainstreaming, but after this degree, I had a much deeper understanding of gender, about the sociology and the power relations between men and women. In my opinion, studying gender, culture, and development is like studying social sciences. My research thesis was on domestic violence. I was curious to learn about the causes and consequences of domestic violence among couples within my own society. At the time of this research, there were just a few studies on this topic in Rwanda, in particular, a number of attempts by undergraduate students. That is one of the factors that motivated me to explore the causes of domestic violence that is confined to the household level but has a wider impact. Being a mother of four children and a student while I was pursuing my master's was not an easy task. It necessitated dedication and extra energy. I am grateful that my family encouraged me and supported me. I am a member of the Forum for African Women Educationalists (FAWE) Rwanda Chapter with a vision for promoting the education of girls.

Role models

My teachers have been my greatest role models and mentors. I am now pleased to be a mentor for young undergraduate girls studying in universities. One of them gained an award for her outstanding performance for her master's thesis in China. I also give advice to girls who drop out of school due to teenage pregnancy on how they can go ahead with their lives and strive to continue with their education.

About the future

After acquiring knowledge and skills in the area of gender, my passion is to help my community understand the concept of gender equality and its relevance to sustainable development, as well as the prevention and management of gender-based violence. Given the opportunity, I would like to do further research in social sector fields, especially in gender. When an opportunity arises, I will pursue a PhD in Gender Studies.

Notes

[1] Extract from an interview with Sifa Bayingana by A Escrig-Pinol and S Randell in 2011, updated in 2019.

Image: Simon Nsabiyeze

Simon Nsabiyeze's story[1]

Thesis: 'The Catholic Church's response to adversity: A study on the involvement of men and women in relief and development work through two CAFOD funded projects in Great Lakes'.

Childhood and early education

I am 41 years old, the third of eight children, five girls and three boys, and was born and raised in Rwanda. My parents were from the same village, my mother a cultivator and my father a civil servant. My grandparents were in a large, happy family. My grandfather worked for missionaries, and I was schooled in Catholic schools. I was a good student throughout my education.

Career and higher education

I studied psychopedagogy in secondary school and was recruited to work as a teacher of French and Psychology and in charge of discipline before I completed a bachelor's degree in 2004 and then a Master's in Psychology in 2007 at the National University of Rwanda. I joined the gender studies program for my second master's degree because I wanted to increase my understanding of phenomena and problems I had encountered in life and at work, especially with widows, orphans and other vulnerable people. I also wanted to understand, among others, why and how some men behave badly when their wives are strong and independent like mine. There was a component of culture in gender studies and I had a research interest in the Rwandan culture and post-traumatic stress disorder. I had jointly published in the area during five years of practicing therapeutics and psychotherapy, amongst other books. My thesis dissertation in the social sciences was on the involvement of men and women in the relief and development work of the Catholic Church. While I was studying I was also the Country Program Manager and Gender Focal Point for the Catholic

Agency for Overseas Development (CAFOD), managing the Rwanda sub-office, coordinating funding for 12 local organisations with a small team of colleagues and giving support to two projects in the east of the Democratic Republic of Congo (DRC) and Burundi.

In 2016–2017, I completed a Diploma in Humanitarian Diplomacy where I studied humanitarian diplomacy and aid effectiveness. My dissertation focused on challenges and successes in aid delivery to Chadian returnees from the Central African Republic (CAR). This was one of the courses that opened my lens wider and deepened my understanding of international and humanitarian affairs, equipping me to perform my responsibilities in the changing humanitarian industry. I aimed high for senior international job positions in humanitarian work. Over the last 14 years, I have worked with international organisations that deployed me in Rwanda, DRC, CAR, Chad, Ethiopia, South Sudan and Mozambique. I am currently working in Chad with the United Nations Office for the Coordination of the Humanitarian Affairs, where I am in charge of a sub-office in the South of Chad, dealing with the consequences of the CAR crisis.

I have been involved in managing teams of national and international colleagues of between 10 and 200 and a budget portfolio of up to US $5 million per year. As a psychologist, a participative and empowering leader, I have a situational leadership approach, due essentially to my belief that my team has diverse and enormous potential that has to be given opportunity to blossom. I try to promote listening, problem-solving and ownership, enhancing creativity, building on diversity, ensuring accountability but also promoting each and everyone's potential and performance, engaging and motivating my team and celebrating success. I have faced huge challenges as a leader in a context where humanitarians and peacekeepers are sometimes victims of varied accusations and humanitarian access challenges. Leaders in humanitarian work are expected to perform and deliver sometimes where governments and other traditional systems have failed or are failing in their mandates. This requires negotiation skills, diplomacy, conflict management, dealing with intimidation and managing the security and safety of staff. Working in both rebel and government held territories in countries like CAR and South Sudan, and keeping neutrality and humanitarian principles is not an easy task and I have been involved in situations of nearly being kidnapped, including my team taken as hostages and later released after negotiations.

Trained in gender, gender sensitive and being a feminist, I am troubled by how women and children, especially young girls, are treated in most of the places I have worked. I have also lived many joys in my leadership. As a humanitarian, for example, while with Save the Children, I was always joyful and felt energised to continue my work despite challenges when, as a result of my team's efforts, one or more children were removed from the long list of the millions of children worldwide who go hungry every day, who are malnourished, who do not have access to education or health services, whose rights are violated and who are voiceless.

Personal life

I married Ernestine Narame in 2006. We have two children, Amanda and Romeo, now 12 and 9, schooling in Switzerland where Ernestine is concluding PhD studies at University of Lausanne. Her thesis, entitled 'The Schooling Paths and Socio-emotional Development of Children raised by Single Women in Rwanda', is a continuation of her thesis for the Master's in Gender and Development degree, in which we enrolled together. Amanda won a yellow belt in karate at the time she belonged to a kids' club in her home country; she is a fan of piano and swimming. Romeo plays in a local basketball club and is a good swimmer. His hobby, as with many kids of his age, is building Lego, and with the aspiration of becoming an aviation engineer, he builds them with immense passion and talent. I am very proud of my 'amazing family, growing, united and in love' and we do all that is possible to ensure we have time with our children.

Leaving my children and wife behind constitutes a huge challenge in my life. I keep in close contact with my family, especially the three women pillars of my life: my wife and my daughter daily and my mother weekly, as they constitute my source of energy and resilience. I confirm that 'besides every successful man, there is always a woman's support'. I visit them every two months during my rest and recovery breaks and annual leave.

Role models

I have had two role models. One is an uncle. Even though he was not an academic, he liked reading and being up to date. He had a very happy family and was in a good relationship and a friend to everyone. He managed conflict and contributed to his children's education, accompanying them to school when possible, and going with them to mass. This was different from what I saw in some others and it inspired me as a good example and the kind of family I wanted when I had my own. My other role model is a priest who was one of my neighbours when I grew up and I always wanted to be like him. We belonged to the same choir when he was in major seminary and he inspired me in terms of both intelligence and religion.

Looking forward

Above all, I aspire to be more, not to have more!

Notes

[1] Autobiography written by Simon Nsabiyeze in 2011 and updated in 2019.

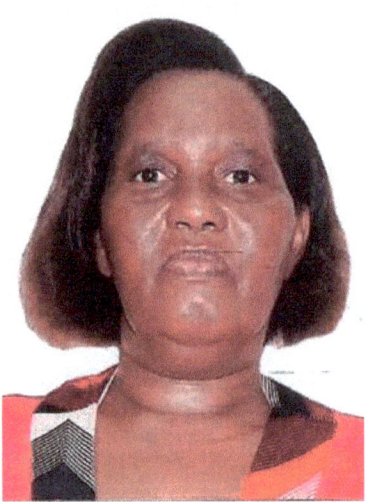

Image: Violet Kabarenzi

Violet Kabarenzi's story[1]

Thesis: 'Causes and risk factors for violence against women by intimate partners identified by abused women in Runyonza Village, Rwanda'.

Childhood and early education

I was born in Uganda, in a family of three boys and five girls. My parents, Mrs and Mr Oliva and Daniel Karemera, were priests in the Anglican Church. I owe my compassion and commitment to social justice to them; they socialised me to value humankind without discrimination. This has impacted on my dedication to the promotion of gender equality. I went to primary school at Rwengoro Primary school, Mt. St. Mary's Namagunga for secondary school.

Career and higher education

I attended the National University of Lesotho at the tertiary level and hold a Bachelor of Commerce degree specialising in management. In my earlier career, I served as a secondary school teacher in economics and accounting in different schools in Kenya and Lesotho. From 1998 to 2003 I was head of the gender training division in the Ministry of Gender and Women in Development in Rwanda, the Ministry that has evolved to become the Ministry of Gender and Family Promotion. I took the opportunity to facilitate the development of the gender training manual that was used widely to train about gender concepts and gender and development. From April 2003 to July 2006, I had the opportunity to serve as the head of gender and media, and later as head of women in technology and community development at the Kigali Institute of Science and Technology, KIST. During this period, I facilitated projects for promoting girls' education in science and technology through capacity building and mentoring programs. I also initiated KIST's outreach programs for women's empowerment through dissemination of appropriate technologies, including energy saving technologies and imparting skills in food technology and entrepreneurship skills. While at KIST I also participated in development of KIST's equality and diversity policy.

In 2011 I was a Gender Projects Officer in the Rwanda National Police with a special focus on prevention and response to gender-based violence. During my service in the Rwandan National Police, I was a member of the coordination committee that organised the Kigali International Conference on the role of security organs in ending violence against women, held in October 2010. An outcome of the conference was the adoption of the Kigali Declaration by Africa region security organs to end violence against women.

In recent years, I have been doing research as a consultant. I undertook a participatory gender audit report on tea companies in Rwanda on behalf of the Gender Monitoring Office (2016), developed the Rwanda Ministry of Infrastructure Gender Mainstreaming Strategy (2016) and coordinated and monitored the Women Economic Empowerment study in Rwanda (2018). Currently, I am working with Kvinna till Kvinna Rwanda, an international women's rights organisation as a program officer. I am responsible for supporting partners to prepare grant proposals, report writing, monitoring and organisational capacity building. I also participate in organising networking forums at national, regional and international levels.

Role models

I have two role models. First, Dr Jolly Mazimpaka, who was my literature teacher from senior one to senior four. She inspired me through the compassion she displayed in her work and using a student empowering teaching methodology. She had the power to take you along and that has a lasting impact. She puts a human touch into whatever she is doing. My second role model was Dr Josephine Odera, who was the Regional Program Director for UNIFEM, CARO, while based in Kigali. She was out to do the best possible to promote gender equality, not just as part of her job but with the commitment to bring change. She spread her energy to reach out to the influential for policy change without forgetting the community for their empowerment and encouragement. She valued knowledge and combined Godly values with respect for humankind and a heart to serve while a leader.

Looking ahead

For my future I am committed to further research into women's issues, especially in the areas of violence and peacebuilding as key constraints for women's development and full participation in development and enjoyment of their human rights.

Notes

[1] Autobiography written by Violet Kabarenzi in 2011 and updated in 2019.

Image: Viviane Kalumire Furaha

Viviane Kalumire Furaha's story[1]

Thesis: 'Sexual risk behaviors and HIV/AIDS risk: Perceptions of National University of Rwanda students'.

Childhood and early education

I am 36 years old, third in a family of eight children comprising four boys and four girls, with only two years age difference from each other. I was born in Bukavu, a town in Eastern Democratic Republic of Congo (DRC) and was raised in the Roman Catholic Church tradition. I was very close to my siblings, and my big sister was my best friend. My family, especially my mother, was very spiritual; a wonderful, loving, compassionate woman whose values built in me my passion to advocate for vulnerable women and girls and thus led to my career in gender and development, while my father forged in me the 'Go get it!' attitude. My parents owned a business together and were incredibly hard working. They did not have the chance for enough education, my father completing elementary school and my mother high school. However, they ended building up a wholesale business and became successful, thus allowing their children to have the opportunity to study in very good schools, since they both believed that a good education was the way to succeed in life. Having successful entrepreneurial parents that started from zero gave me the strong belief and confidence that nothing is impossible. My father was very strict, especially with school and my choice of friends, monitoring everything his children did, and we had lot of restrictions. My life was between the school, home, library and church. It was like we were in an army camp with him being the chief commander. He said: 'I put you in nice schools, but it depends on you to take advantage of the opportunities. It is your own life and you are responsible for it'.

The first tragedy of my childhood was my first experience with domestic violence when my dad beat my mother who, for the first time, ended up in hospital. That day changed the image I had of my father. Despite all his restrictions in our education, I used to look at him as a role model and suddenly he began to be violent to my mum over nothing: that changed everything for me. Then, from October 1996, my family experienced a tragic war and its consequences in DRC during which women and girls faced serious gender-based violence (GBV), especially rape as a weapon of war. This was the end of my somewhat happy and stable childhood. I lost close family members and experienced different traumas that impacted on my health, family and social life. The most life-changing event was to get HIV from the sexual abuse I was a victim of, after which I just struggled to survive in a world controlled by men. These different situations impacted my adulthood terribly, because I lost trust in men.

Furthermore, I emotionally struggled for a long period with the lack of paternal affection during my childhood and early adulthood. This made me make poor choices regarding male partners and getting involved in intergenerational relationships.

I completed elementary and high school at College Alfajiri, a Jesuit school that originally was just for boys but later admitted a few girls. In a class of 30 students there were only two or three girls. I knew I had to perform very well and worked hard. While in elementary school I was a fervent reader and was amazed by reading the story of Madam Marie Curie. She seeded in me the passion for sciences and research from an early age. Furthermore, under the influence of a family friend, who was a pharmacist, I decided to take biology and chemistry as my main subjects for my last three years in high school.

Career and higher education

In 2001 after graduating from high school I left DRC to go to Rwanda. I developed a coping mechanism in order to forget all these things that had happened to me: silence. I was not talking, nor had I mentioned any of my traumatic experiences to my university friends. I was pretending everything was ok and was living as a normal young woman. But it was not easy.

I went on to study pharmacy at the National University of Rwanda (NUR). I found that I enjoyed and learned more through tutoring my classmates, and thus discovered the teaching talent that led later to my academic career. During that period, my friends saw me as a strong and influential woman, however, what they did not know was the secret of sickness, war, sexual abuse, GBV and patriarchal norms that was eating me up.

In 2006, psychologically and physically weakened by all the traumas I had been through since 1996, I suffered severe depression with memory loss mixed with psychosis in my fourth year at university and was put into a psychiatric hospital for six months. I began to develop many HIV-related sicknesses and attempted suicide. While I was recovering, my counsellors and social workers, one also a woman living with HIV, suggested I join a group of educated women leaders living with HIV. We founded a local NGO, Rwandan Women Living with HIV/AIDS and Fighting Against It (FRSL+/RW). These activities helped me regain confidence in myself to enjoy life again. I felt useful for society since I could speak out for the rights of people who suffered like me.

I went back to NUR and in 2009 graduated in pharmacy with honours. In 2011, while working as a Tutorial Assistant and doing advocacy work with FRSL+/RW, 80% of my co-workers were men and some supported my professional development, thus I regained trust in men. I enrolled in the Master of Gender and Development to gain more knowledge and skills in order to enhance my ability and efficiency as a women's rights and health-for-all advocate. I won the first Shirley Randell Award for Excellence as the top student of my year.

I worked and trained for NUR, the United States Agency for International Development, the International Community of Women Living with HIV (ICW), UN Women, the Global Fund and the Joint United Nations Programme on HIV/AIDS amongst others. When I relocated to the United States of America, I prepared for the USA Foreign Graduate Equivalency Exam of the National Association of Pharmacy Board so that I could be certified as a Pharmacist and get my license to practice pharmacy in the United States. I am a Social Enterprise strategist and a certified Trainer, Speaker and Coach with the John Maxwell Team, taking leadership, business, marketing and sales courses. I co-founded and currently serve on the AFROCAB Executive Steering Committee, a pan-African organisation that provides valued, significant and independent contributions in HIV, TB and other HIV co-morbidity, drug development, research, treatment, prevention and diagnosis. I am currently working as a health professional with a leading National Community Pharmacy in the United States, as well as a Youth Development and Women's Empowerment Activities Facilitator at Fairfax County, Virginia State, USA.

In 2013, I co-founded a nongovernment organisation IMARA-Women Empowerment Foundation to advocate for the social, economic and health rights of vulnerable women and girls in the Democratic Republic of Congo, essential to their dignity and empowerment. I am currently establishing an innovative global social enterprise and authentic African fashion brand: IMARA Social Enterprise, a catalyst for socio-economic empowerment of women in Sub Saharan Africa, to break through the inter-generational cycle of poverty by providing them with the tools and support to reclaim their own futures and flourish as independent entrepreneurs, driving development in their communities. In 2016, I started a coaching and training business (Furaha Transformational Leadership) and developed commercial acumen to promote and develop my business and build up my professional network. I provide marketing tools and training for business owners and non-profit leaders by helping them foresee and pave the way while helping them to set and achieve goals and overcome limiting paradigms through coaching. I am passionate about research and since my graduation my publications have included many scientific peer-reviewed articles, and books.

Personal life

Reading has been one of the activities that has highly impacted the quality of my results, from recreational reading as a child to higher literacy and languages development as an adult. As a teen and young adult, reading was a great coping mechanism in traumatic situations and helped me to develop into a resilient strong woman. My daily reading habit for personal and business growth is helping me to leverage the wisdom and experiences of successful mentors and leaders and being smarter with feelings. Emotional Intelligence factors such as self-awareness, positive self-image, self-discipline and empathy add up to a different way of being smart and they aren't fixed at birth. Shaped by childhood experience, emotional intelligence can be nurtured and strengthened throughout adulthood with immediate benefits to our health, relationships and work.

Having a child of my own totally changed my life perspective. My daughter made me more focused in my spiritual, emotional and professional life. Before having her, I was sometimes 'just playing with life', but now I am aware I am responsible for a human being. Despite all my flaws, God trusted me and made me a steward of this precious princess on the Earth. So now I think twice before taking any decision: what impact will it have not only on my life but on her life too? I want to be a role model for my daughter. She is still little, but she is really changing my life for the better.

Role models

My role models while growing up were mostly from the books I was reading, and even today, when I have real mentors and role models, I am still teaching what I learned from people who paved my way through their writing. I developed the love of reading books as a child and became inspired by the lives of my role models and heroes who were instrumental in my choice of subjects to study: sciences from Marie Curie, and how to deal with life issues and become a good leader from Nelson Mandela, Mother Theresa, Helen Keller, Maya Angelou and Jeanne d'Arc.

There are many other role models in my life that I reach out to. For my academic career, Professor Kadima Justin and Peter Salah from the University of Rwanda are great role models and mentors. I always look up to Professor Shirley Randell as my gender and development expert mentor, I follow her work, publications and social media and get guidance from that. Lillian Mworeko, the ICW East Africa coordinator, is a great role mode as an executive woman living with HIV advocate. I have other role models in specific areas. In turn, I coach my mentees.

Notes

[1] Extract from an interview with Viviane Kalumire Furaha by A Escrig-Pinol and S Randell in 2011 and updated in 2018.

Index

A

African feminism   30
African scholarship   46–47, 49, 71
AIDS
    See HIV/AIDS
Australian Agency for International Development (AusAID)   7, 13

C

Canadian International Development Agency (CIDA)   130, 144, 146
Centre for Gender, Culture and Development (CGCD)   5–14
  funding   6–7, 8, 12, 13
  future plans   13
  genesis   5–6
  scholarly impacts   11–13, 28–29, 35–37, 49
  staff and volunteers   7–9
  students   10, 11, 24, 35–36, 46, 57–59
children   78, 100, 165, 238, 241–242
    See also schools
CIDA
    See Canadian International Development Agency (CIDA)
Constitution of Rwanda   4, 255

D

development
  education and   29, 79–80, 81–82, 270
  gender equality and   22, 30–34, 87
  gender-based violence and   96–101
  theories of   95–96
domestic violence   100, 114, 288, 299–300

E

economic development
    See development
education
  'banking method' (Paulo Freire) 20
  benefits of 78
  as development tool 29, 79–80, 81–82, 270
  female participation 79–87, 100, 198, 206, 270
  as a human right 78–79, 80–81, 86
  research and study skills 46, 71
  Rwandan government policy 29, 54–55
  science, technology, engineering and mathematics (STEM) 54–55, 77–78, 79–87, 300
empowerment 58, 67, 110, 126, 250

F

family 58–59
FAWE (Forum for African Women Educationalists) 12, 138, 189, 206, 288
feminism 23, 29
  African 30
  post-colonial (PCF) 30–31, 95–96, 98–99, 100–101
feminist pedagogy 17–23, 66–68
feminist research and scholarship 27–37, 47–48, 55–57, 60
Forum for African Women Educationalists (FAWE)
  See FAWE

G

gender
  in conflicts and peace talks 223, 224–225
  development and 22–23, 30–37, 87
  educational opportunity and 79–87, 198, 206, 270
  invisibility of women's labour 32–33
  scholarly publishing and 47
  socially constructed gender roles 21–22, 31, 45, 114, 122, 154, 206
  stereotypes 45, 81, 134, 198, 270
gender-based violence 93–94, 96–102, 153–154
  in conflicts and war 223, 224–225, 300
  definition 96
  development and 96–101
  domestic violence 100, 114, 288, 299–300
  economic control as 48
  gender equality impeded by 31
  responding to 215–216, 221–222, 223, 296
  sexual violence 100, 221–222, 223, 238–239, 300
gender equality and women's empowerment (GEWE) 3–5, 9, 100, 254, 284
Gender Equity Index 23
Gender Monitoring Office (GMO) 70, 118, 130, 180, 202, 255, 261, 266, 296
gender policy 4, 34
Government of Rwanda (GoR)
  See also Gender Monitoring Office (GMO); *See also* entries beginning Ministry of ...
  education policy 29, 54–55
  gender equality 4, 32–33, 285
  gender expertise training 12
  scholarship and research permits 35

H

health   87, 100, 185, 206, 210, 232, 279
  See also HIV/AIDS; See also Ministry of Health
HIV/AIDS
  graduate stories (career involvement)   144, 153, 186, 197, 216, 217, 284
  graduate stories (personal)   10, 178, 300
human rights   78–79, 80–81, 86, 97–99, 100, 101

K

Kigali Institute of Education (KIE)   8, 28, 44, 45–46
  See also Centre for Gender, Culture and Development

L

language   18, 44–45, 46, 67
leadership   21, 36, 60, 292

M

Master in Social Sciences (Gender and Development), formerly the Master in Social Sciences (Gender, Culture and Development)   44–45, 48–49, 49, 56–57
MDGs (UN Millennium Development Goals)   22–23, 24, 80, 100
  See also SDGs
mentoring   59
MIFOTRA
  See Ministry of Public Service and Labour
MIGEPROF
  See Ministry of Gender and Family Promotion

Ministry of Agriculture   254
Ministry of Environment   254
Ministry of Family and Social Affairs   254
Ministry of Foreign Affairs   217
Ministry of Gender and Family Promotion (MIGEPROF)   180, 255, 266, 270, 295
Ministry of Health   189, 197, 279, 284
Ministry of Justice   117
Ministry of Local Government   223
Ministry of Public Service and Labour (MIFOTRA)   122, 169, 223, 228

N

National Electoral Commission   239
National Itorero Commission   228
National Unity and Reconciliation Commission   144, 228, 274, 278
National University of Rwanda (NUR)   12, 189
National Women's Council   254
Norwegian Agency for Development (NORAD)   6–7, 8, 10, 13, 179, 194

P

patriarchy   31, 266
post-colonial feminism (PCF)   30–31, 95–96, 98–102
primary schooling   29, 83
Public Service Commission (PSC)   122

R

rape   100, 221, 223, 238
RAUW
  See Rwanda Association of University Women

reconciliation   65, 69, 71–73
research and study skills   46, 71
research graduates   12
research grants   12
research methods   55–57, 60
resilience   57–58
RPF
    See Rwanda Patriotic Front
RWAMREC
    See Rwanda Men's Resource Centre
Rwanda Association of University Women (RAUW)   5, 122
Rwanda Civil Society Platform (RCSP)   144
Rwanda Men's Resource Centre (RWAMREC)   144, 173, 180
Rwanda National Police   12, 296
Rwanda Patriotic Front (RPF)   113, 145, 254
Rwanda Women's Network Organization   239
Rwandan Constitution   4, 255
Rwandan government
    See Government of Rwanda (GoR)
Rwandan Women's Parliamentary Forum (RWPF)   4–5

S

schools   29, 83
science education   54–55, 77–78, 79–87, 300
SDGs (UN Sustainable Development Goals)   34, 86–87, 100
secondary schooling   29, 83
sexual and reproductive health   185, 206, 210
    See also HIV/AIDS
sexual violence   100, 153–154, 221, 223, 238
social change   48–50, 58

STEM education (science, technology, engineering and mathematics)   54, 77, 79–87

T

teaching methods   17–23, 66–68
tertiary education   29, 81–85
transitional justice (TJ)   65, 68–74

U

United Nations
  2030 Agenda for Sustainable Development (SDGs)   34, 86–87, 100
  Declaration on the Elimination of Violence against Women   98
  Millennium Development Goals (MDGs)   22–23, 24, 80, 100
  World Conference on Human Rights   98
United Nations Development Program (UNDP)   129, 130–131, 223, 254
United Nations Educational, Scientific & Cultural Organisation (UNESCO)   11, 46, 81
  UNESCO Institute of Statistics (UIS)   82
United Nations Fund for Population Activities (UNFPA)   174, 266, 287
United Nations Fund for Women (UNIFEM)   4–5
United Nations High Commissioner for Refugees (UNHCR)   216, 218, 259, 287
United Nations International Criminal Tribunal for Rwanda (UN-ICTR)   158
United States Agency for International Development (USAID)   144, 173, 180, 216, 232

United States of America
  gender equality statistics   24, 82–83, 85
  Support for CGCD   9, 12
university education
      See tertiary education

V

violence
      See gender-based violence

www.ingramcontent.com/pod-product-compliance
Lightning Source LLC
Chambersburg PA
CBHW061246230426
43662CB00021B/2439